Posthumorism

Posthumorism

The Modernist Affect of Laughter

Frances McDonald

BLOOMSBURY ACADEMIC
LONDON • NEW YORK • OXFORD • NEW DELHI • SYDNEY

BLOOMSBURY ACADEMIC
Bloomsbury Publishing Plc
50 Bedford Square, London, WC1B 3DP, UK
1385 Broadway, New York, NY 10018, USA
29 Earlsfort Terrace, Dublin 2, Ireland

BLOOMSBURY, BLOOMSBURY ACADEMIC and the Diana logo
are trademarks of Bloomsbury Publishing Plc

First published in Great Britain 2022
This paperback edition published 2023

Copyright © Frances McDonald, 2022

Frances McDonald has asserted their right under the Copyright, Designs
and Patents Act, 1988, to be identified as Author of this work.

For legal purposes the Acknowledgments on pp. ix–x constitute
an extension of this copyright page.

Cover design: Eleanor Rose
Cover image © "Kleine Sonne" (Little Sun) by Hannah Höch, 1969. © DACS 2021.

All rights reserved. No part of this publication may be reproduced or
transmitted in any form or by any means, electronic or mechanical, including
photocopying, recording, or any information storage or retrieval system,
without prior permission in writing from the publishers.

Bloomsbury Publishing Plc does not have any control over, or responsibility for,
any third-party websites referred to or in this book. All internet addresses given
in this book were correct at the time of going to press. The author and publisher
regret any inconvenience caused if addresses have changed or sites have ceased
to exist, but can accept no responsibility for any such changes.

A catalogue record for this book is available from the British Library.

A catalog record for this book is available from the Library of Congress.

ISBN: HB: 978-1-3502-6461-8
PB: 978-1-3502-6465-6
ePDF: 978-1-3502-6462-5
ePUB: 978-1-3502-6463-2

Typeset by Integra Software Services Pvt. Ltd.

To find out more about our authors and books visit www.bloomsbury.com
and sign up for our newsletters.

To my mum and dad

Contents

List of Illustrations	viii
Acknowledgments	ix
Introduction	1
1 Gestalt Looking: Nathanael West's "Ha Ha"	35
2 George Bataille's Affectology	61
3 The Grain of Hélène Cixous's Laugh	87
4 Atomic Laughter	115
Digital Posthumorism	143
Bibliography	159
Index	172

Illustrations

1 "E = MC³" by Forrest Myers © 1963. Reproduced with the permission of the artist and Paula Cooper Gallery, New York   1
2 "Atomic Laughter" by Andreas Müller-Pohle © 2002. Reproduced with the permission of the artist   115

Acknowledgments

This project started life as a dissertation at Duke University. I could draw a map of all the places I wrote it—the tiny nook on the third floor of Lilly Library, the table with the sparking outlet at The Federal, Whitney's back porch. And along with the geography, the soundtrack: every album by The National, and, when things got particularly dire, my "everything will be okay" playlist, which starts with "No Questions Asked" by Fleetwood Mac and ends with the live version of "Don't Let the Sun Go Down on Me." I want to thank all my friends who typed opposite me during those years, and especially to Brenna Casey, Sean Mannion, and Gordon Getzinger. I also need to thank my mentors at Duke, whose early guidance helped shape this project in ways large and small. I am extremely grateful to Tom Ferraro, who first sparked my interest in laughter by pressing a copy of *The Day of the Locust* into my hands. My sincere thanks, too, to my dissertation director Priscilla Wald. Our conversations about laughter, which took place in corridors and forests, across Thanksgiving dinner and the Atlantic Ocean, were a distinct pleasure that I shall not forget.

At the University of Louisville, I took the dissertation apart and rebuilt it, sentence by sentence. I could not have done so without the encouragement of Aaron Jaffe, who not only convinced me to submit this manuscript to publishing houses but also came up with the term "posthumorism." I owe him an enormous intellectual debt, which I shall try to repay in the form of strong Bloody Marys and weak karaoke performances. I am thankful, too, for my friends here. I feel terribly lucky to know Kristi Maxwell—she's one of those people who deeply commits to everything she does, from itinerary-building to cruciverbalism. It's this quality, I think, that makes her such an exceptional friend, poet, teacher, and scholar. My love and gratitude too to Beth Henson, Zoe Bridges-Curry, John Bigbooté, and Sarah Martin—it's impossible to record all the gifts I've received from you, but here are a few: the long Cherokee walks that we started taking once we knew I was leaving; the wedding planner that I've used either zero or three times, depending on how you look at it; a new appreciation for the inexplicable lives of fruit; and basically half my wardrobe.

The University of Louisville has been a wonderful place to complete my research. I would like to thank my colleagues, and in particular Susan Ryan and

John Gibson, for their unwavering encouragement and support over the last five years. It was under John's directorship that I received financial and intellectual support from the Commonwealth Center for the Humanities and Society, for which I am grateful. I am indebted too to the Society of Critical Exchange, and to the members of its 2019 Winter Theory Institute with whom I shared my exploratory research on digital posthumorism. My thanks, too, to the Ekstrom library staff for everything they have done to support this project. And, at Bloomsbury Academic, I would like to thank Ben Doyle and Laura Cope.

My friend Whitney Trettien gets her own paragraph. We wrote our dissertations together, and then we wrote our books together. In between, we set up *thresholds*, a creative-critical zine that published and so made public the messy, collaborative nature of all writing. Some of my favorite memories are of us doing this work. I see us surrounded by half cups of coffee in a cottage in Scotland or pouring over scribbled designs in a hermetically sealed New York hotel room or segueing effortlessly from a discussion about Skyler White to a discussion about user navigation on a wintery hike through Duke Forest. There are these scenes and hundreds more.

Finally, I extend my love and gratitude to my family. To Ben, who helped me with these pages by reminding me of everything that exists outside of them. To my mum and dad, whose support has never thinned, despite being stretched over four thousand miles for close to a decade. And to my sister, who once told me with a barely concealed glee that postmodernism was "disgusting" but whose literary hand-me-downs are responsible for me writing this sentence today.

***

A shorter version of Chapter 1 appeared as "'Ha-ha and Again Ha-Ha': Laughter, Affect, and Emotion in Nathanael West's *The Day of the Locust*," in *American Literature* 88, no. 3 (2016): 541–68. It is reprinted here with permission from Duke University Press. A section of Chapter 4 was first published as "The Last Laughs of Doomsday Humor" in *Apocalypse and American Literature*, edited by John Hay (Cambridge: Cambridge University Press, 2020), 281–92. It is reprinted here with permission from Cambridge University Press.

Introduction

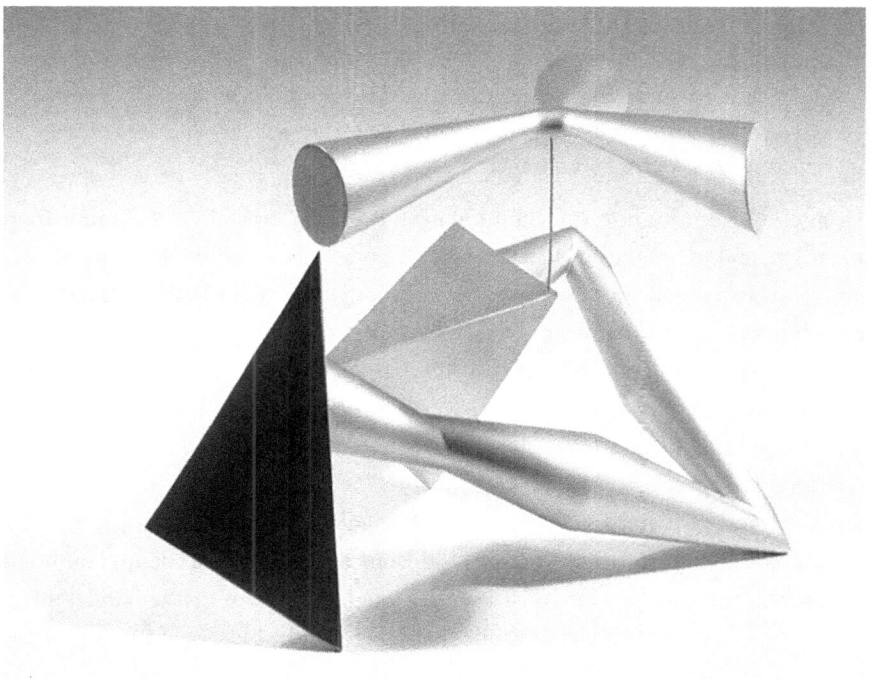

Figure 1 "E = MC³" by Forrest Myers © 1963. Reproduced with the permission of the artist and Paula Cooper Gallery, New York.

Laughter without Us

What is the shape of a laugh? How would you sculpt one from plastic or glass? Perhaps you are picturing the human body caught in a spasm of laughter—a ridged throat and a red, round mouth. This is to be expected but try, now, to extract laughter from the fleshly coordinates of the human body. What shape is *this* laugh? What materials would you use to give it form? Do you envision a monumental stone curve? A fibrous lattice? A soft, labial fold? In an extraordinary essay from 1966, the American artist Robert Smithson asks after the formal dimensions of a laughter without us. The essay focuses on the Manhattan-based art collective the Park Place Group. Like the massive obsidian monolith that sits stark and strange at the heart of Stanley Kubrick's *2001: A Space Odyssey*, the Park Place Group's minimalist sculptures are abstract and alien—they baffle the eye with their inhuman proportions and their hard, brilliant surfaces. What these monuments give form to, Smithson proposes, is laughter:

> Laughter is in a sense a kind of entropic "verbalization." How could artists translate this verbal entropy, that is "ha-ha," into "solid-models"? Some of the Park Place artists seem to be researching this "curious" condition. The order and disorder of the fourth dimension could be set between laughter and crystal-structure, as a device for unlimited speculation.[1]

Unhitched from humor and the human, the "ha-ha-crystal" is the sound that meaning-making makes as it edges into the black. For Smithson, it signals the arrival of expanded modes of perception that would allow artists "to face the possibility of other dimensions, with a new kind of sight."[2]

In search of concrete examples of the ha-ha-crystal, Smithson alights upon the abstract sculptures of Forrest Myers. In Myers' unsmiling geometries of aluminum, plastic, and glass, Smithson senses the presence of a laughter that has been stripped of its human coordinates: "Myers sets hard titter against soft snickers, and puts hard guffaws onto soft giggles. A fit of silliness becomes a rhomboid, a high-pitched discharge becomes prismatic, a happy outburst becomes a cube, and so forth."[3] To render laughter as pure mathematical form, Myers must extract it not only from the human body, but also from any sense of humor—the "silliness" or "happiness" that might have provoked (and so explained) the act of laughter are now available to us only as lines and surfaces, angles and vectors. On this point, Smithson is adamant. "We must not think of Laughter as a laughing matter," he writes, "but rather as the 'matter of laughs.'"[4] Playing on the double meaning of "matter," Smithson here asks us to conceive of laughter not in terms of humor (a "laughing matter"), but in itself as a material substance; a little later in the essay, he goes further to describe laughter as a particle state, as "laugh-matter and/or antimatter."[5]

At stake in Smithson's ha-ha-crystal is a way of thinking about laughter without humor, without humans, and without humanism. Smithson's anti-humanism is well known—his most celebrated artwork, the colossal earthwork sculpture

Spiral Jetty (1970), reflects his enduring theory that geometric abstraction will provide an escape hatch from the "diseased words and out-moded criteria" of humanism.⁶ "In the Spiral Jetty," he writes, "the surd takes over and leads one into a world that cannot be expressed by number or rationality. Ambiguities are admitted rather than rejected, contradictions are increased rather than decreased—the *alogos* undermines the *logos*. Purity is put in jeopardy."⁷ Stemming from the Arabic *jidr asamm*, meaning "deaf root," the word *surd* is rarely used outside of the specialized fields of mathematics and phonetics. In mathematics, it is a real number that has an infinite number of digits after the decimal point. In phonetics, it is a consonantal sound that is uttered not by the voice but by the breath, for example, *f, k, p, t*. These two definitions meet in the figure of laughter, which Smithson conceptualized as an infinite exhalation of breath, as "verbal entropy."

Smithson's ha-ha-crystal might be eccentric, but it has many bedfellows. Modernity is strewn with examples of humorless, human-less laughter, which is defined by a double movement: on the one hand, its ability to crack up and destroy humanist criteria, and on the other, its opening onto new horizons of perception. Take, for example, the famous opening lines of *The Order of Things* (1966), in which Michel Foucault describes the burst of laughter that accompanied his reading of an "impossible" taxonomy by Jorge Luis Borges:

> This book first arose out of a passage in Borges, out of the laughter that shattered, as I read the passage, all the familiar landmarks of my thought—our thought, the thought that bears the stamp of our age and our geography—breaking up all the ordered surfaces and all the planes with which we are accustomed to tame the wild profusion of existing things, and continuing long afterwards to disturb and threaten with collapse our age-old distinction between Same and Other.⁸

I take up this passage in more detail in Chapter 4, but for now it's enough to notice Foucault's investment in laughter as a technique for hacking into and blasting free from humanism, which he imagines as a gigantic sorting machine that relentlessly organizes things into one of two categories: "Same and Other." Elsewhere, Foucault imagined a new style of critical thought that would keep step with the "wild profusion" that throbs in the sidelines of humanism. Such thinking, Foucault said, would "light fires and watch the grass grow"; it would "bear the lightning of possible storms."⁹ *Posthumorism* acknowledges posthumorist laughter as a critical agent in this "rewilding of theory," to borrow a term from Jack Halberstam and Tavia Nyong'o.¹⁰ A wild theory, in Halberstam and Nyong'o's account, is one that shrugs off "sovereign expectations of autonomous selfhood" in order to better attune itself to the disordered and asymmetrical rhythms of the world.[11] Posthumorism (and *Posthumorism*) participates in this project; it too seeks to shrug off sovereignty in favor of new styles of being and belonging.

Modernist Posthumorism

Written almost entirely as prose poetry, Friedrich Nietzsche's *Thus Spake Zarathustra* (1883–91) contains the first literary instance of posthumorist laughter. Like Smithson and Foucault after him, Nietzsche is interested in how the material state of laughter might transport its host into a philosophical wild zone where the tenets of humanism no longer hold. About halfway through the book, Zarathustra, a self-proclaimed prophet of laughter, recounts the parable of a shepherd who bites off the head of a "heavy black snake," the thickened coils of which represent the chokehold of every human system.[12] Upon decapitating the snake, the shepherd is overwhelmed by laughter, which Zarathustra takes as a sign of his affirmative transformation into something entirely other, for which the oft-misunderstood term "Übermensch" serves as placeholder. "No longer shepherd, no longer human—one transformed, illuminated, *who laughed*! Never yet on earth has a human being laughed as *he* laughed. O, my brothers, I heard a laughter that was no human laughter, and now a thirst gnaws at me."[13]

A few chapters later, Zarathustra's gnawing thirst is sated as he, too, is overcome with laughter:

> My wise yearning cried and laughed from out of me—born upon mountains, a wild wisdom verily!—my great, wing-beating yearning! And often it tore me away and up and out and in the midst of laughing; and then indeed I flew quivering, an arrow, through sun-drunken rapture: —out into far futures no dream as yet had seen, into hotter souths than artists had ever dreamed of: where gods in their dances are ashamed of all clothes:—for I now speak in parables and like poets hobble and stutter.[14]

Seized by laughter, Zarathustra ceases to hold a fixed position in time and space as humanism, and classical physics, would have him do. He abandons his post to become an arrow in flight; pure, impersonal passage. It is worth pointing out here the illegibility of Zarathustra's laughter, which fails to function as a sign of a particular emotion or sense of humor. It is insufficient to say that the laughter that spills forth is a figuration of *Zarathustra's* joy, *Zarathustra's* anxiety, *Zarathustra's* triumph, or whatever; in fact, the precise opposite is true—the movement of laughter is the movement away from interiority. Nietzsche dramatizes this strenuous experience through the rhythmic pulse of accumulative threes. The poetic quickening of "away and up and far," "I flew, quivering, an arrow," and "to speak in parables and to limp and to stammer" compels the reader to use the conjunction or comma as a pirouetting block from which they might fling themselves forward through language as Zarathustra does through his "sun-drunken" skies. It is this quality of over-exertion, of "high-affect performance," that prompted Sianne Ngai to characterize Nietzsche's writings as inherently "zany."[15]

It is not an exaggeration to say that in *Zarathustra*, Nietzsche invented not only a new, "zany" style of philosophical discourse, but also a new gesture of laughing. I call this strain of laughter *posthumorist* to mark its radical disinvestment from humor, the human, and humanism. Posthumorist laughter is not only modern, but also modernist. To understand it as such, we must give up on the increasingly tenuous notion that modernism lives in the pocket of humanism. From Susan Stanford Friedman's "planetary modernisms" and Paul SaintAmour's conceptualization of "weak modernism," to Guy Stevenson's "anti-humanist modernisms" and Aaron Jaffe's more cosmically bound "modernist inhumanisms," scholars have in the last decade done important work in blasting open modernism's geographic, historical, affective, and aesthetic boundaries.[16] As Jaffe in particular has argued, the story that is most often told about modernism forgets its preoccupation with the impersonal, the weird, and the alien; but modernist texts, both canonical and fringe, are swarming with all sorts of *in*humanisms, including "reports of anonymous being, nocturnal ontology, circulating sap, poisonous radiation, alien ecologies, machinic ventriloquism, dwindling existence, untenable talk, promethean shame, scalar pathos, kind pessimism, precarious foregrounds, and extinct backgrounds."[17]

If modernism is, as Jaffe has argued, "a force field for all matter of thinking without humans," then posthumorist laughter is one of its most prized tools in undertaking such an enterprise.[18] This book in its entirety will testify to this fact, but for now let's take a whistle-stop tour through a few regions of modernist posthumorism as a way of acquainting ourselves with our object. Our first stop is pataphysics, the avant-garde pseudoscience developed by Alfred Jarry in the early 1890s. In his "neo-scientific novel" *Exploits and Opinions of Dr. Faustroll, Pataphysician*, Jarry defined pataphysics as an experimental branch of science that "will examine the laws governing exceptions, and will explain the universe supplementary to this one; or, less ambitiously, will describe a universe which can be—and perhaps should be—envisaged in the place of the traditional one."[19]

In Jarry's novel, the eponymous pataphysician Dr. Faustroll and his companion, a baboon named Bosse-de-Nage, set out on a perilous voyage to locate this new universe.[20] Their journey extends far beyond the spheres of science and metaphysics, and ends in the thickened realm of eternity where Dr. Faustroll's measuring devices cease to function. "Imagine the perplexity of a man outside time and space, who has lost his watch, and his measuring rod, and his tuning fork," he writes, "I am no longer on earth."[21] Faustroll coins the portmanteau "ethernity" to describe the tactility of this infinite non-space, which takes the form of an ethereal luminescence that is "as elastic as jelly."[22]

We do not have to wait until the end of the book to reach ethernity, however. It is contained already in Bosse-de-Nage, or perhaps more specifically, in Bosse-de-Nage's laughter, a "tautological monosyllable" that repeats twenty-one times.[23] With only a few exceptions, the formula Jarry uses to figure Bosse-de-Nage's laughter is always the same: it is an enigmatic "Ha Ha" that erupts apparently at random but is always looped into the process of signification by the narrator. Here are a few examples, but there are many more:

"Ha, ha!" said Bosse-de-Nage, without further commentary.
"Ha ha!" he growled, to express his fury.
"Ha ha!" interposed Bosse-de-Nage by way of digression.
"Ha ha," agreed Bosse-de-Nage wholeheartedly.[24]

The most common signal phrase the narrator uses in these moments is "he said," which cuts to the heart of the joke; the narrator cannot help but take de-Nage's laughter for meaningful human speech, when it is precisely the opposite; it is a "tautological monosyllable" uttered by a "dog-faced baboon."[25] Like Smithson's entropic ha-ha-crystal, de-Nage's tautological Ha Ha ramps up ambiguity and contradiction in the service of difference; as Jarry observes, "[Ha Ha] pronounced quickly enough, until the letters become confounded, is the idea of unity. Pronounced slowly, it is the idea of duality, of echo, of distance."[26]

After de-Nage's violent death, Jarry dedicates a chapter to his laughter. Titled "Concerning Some Further and More Evident Meanings of the Words 'Ha Ha,'" the commentary dwells particularly on the orthography of pataphysical laughter—how does one write the inhuman infinity of the baboon's eternally looped Ha Ha? The narrator proposes that we render it on the page not as "Ha Ha," but as "AA." Anticipating Derridean deconstruction by a good sixty years, Jarry explains that the doubled letter would help formalize the fact that pataphysical laughter *is* différance: "A juxtaposed to A, with the former obviously equal to the latter, is the formula of the principle of identity: a thing is itself. It is at the same time the most excellent refutation of this very proposition, since the two A's differ in space, when we write them, if not indeed in time."[27] In his valuable gloss of this passage, Christian Bok describes de-Nage's Ha Ha as "a laugh track for the sophistry of différance, the limit between differing and deferring … [it dramatizes] the *syzygia* of physics in a universe of undecidable uncertainty."[28] In other words, de-Nage's Ha Ha is a synecdoche of *ethernity*—it is itself a foray into the surd world that exists on the outskirts of humanism. Jarry confirms this in the book's last chapter, which offers a final word on the orthography of pataphysical laughter. The narrator is calculating an algebraic formula for God, where "a is a straight line connecting 0 and ∞." Viewed side by side, the reader cannot help but notice that the alphabetical letter "a" resembles one half of the infinity symbol. Place a mirror against its right-hand side, and "a" becomes "∞." Bosse-de-Nage's laughter, then, goes through a third mutation: from "Ha ha" to "AA" to "∞."

With a passage from *Dr. Faustroll* acting as its epigraph, René Daumal's 1929 essay "Pataphysics and the Revelation of Laughter" offers further insight into the gesture of pataphysical laughter, which Daumal describes as "headlong rush" between opposites that causes the human ("that lucky Earthling") to "explode."[29] Daumal dramatizes this experience in verse form:

I am Universal, I burst;
I am Particular, I contract;
I *become* the Universal, I *laugh*.[30]

Here, laughter's rhythmic force hurls its host between the dialectic's poles with such violence that the system breaks apart, and the laugher is jettisoned into a state of radical flux where a new "instantaneous and fluid" style of communication becomes possible.[31] As Marcel Schwob put it in his own contribution to the literature of pataphysical laughter, "to laugh is suddenly to find oneself disregarding laws: did we then really believe in the world order and a magnificent hierarchy of final causes?"[32]

Closely related to pataphysical laughter is the ecstatic laughter that marked the drug writings of several prominent modernists, including Daumal (carbon tetrachlorine), William James (nitrous oxide), Walter Benjamin (hashish), and Henri Michaux (mescaline). In a trip report from 1927, for example, Walter Benjamin drew a connection between laughter and "the extraordinary mental vacillation" that accompanied his intoxication.[33] "Stated more precisely," he writes, "laughter is connected with … great detachment [and with] irresolution."[34] As Jarry and Daumal both experiment with different aesthetic forms to represent the dialectic-bursting experience of posthumorist laughter (∞, verse) so too does

Benjamin, who paradoxically presents laughter not only as a shattering shard, but also as a "phenomenon of long horizontal extension" that finds literary form in extremely long sentences, and architectural form in the Arcades.[35] Years later, laughter would find its way into his *Arcades Project* in the form of a scribbled fragment: "Laughter is shattered articulation."[36]

Laughter's paradoxical status as both fragment and extension is present, too, in Henri Michaux's writings, where laughter causes the poetic line to stutter and distend, depending. In "Immense Voice," a poem that was written a few years before his famous mescaline experiments, Michaux marshaled posthumorist laughter to break the spell the titular "Immense Voice" holds over the speaker. In the final stanza, a burst of unruly laughter thrusts the Immense Voice aside and casts the speaker into ecstatic territory beyond language:

> Immense voices that drink that drink that drink
> I laugh, I laugh alone in another in another in another, secretly
> I laugh, I have a laughing gun my body gunned I, I have, I am elsewhere! elsewhere! elsewhere![37]

As with the pataphysicians before him, Michaux becomes embroiled in a confrontation between identity and difference. Laughter escorts his "I" through "another" and "another" before extinguishing it in a radical "elsewhere." Accessing this "elsewhere" is the objective, too, of his later mescaline experiments, themselves riddled with laughter.[38] It is there that he is able to articulate most clearly his revelation that "everything in thought is somehow molecular ... Particles in perpetual associations, dissociations, reassociations, swifter than swift, almost instantaneous."[39]

These conjoined ideas—that identity is difference, and that the world and everything in it is thickly material—are at the heart, too, of William James's nitrous oxide experiments, which he documented in a three-page postscript that he appended to an 1880 essay on Hegel, which was published in *Mind* on April Fool's Day, 1882. In the essay's main body, James describes Hegelianism as a "complex hocus-pocus of triads" cooked up by a despot of a man who wanted above all to gather the whole world in his "all-devouring theoretic maw."[40] In the postscript, though, James reverses his position. His recent experiments with laughing gas, he says, have altered his opinion of Hegel. Its "first result," he writes, "was to make peal through me with unutterable power the conviction that Hegelism was true after all, and that the deepest convictions of my intellect hitherto were wrong."[41] The second stage boosts James past the dialectic and into untrammeled ground:

Whatever idea or representation occurred to the mind was seized by the same logical forceps, and served to illustrate the same truth, and that truth was that every opposition, among whatsoever things, vanishes in a higher unity in which it is based; that all contradictions, so called, are but differences; that all differences are of degree; that all degrees are of a common kind; that unbroken continuity is of the essence of being; and that we are literally in the midst of *an infinite*, to perceive the existence of which is the utmost we can attain.[42]

The "higher unity" that is the culmination of dialectical reasoning is only the midpoint of James's intoxication, and so does not warrant a clean grammatical stoppage point. Instead, the mounting clauses cause the sentence to pick up speed and barrel over and away from Hegelianism toward a material "infinite" in which the whole world is ensnared.

As we have come to expect, James gains access to this ineffable zone by way of a violent burst of posthumorist laughter:

> Reconciliation of opposites; sober, drunk, all the same!
> Good and evil reconciled in a laugh!
> it escapes, it escapes!
> But—
> What escapes, WHAT escapes?[43]

At first, it appears as if laughter is in the service of the dialectic, reconciling as it does several opposites. But, as with Daumal's rigorous bursting and contracting, the rhythmic force of James's laughter ultimately casts him into a wild tumult where differences proliferate. Notice how, as with Benjamin and Michaux after him, James's style stutters and fragments before opening onto an extensive plain across which the undefined "it" skitters and escapes from view.

These experiments belong to a vast and varied archive of posthumorist laughter that spans at least a century and several continents. We might add to pataphysics and the psychedelic trip report Velimir Khlebnikov's "Incantation for Laughter," an iconic zaum poem in which laughter makes language lumpen and strange; and the famous final scene of Djuna Barnes's *Nightwood* in which Robin, our protagonist, drops suddenly to her knees and begins "barking in a fit of laughter, obscene and touching."[44] The point of this book, though, is not to offer a refurbished account of twentieth-century laughter as it maps onto modernism. This has already been done by Anca Parvulescu, whose landmark study *Laughter* compiled a formidable array of "twentieth-century laughers" from Khlebnikov to the Dutch filmmaker Marleen Gorris.[45] Although *Posthumorism* is interested in laughter as a modernist gesture—and more specifically, as a surd of modernist inhumanism, to return to Smithson—its argument tightens around a particular aesthetic problem. How does one represent posthumorist laughter? How does one compose in language or light that which is radically exterior to the human, and to humanism?

We've already begun to do this work. Nietzsche's zany prose, Jarry's infinity symbol, and the interplay between the fragment and extension (as seen in the writings of James, Benjamin, and Michaux) are all examples of how language might buckle and bend under the pressure of posthumorist laughter. In all the examples listed so far, laughter projects its host into unpresentable dimensions. And in every case a consensus is reached: that which cannot be seen or measured can still most certainly be *felt*. Robin's laughter in *Nightwood* is "obscene," yes, but it is also "touching," where touch, as Eve Sedgwick teaches us, carries the double meaning of "tactile plus emotional."[46] Nietzsche makes a similar appeal to sensation in *Thus Spake Zarathustra*, as does William James in his nitrous oxide note, which is steeped in affect. To edge out into the laughing penumbra of the human, attests James, is to be touched, it is to be "literally bathed in sentiment."[47] Posthumorism, we might say, is the process of resculpting language so that it might better capture the experience of touching and being touched by that which is exterior to the self and the human.

***

Touching. Feeling. Form. Antihumanism. These are the four theoretical poles of this project. Actually, let's take a cue from Aaron Jaffe to envision these not as separate poles but as intersecting circles in a Venn diagram, with the Reuleaux triangle serving as the X that marks the spot of posthumorist laughter.[48] This dense convergence point (or one very like it) is what Jaffe, channeling William S. Burroughs, calls the "Interzone," and it is from here, he argues, that an "expanded hermeneutics of modernist studies" can be bodied forth.[49] "The middle part of the diagram," he writes, "[marks] a critical zone for inhuman cruft, matter, objects, affect, bodies, media, organs, intensities, orientations, genres and gestures within literary-aesthetic modernity."[50] It's not just posthumorism that lives in the middle; *Posthumorism* does too. It skates across the conjoined latticework of radical formalism, affect studies, and posthumanism to reimagine modernism as a "wild profusion of things," to return to Foucault, loosed from the "ordered surfaces" of its disciplinary scaffolding.[51] The figure of the middle resonates with the feminist and queer methodologies that undergird this project. I'm thinking here of Eve Sedgwick's commitment to "the crucial middle ranges of agency" that exist between Self and Other, and between you and me—as we shall see in just a moment, this in-between space is the space of affect.⁵² And all these thickly teeming middles in turn invoke Donna Haraway's ongoing demand that we reimagine our scholarly work as "material-semiotic composting, as theory in the mud, as muddle."⁵³

In this book, a host of posthumorists muddle together, from Axelos to Zarathustra. In this dense, imploded zone, there is one point that is perhaps the most compacted of all: Wyndham Lewis's theory of laughter as he explicated it in "Inferior Religions" (1917) and "The Meaning of the Wild Body" (1927).⁵⁴ In these two brief essays, Lewis imagines laughter as the only extant trace of the "Wild Body":

> The Wild Body, as understood here, is that small, primitive, literally antediluvian vessel in which we set out on our adventures. Or regarded as a brain, it is rather a winged magic horse, that transports us hither and thither, sometimes rushing as in the Chinese cosmogonies, up and down the outer reaches of space. Laughter is the brain-body's snort of exultation. It expresses its wild sensation of power and speed; it is all that remains physical in the flash of thought … The Wild Body is this supreme survival that is us, the stark apparatus with its set of mysterious spasms: the most profound of which is laughter.⁵⁵

For Lewis, the feral snort of laughter is proof that we have never been human. Elsewhere, he imagines laughter as a little red flag that records our true ontological status as things; "All men are necessarily comic: for they are all *things*, or physical bodies, behaving as *persons*."⁵⁶

Although at one point he asks us to think of laughter as "sculptural, isolated, and essentially simple," Lewis's two essays are themselves rich muddles for thinking and writing laughter. In them, he imagines laughter as simultaneously "unchangeable" and "elastic" (as per my analysis of Nathanael West's "self-reflexive" and "grotesque" laughs in Chapter 1), as a "mysterious spasm" that shatters Freudian logic (as does Georges Bataille in Chapter 2), as key to an exuberant formal style that he figures as a "winged, magic horse" (as does Cixous in Chapter 3), and, finally, as a "bomb" that obliterates the foundational structures of humanism (as does "atomic laughter" in Chapter 4).⁵⁷ The striking resemblances between Lewis's literary depictions of laughter and the strategies used by my primary interlocutors in this book are no coincidence. As a "wild sensation" that refutes the humanist principles of order, reason, and progress, Lewis's laughter straddles the same theoretical zones of affect, formalism, and posthumanism that structure this book in its entirety; it is a concentrated form of both posthumorism and *Posthumorism*.

If Laughter Is an Affect

Posthumorism connects modernist experiments in posthumorism with contemporary studies in affect. My grounding claim is that posthumorist laughter is an affect, and that experiments in writing it are therefore experiments in giving form and shape to affect. Taking a cue from Gilles Deleuze and Félix Guattari, *Posthumorism* understands affects as material forces of sensation that originate outside, and function on scales that exceed, the individual human. Affects—like all matter, for that matter—are impersonal and inhuman. Deleuze and Guattari's affect theory is bound to a theory of art, indeed, part of their larger argument (expressed most plainly in *What Is Philosophy?*) is that affects are realized only through great feats of artistic experimentation, as the writer "twists language, makes it vibrate, seizes hold of it, and rends it in order to wrest the percept from perceptions, the affect from affections, the sensation from opinion."[58] Great artists use their materials not to craft a resemblance to the world, but to bring before us the pure sensation of an object or event. Deleuze and Guattari offer a sampler of two such efforts, both culled from modernist literature:

> Ahab really does have perceptions of the sea, but only because he has entered into a relationship with Moby Dick that makes him a becoming-whale and forms a compound of sensations that no longer needs anyone: ocean. It is Mrs. Dalloway who perceives the town—but because she has passed into the town like "a knife through everything" and becomes imperceptible herself. Affects are precisely these nonhuman becomings of man.[59]

Both examples turn on moments in which characters strain from their own bounded specificity to touch the nonhuman texture of life itself. In these moments the garrulous "I" is thrown into abeyance, which in turn forces a grammatical rotation away from the perspective of the perceiving subject: *affection* is exchanged for *affect*.

Posthumorist laughter indexes this otherwise imperceptible movement from emotion to affect, personal to impersonal, human to nonhuman. As the scene from *Zarathustra* helped make plain, posthumorist laughter does not belong to the individual but is instead an autonomous force that passes through and momentarily dislocates a person from their subjectivity. In this moment of dislocation, laughter forges an aperture in which an alternative mode of existence, impersonal yet singular, may come rushing in. The suspicion that laughter does not belong to us has a B-movie glow to it that we will see refracted through every scene under consideration here, from the sci-fi surfaces of Smithson's ha-ha-crystal through the body horror blur of Nathanael West's grotesque laughter to the inhuman shriek of "atomic laughter" as it is defined in the penultimate chapter. To be overrun by a somatic sound that deforms our meaning-making systems is the stuff of horror, to be sure. But the point of *Posthumorism* is that our intrepid travelers come back from this strange milieu carrying with them what Smithson calls a "new kind of sight."[60] This recalibrated vision does away with the dialectic to spotlight instead the intimate and always material ways in which people and things are entangled with one another.

Insofar as *Posthumorism* claims laughter as an affect, it makes a methodological intervention in affect studies, which tends to conceive of its object in one of two ways. Following Brian Massumi's extended riff on Deleuze and Spinoza, one group of scholars understand affect as an unqualified intensity that is always in excess of language, consciousness, and signification. As is well known, Massumi argues for a hard distinction between affect and emotion, where the latter is defined as a heavily processed affect. In other words, emotion is affect, interpreted. As he explains it in his 1995 essay "The Autonomy of Affect,"

> An emotion is a subjective content, the sociolinguistic fixing of the quality of an experience, which is from that point onward defined as personal. Emotion is qualified intensity, the conventional consensual point of insertion of an intensity into semantically and semiotically formed progressions, into narrativizable action-reaction circuits, into function and meaning. It is owned and recognized. It is crucial to theorize the difference between affect and emotion. If some have the impression that affect has waned, it is because affect is unqualified. As such, it is not ownable or recognizable.[61]

Massumi's account of affect forgets the concreteness of Deleuze and Guattari's literary examples to insist instead upon affects' radical formlessness and attendant unpresentability. To preserve this quality, Massumi eschews structure ("the place where nothing ever happens") in favor of a certain vagueness; in the study of affects, he writes, "vague concepts, and concepts of vagueness, have a crucial, and often enjoyable role to play."[62]

A second group of affect theorists take as their navigational stars not Deleuze and Guattari but Raymond Williams and Eve Sedgwick. These projects use "affect" as a strategic alternative to "emotion" to investigate how large-scale cultural moods (or "structures of feeling" to use Williams' term) shape and direct the everyday lives of nations, communities, and collectivities.[63] As surely as Massumi rejects structure and structuralism, these projects cleave to them. Sedgwick's late writings on queer shame are rooted in the affect theory of Silvan

Tomkins, an American psychologist for whom "affect" referred to a biologically based system of "hard-wired, preprogrammed, genetically transmitted mechanisms" that together constituted the *langue* of human feeling.[64] Noting the strong resemblance between Tomkins's affect theory and Sausurrean linguistics, Sedgwick positions her own study as part of a larger effort to recover structuralist methods from under the treads of post-structuralism. She explains:

> Part of our aim is to describe structuralism not as *that mistaken thing that happened before poststructuralism but fortunately led directly to it*, but rather as part of a rich moment, a rich intellectual ecology, a gestalt (including systems theory) that allowed it to mean more different and more interesting things than have survived its sleek trajectory into poststructuralism.[65]

Glossing Tomkins, Sedgwick elsewhere defines affect as a fixed structural arrangement that can manifest itself in any number of ways: "[A]ffects can be attached to things, people, ideas, sensations, relations, activities, ambitions, institutions, and any number of other things, including other affects. Thus, one can be excited by anger, disgusted by shame, or surprised by joy."[66] Sedgwick's structuralism is still felt in contemporary studies of affect, which tend to isolate a feeling—happiness (Ahmed), mourning (Eng), or in the case of Berlant's *Cruel Optimism*, the promise of the good life—and read it as a fixed social relation that can *feel* any number of ways.[67] As Berlant puts it, "the emotions vary, while the affective structure remains."[68]

Although Massumi and Sedgwick are proxies of two very different affect theories, they share an itching impatience with psychoanalytic discourse and its insistence of the first-person declarative as the gold standard for how we testify to, think about, and analyze feeling. The psychoanalyst's leading question, "Now tell me, how do you feel?" presumes that feeling is (1) personal and (2) narratable, but as affect theorists from both camps are wont to tell us, there are speeds and styles of feeling that are neither. Affect theory is founded on this negative gesture, and it has struggled in the intervening years to build a positive model of its critical object. This is most obviously true in the case of Massumi's affect theory, which defines affect in terms of emotion, which is to say, in terms of what it is not. As Eugenie Brinkema has sharply noted,

> one of the symptoms of appeals to affect in the negative theoretical sense—as signaling principally a rejection: *not* semiosis, *not* meaning, *not* structure, *not* apparatus, but the felt visceral, immediate, sensed, embodied, excessive—is that "affect" in the turn to affect has been deployed almost exclusively in the singular, as the capacity for movement of disturbance in general.[69]

Although Massumi's often maddeningly vague formulations are a prime target for such critiques, the problem of positively locating specific affects is felt on both sides. In *The Long Revolution* (1961), for example, Raymond Williams develops his influential notion of structures of feeling, those "social experiences *in solution*" that, like Massumi's intensities, exist on very cusp of articulation and measurability.[70] As its name suggests, a structure of feeling lends itself to a structuralist analysis—Williams suggests that we can apprehend them only by casting our eye across a large set of texts (both literary and nonliterary) in search of a common configuration or pattern of elements. This method cannot help but conceive of both affect and form in broad strokes—a tectonic shift in feeling becomes identifiable, for example, in the arrival of a new literary genre such as the "Welsh industrial novel," or the "new novel of Sarraute or Robbe-Grillet."[71]

Posthumorism trips up these two operating systems in interesting ways. As a contagious convulsion that torques the face, vibrates the air, and scars the page, its laughter is too brutishly present to qualify as an affect in the soft-focus sense suggested by Massumi. And while laughter can certainly take hold of and move through a social body as a contagious force that can feel any number of ways, it is ultimately of a different species to the second camp's critical objects, which roughly map onto the existing taxonomy of human emotions. Posthumorist laughter might also seem too, well, *weird* to sit comfortably with such company, which is mostly drawn to the low-key throb of everyday feelings for what they can tell us about life under capitalism. To recognize laughter as an affect is to slip, then, between these two camps and their attendant methodologies. *Posthumorism* conceives of affects neither as formless intensities as per Massumi, nor as a fixed structural relation that invites a set of *why* questions like "Why do we feel bad?" or "Why do we desire that which harms us?" Instead, it re-roots itself in Deleuze and Guattari to recognize affects as radically material, radiantly inhuman forces that are realized in and through experimental artistic practices. Posthumorist laughter is a valuable case study in the study of affect precisely because it can and does take on literary form, although to achieve this, writers must design ways to short-circuit language's representational abilities.

Others share my conviction that affects can take specific textual forms. Eugenie Brinkema's book *The Forms of the Affects* discovers affects in the minute formal aspects of the filmic body, in its light, lines, curves, and colors. Her close reading of the survival horror film *Open Water*, for example, locates the cinematic form of anxiety in the interrupted horizontal line that serves as the break between sea and sky. Sianne Ngai is similarly attentive to the forms affects take. In *Ugly Feelings,* she defines affects as a set of feelings that forever equivocate between the subjective and the objective. Because of the centrality of ambivalence to Ngai's take on affect, she won't say, as Brinkema does, that an affect can take on a pure, objective form. Instead, she discovers various formal equivocations in both literature and cinema that she argues concretely render the back and forth that constitutes affect. In a reading of Coppola's surveillance thriller *The Conversation*, for example, Ngai locates the cinematic form of paranoia in a shifting, shifty style of filmmaking that flickers between "first- and third-person enunciations within a single shot."[72] Medium matters. As a human body moves and communicates differently in water than it does on land, so affects behave differently in literature than they do in film. *Posthumorism* restricts its focus mostly to literary portraits of laughter to investigate how a group of writers make use of their materials—poetic language, grammar, syntax, and orthography—to render posthumorist laughter on the page or screen.

Our motivating question now carries tucked within it at least two others. When we ask, "What is the shape of laughter?" we are also asking, "What is the shape of an affect?" and more broadly, "What is the shape of writing after humanism?" To claim modernist experiments in laughter as early adventures in affect theory is to recover a large and largely unexpected archive of writings that each offers their own answer to these three questions. As we shall see, writing laughter as an affect in language, rather than as the affectation of a human being, is no easy enterprise. How do we say laughter? To figure laughter as something other than an expression and index of the human, writers must rewire language's conventions and structures. Again and again and in different ways, Nathanael West, Georges Bataille, and Hélène Cixous, as well as a host of other posthumorists, use the material burst of laughter to stall the sentence, the signal, the image, and the imaginary. When this signal-jamming is at its sharpest and most formidable, the posthumorist no longer needs to narrate or transcribe laughter—there are no more "he laughed" or "ha-ha"s. Instead, they discover a way to pass laughter through language, to intone language with the gesture of laughing. They learn how to *make the language laugh*.[73]

On Affectology

I call this posthumorist practice *affectology*. An affectology is a set of formal techniques that reconfigure a medium so that affects can pass directly through it without distortion. Its defining gesture, then, is the resequencing of the ordinary power relations between language and affect; in an affectology, language is disfigured in the presence of affect, and not the other way around. This reversal means that there are no more "I feel" statements that translate affect into emotion (as in "I feel happy" or "I feel sad"); instead, the author carries out a series of experiments to solicit affect without summoning the individual, or the human. Every affectological operation is therefore an exploit in the sense meant by Alexander Galloway and Eugene Thacker—it is a spanner thrust in the anthropological machine's language center.[74] Of course, the problem of how to give form to that which lies outside the human is not limited to writers of affect.[75] For the past thirty years or so, critical theory has been slowly rotating toward that same uncanny milieu from which posthumorism springs, and it has discovered there a whole array of other nonhuman forces and systems, from Timothy Morton's "strange strangers" to Karen Barad's "self-touching electron."[76] While *Posthumorism* takes as its focus the experimental writing of affect, its findings are relevant too to the writing of other nonhuman objects and events.

The process of passing affect through language is necessarily experimental and artistic, and so all affectologies are creative-critical. Consider, for example, Kathleen Stewart's landmark work in affectology, *Ordinary Affects* (2007). Stewart understands that the task of theorizing affect is the task of finding compositional strategies capable of rendering its textures and forms on the page. In the introduction, she describes her project:

> This book tries to slow the quick jump to representational thinking and evaluative critique long enough to find ways of approaching the complex and uncertain objects that fascinate because they literally hit us or exert a pull on us. My effort here is not to finally "know" them—to collect them into a good enough story of what's going on—but to fashion some form of address that is adequate to their form; to find something to say about ordinary affects by performing some of the intensity and texture that makes them habitable and animate.[77]

Stewart hesitates to accept logos—its acquisition and accumulation—as the end-goal of criticism. Instead, she understands herself as enacting a performative style of storytelling that shapes itself in response to, rather than in spite of, its critical object. Stewart's own affectology hinges on an aesthetics of slowness. As she explains in the above passage, *Ordinary Affects* aims to decelerate the reader's eye so that they might tarry a while among the affects that charge ordinary life. A batch of affectological techniques help achieve this effect, but I'll focus here on just two: first, the various hedging tactics that interrupt the book's forward propulsion, and second, Stewart's experimental remediation of the still life as a literary form.

Ordinary Affects is riven with hedging devices, but perhaps the most prominent are the parentheses that litter its pages. Repeatedly in the book, Stewart uses brackets to jimmy open sentences and wedge in narrative alternatives, most often in the form of the construction "or not," as in, you're "getting messed up and recovering (or not), looking for love (or not), trying to get into something, or trying to get out of something."[78] That word "something" repeats with some regularity in the book and constitutes a second form of hedging. Stewart knows that we cannot skim-read a something; its non-specificity impedes our easy recognition of its contents, which are liable to change depending on the context. Stewart uses the word to craft what I call dangling similes, which are similes that are without a concrete referent. An example appears in the book's opening few lines: "Something surges into view like a snapped live wire."[79] Stewart does not articulate what this "something" is—we cannot definitively say whether it refers to a sudden wave of undirected fear (or not), a glimpse of a face in a house window (or not), or a flutter of leaves on the pavement (or not). Stewart's "something" models her preference for description over analysis: we are asked to give up our desire to know the thing itself and instead pay sustained attention to what it is *like*, how it behaves in and acts on the world.

Stewart further decelerates the reader's eye through her development of another affectological technique: the remediation of the still life as a literary form. "In painting," she says, "a still life is a genre that captures the liveness of inanimate objects (fruit, flowers, bowls) by suspending their sensory beauty in an intimate scene charged with the textures of paint and desire."[80] Stewart is attracted to the still life because she sees its will to inaction as paradoxically creating a field of "vibratory motion."[81] Nothing frozen can stay. In the visual arts, the still life suggests movement, or more specifically, the moment unto movement, the move-to-movement. Plums jostle and water globules quiver, and we watch and wait for the fruit to rot and the liquid's surface to tremble. In *Ordinary Affects*, Stewart uses the still life to give material form to affects' potentiality. The book is held together by unpopulated scenes that are nevertheless charged with the momentum of past movements: "a living room strewn with ribbons and wine glasses after a party," "a chair overturned."[82] Like that *something*, these still lifes are under-determined to such a degree that they cause, according to Stewart, a "simple stopping" that enables the reader to register the weird dimensions of a scene without us.[83] (Hélène Cixous's affectology shares a similar synesthetic imagination, whereby one medium is made to mimic the sensual forms and sensory effects of another; more on which in Chapter 3.)

Stewart gets closest to articulating the critical value of affectology in an earlier essay, where she explains that "writing culture through emergent forms means stepping outside the cold comfort zone of recognizing only self-identical objects."[84] The cold critic conceives of the text (and the world) as a reflective surface, and so can only ever see themselves, *mise en abyme*. The project of *Ordinary Affects* is to reverse this scholarly disposition by developing slow forms of writing and reading that are capable of recognizing affects without compacting them into neat units of knowledge. Stewart warns us that subscribing to her affectology might result in withdrawal symptoms—a pang, perhaps, for the "cold" feeling of omniscience that comes with our cultivation of a bird's eye view, or the "comfort" that accompanies our sense of interpretative closure. There can be no omniscience and no closure here (indeed, the last vignette of her book is titled "Beginnings"). This open-endedness is the sign of a successful affectology that, rather than forcing its object of study to accord to its own intransigent forms, attempts to evoke and inhabit an affect or affects as they begin to unfold.

Posthumorism is intended as a commentary on, rather than a contribution to, affectology. Its project is to analyze through slow, sustained close readings the specific ways in which a handful of posthumorists use laughter to reshape literary language and critical discourse. This approach distinguishes *Posthumorism* from other scholarly studies of twentieth-century laughter, which tend to mimic laughter's qualities of fragmentation and extension by moving horizontally between several texts, rather than digging down into a few.[85] The two most well read of these are Diane D. Davis's *Breaking Up (at) Totality* (2000) and Anca Parvulescu's *Laughter: Notes on a Passion* (2010). In Davis's *Breaking Up*, we encounter together for the first time some of the biggest names in posthumorism, from Nietzsche and Bataille to Derrida, Foucault, Kristeva, and Cixous. A decade later, Parvulescu supplemented Davis's archive with a flurry of other scenes of laughter that go both long (Erasmus, Thomas Hobbes) and wide (the letters of the Earl of Shaftesbury, the Dutch film *A Question of Silence*). This kind of archival work is always difficult, but it is especially so in the case of laughter, which is by nature fleeting. Posthumorist laughter often appears only as a single passage in a much larger work—Foucault's Preface to *The Order of Things* is a good example of this. (It's also striking how often posthumorist laughter can be found lurking in ancillary texts; in prefaces and afterwords, footnotes and addendums).[86] To trace the burst of laughter as it erupts across the face of the twentieth century, the researcher must craft what Jack Halberstam has in another context called "scavenger methodologies."[87] The scavenger raids any and every aesthetic form, critical method, and academic discipline to create a singular, inclusive archive that extends across great distances.

Although *Posthumorism* does contribute a few extra texts to the archive of twentieth-century laughter, it does not share Davis and Parvulescu's archival aspirations. Instead, it hooks posthumorist laughter up to affect studies. This reorientation of critical focus sees a reorientation in method: the drift of fragments is hereby exchanged for the detailed case study. If the posthumorists are right and laughter opens onto new ontological and epistemological modes based in entanglement rather than separability, then the question of form becomes crucial. How are we to recognize the dimensions and movements of these new modes if not through their forms? Scholars of affect are quick to point out that their critical object necessitates a shift in how we apprehend the world; to catch affect in the act we must train our eye on the transversal spaces between people, rather than the people themselves, and to the swollen moment before an action, rather than the action itself.[88] But this new style of looking is rarely leveraged into a new style of writing and reading. Kathleen Stewart, of course, is an important exception, as is Eve Sedgwick, whose willingness to disturb the conventions of academic writing in pursuit of a non-dualistic mode of expression thrills me. *Posthumorism* moves between posthumorist fiction and philosophy to add three more exceptions to the pile: Nathanael West's final novel *The Day of the Locust*, Georges Bataille's *Atheological Summa*, and Hélène Cixous's *The Book of Promethea*. The final chapter passes freely between literature and theory through connected close readings of selections by Michel Foucault, Kurt Vonnegut, and Stanley Kubrick, and the book's coda sails into the uncanny digital spaces of YouTube and Reddit to discover what "writing" laughter online looks like.

In the Shadow of the Asylum

As its name suggests, one of the primary gestures of posthumorism is its rejection of humor as a heuristic for understanding laughter. There are no humorous stimuli that can explain Smithson's ha-ha-crystal or Wyndham Lewis's sculptural snort. The shared etymology of *humor* and *human* is instructive here: since antiquity, philosophers and scientists have used humor to confirm our status as rational, thinking beings, from Aristotle's famous claim that humans are "the only animal that laughs" to Darwin's notes on laughter as an expression of human emotion.[89] For centuries, these writings were scattered as so many fragments across so many texts, but in the early years of the twentieth century, scholars started to assemble them into one traversable field of knowledge. Three theories would come to dominate and so organize this nascent field, each of which reinforced a model of subjectivity based in rational self-containment: the superiority theory, the incongruity-resolution theory, and the relief theory. Superiority: I laugh because you have failed, and I am not you. Incongruity-Resolution: my laughter is the cry of victory at detecting and resolving an incongruity that threatened my Weltanschauung. Relief: I laugh because in a moment of danger I consolidated myself; I remain untouched and unharmed.[90] That humor studies emerged in tandem with posthumorist laughter is therefore no coincidence; its goal was to guard the connections between laughter, humor, and humanism that Nietzsche and others sought to break. It is humor studies that conscripts laughter to the humanist project, and it is from humor studies that posthumorist laughter, and *Posthumorism*, seeks to escape.

Published in 1900, Henri Bergson's *Laughter: An Essay on the Meaning of the Comic* served as both herald and model for the emergence of humor studies in the twentieth century. Bergson anticipates this in his introduction, where he explains that his observations would have "less bearing on the actually comic than on the field within which it must be sought."[91] What is immediately striking about *Laughter* is the cool elegance with which it disposes of laughter. In his preface, Bergson asks "What does laughter mean?" before admitting the impossibility of answering such a question. Laughter, he explains, has the "knack of baffling every effort, of slipping away and escaping only to bob up again, a pert challenge flung at philosophic speculation."[92] Having flagged laughter as an impossible object, the rest of Bergson's book is dedicated to the careful curation and dissection of the *laughable*. Bergson analyzes a host of comic objects, actions, and situations—the pratfall, the hunchback, and the stutterer, among others—in search of a common principle that answers not his original inquiry into what laughter means, but an alternate question, *why* do we laugh? Bergson's answer to this question posits laughter as an antidote to "a certain mechanical inelasticity" in modern man. It is, he writes, "a social gesture that singles out and represses a special kind of absentmindedness."[93] In his effort to maintain a model of the human being as self-contained and socially productive, Bergson strategically omits other types of laughter—the disjunctive spasms or contagious wails that may disrupt the social or dissolve the individual. Laughter is figured throughout as a jolly policeman dedicated to corroborating rather than corroding the individual.[94] "We have," he writes, "regarded laughter as first and foremost a means of correction."[95]

Following Bergson, humor studies scholars took to politely admitting the intellectual impasse of laughter before redirecting the reader's attention elsewhere. Published in 1928, C.W. Kimmins's *The Springs of Laughter* provides one of the first examples of this maneuver. Mimicking Bergson, Kimmins begins with a rueful confession of the "hopeless task ... to secure anything approaching a common principle" of laughter, before launching into three chapter-length summaries of each dominant theory of humor.[96] By the latter half of the twentieth century this model had become standard fare. A slew of disciplinary handbooks on humor appeared in the 1970s and 1980s, each of which rendered laughter synonymous with the laughable and so evacuated from discussion any of its forms that did not abide by the rational rules of humor.[97] The last and most complete of such handbooks, entitled *The Philosophy of Laughter and Humor*, culminates with an essay by Roger Scruton misleadingly titled "Laughter," which begins with an explicit disavowal of the philosophical value of laughter in itself. "It is not laughter," asserts Scruton, "but laughter at or about something that interests the philosopher."[98] In keeping with the political agenda of humor studies, Scruton casts laughter aside to concentrate on the aesthetic category of "amusement," which he identifies as "a mode of reflective attention" that proves our status as "rational beings."[99]

As humor studies worked to expel humorless laughter from its ranks, the diagnosis of pathological laughter emerged in medical journals. In 1894, the French physician E.W. Brissaud published an article titled "Spasmodic laughing and crying" in which he discussed convulsive laughter as a physiological symptom of cerebral palsy. Less than a decade later, Charles Féré published a diagnosis of *fou rire prodromique*, a phenomenon in which a brainstem stroke is preceded by a sudden burst of laughter.[100] Translated as "pathological laughter," this rare form of apoplectic laughter has become a catch-all symptom of a wide range of nervous and mental diseases, from pseudobulbar palsy to schizophrenia and hysteria. In the 1980s, Donald Black offered a modern definition of the condition as a "laughter that is not proportionate to the emotional stimulus and so is inappropriate, unrestrained, or uncontrollable (forced); alternatively it may exist when laughter is dissociated from any recognizable stimulus."[101] Notice that Black's diagnostic description of pathological laughter is the mirror image of Bergson's normative model of laughter. If Bergsonian laughter brings an absentminded individual "back to complete self-consciousness," then pathological laughter is, to use Black's freighted language, "disassociated" from any humorous stimulus.[102] Bound by their shared perception of what a human being should look, act, and sound like, humor studies and the clinic concatenated into a single disciplinary apparatus that worked to control and contain laughter's inhuman, impersonal properties.

The tension between humor and laughter structures each of my four chapters to differing degrees. The further *Posthumorism* advances, the further away we get from humor studies. Chapter 1 shows the extent to which humor studies has insinuated itself in literary criticism by detailing the critical reception of Nathanael West's *The Day of the Locust*, before providing a model for reading West in terms of his laughter, not his humor. Chapter 2, "Georges Bataille's Affectology," reads the complicated divergence of laughter from humor through Georges Bataille's personal rivalry with André Breton. Their final spat, which prompted the disunion of the Surrealist movement in 1929, was predicated on their irresolvable philosophical commitments: Bataille to a heteroclite materialism that crystallizes in a burst of ecstatic laughter, and Breton to an increasingly self-centered idealism that he would later use to construct his theory of humour noir. Remaining on French soil for a little while longer, the third chapter asks after the laugh of Hélène Cixous, which is not the same thing as the laugh of the Medusa. As with the first chapter, the goal here is to understand Cixous's laughter not as the sign of a subversive sense of humor (as it is so often read), but as an affect that demands the complex recalibration of philosophical discourse. The last chapter argues that American black humor, despite its apparent connection to Breton's concept of humour noir, directly undermines both it and the incongruity-resolution theory of humor, which is the dominant theory in humor studies today. The shattering strain of laughter found within, which I dub "atomic laughter," is the apotheosis of posthumorism.

It's worth saying explicitly that the purpose of this book is not to place a moratorium on discussing humor or comedy, nor is it to detail or otherwise celebrate humorlessness. Rather, its goal is to critique and offer an alternative to humor *studies* as a set of critical methods and protocols for thinking about laughter, and more broadly, about the forms that feeling and thought can take. Humor studies relies on the figures of classical epistemology—the taxonomy, the inventory, the formula—to gain purchase on laughter. And yet, as Robert Smithson's surd anatomy of laugh-shapes suggests, the modernist gesture of laughter cannot be held by these forms—it causes them to rupture and break apart. As Bataille writes: "It makes us laugh to pass very abruptly, all of a sudden, from a world in which each thing is well qualified, in which each thing is given in its stability, generally in a stable order, to a world in which our assurance is suddenly overthrown."[103] While a humor studies scholar might approach laughter from a number of standpoints—historical, sociological, physiological, or anthropological, for example—in the texts with which we concern ourselves laughter *becomes a standpoint* from which we can invent new dispositions toward the world. To be "thrown over" or, in Smithson's tongue, "thrown off" the positional matrix as it is imagined by humor studies and humanism, this is the promise of posthumorism.[104]

Shape, Speeds, Trajectories

Although *Posthumorism* is not itself an affectology, it is still possible to see laughter's shape in its rills and patternings. Take, for example, the book's trajectory, which begins in a London café and ends in the vast, cosmic drift of the internet. This geographic dilation is accompanied by a dilation in thought. The book opens with the cramped perspective of humanism as it is propounded (ironically, or not) by an alien, and its main body ends with the art of planetary thinking as it is theorized by the Greek French philosopher Kostas Axelos and the Martinique poet and scholar Édouard Glissant. Although Glissant only makes his appearance in the last section of the book, the style and movement of his thinking—expansive, errant, and immanent—deeply informs the rhythms of this book. In what remains one of my favorite sentences, Glissant describes the errant as one who "strives to know the totality of the world yet already knows he will never accomplish this—and knows that is precisely where the threatened beauty of the world resides."[105] At the heart of Glissant's work, and at the heart too of posthumorism, is an ethics of unintelligibility that seeks to devise methods of creative-critical engagement that do not enclose or abbreviate difference. *Posthumorism* shares these ambitions. Rather than peddling a totalizing theory of laughter, each chapter is dedicated to examining the particularities of one strain of laughter it unfolds across the open spaces of literature, philosophy, and film.

Posthumorist laughter swells in the gap between literature and philosophy, causing the two to intersect. In its plainest form posthumorist laughter *is* a gap, albeit one that is full to the brim with stuff. The gap is therefore a crucial figure in *Posthumorism*—you will see it return repeatedly in different forms. In Chapter 1, for example, Nathanael West complains that the strangeness of his comedy has caused him to "slip in between all the 'schools,'" but it is precisely in this little ravine that he discovers a way of writing laughter as an affect.[106] In Chapter 2, Georges Bataille theorizes laughter as a radical excess that gestates in the gap between the dialectic's poles. This formulation, as I explain in detail, is very similar to Brian Massumi's theory of affect, which he famously locates in an in-between zone that confounds the binary. Chapter 3 remembers that laughter is a spasm of spit and sound that erupts through the gaps in our faces, as in the Charles Baudelaire poem "The Desire to Paint," which is about a painter's obsession with "the laughter of a wide mouth, red and white and alluring."[107] The chapter focuses not on Baudelaire but on Hélène Cixous, whose affectology is a series of experiments in writing sound that require the author to traffic between senses and media. The climactic final chapter sets all these expressions of the gap in contrapuntal motion with one another to indict and replace the incongruity-resolution theory of humor, which posits laughter as the triumphant sound we make as we close gaps in reason, with the laughter of American black humor, which joyfully occupies and helps to prop open the same.

Thanks to the mutually reinforcing archival work of Davis and Parvulescu, there exists now something like a canon of twentieth-century laughers that includes Nietzsche, Bataille, Foucault, Derrida, Kristeva, and Cixous. *Posthumorism* offers minor readings of some of these major laughs, as well as of some of the more famous laughs from American black humor. The minor, as Erin Manning defines it, is "a gestural force" that deflects an experience, event, or text from the "major key" to open it to the possibility of variation, difference, diversion, and indeterminacy.[108] The effect, says Manning, "is operational. It shifts the field, altering the valence of what comes to be."[109] Each chapter adopts a minor approach that shifts the field in which its specific object is usually situated. Chapter 3, for example, comes to Cixous's laughter not by way of her famous "Medusa" essay, but through her 1983 novel *The Book of Promethea*, thus reversing the tendency among Anglo-American critics to decapitate Cixous's theoretical head from the vast bodily territories of her fiction. Like Siegfried Zielinski's anarchaeology or Svetlana Boym's off-modern, *Posthumorism*'s skewed critical eye causes the landscape of modernism to quake. Concepts tremble and genealogies slide, and a new topographical arrangement of people, ideas, and things fall into view.[110]

Another effect of reading laughter in the minor key is that creative writing and critical theory knit together ever more closely. Viewed along the vector of posthumorism, Nathanael West is a proto-affect theorist as surely as is Georges Bataille, and the shattering laughter with which Foucault opens *The Order of Things* is every bit as fantastical and conjectural as Robert Smithson's ha-ha-crystal. Following the trail of laughter, it becomes increasingly difficult to distinguish literature from philosophy: both draw on each other in their invention of new discursive forms that register new dimensions of experience. The arc of *Posthumorism* records this acceleration—as we approach the book's end, the crossings between art and philosophy become more frequent and less well marked, and when the book does finally end it does so in the voice of Édouard Glissant, for whom all of philosophy is a poetics.

***

Chapter 1, "Gestalt Looking," provides a model for encountering laughter as an affect in literature. As the title suggests, reading for laughter (and, more broadly, for affect) requires that we learn to shift our focus from the inner emotional lives of individual characters to the churning milieu in which the action takes place. As in the duck-rabbit illusion, both frames of reference exist simultaneously—the trick is to learn how to toggle back and forth between the two. The chapter demonstrates how to do this through a close reading of Nathanael West's *The Day of the Locust* (1939), which does its own toggling between emotion and affect through two discrete strains of laughter that occupy the novel. The first strain of laughter, which following Tyrus Miller I call "self-reflexive" laughter, colludes with both humor studies and the culture industry in its attempt to categorically fix and so preserve the subject as a preset, consistent "type." On the page, it looks like this: ha-ha. The second strain of laughter is an impersonal affect that blusters unchecked through an individual, breaching ontological and bodily borders as it goes. While West's expression of affect does have positive dimensions, this grotesque laughter ultimately fails to generate new models of subjectivity or sociality, registering instead as a terrifying dispossession of sense and self.

Chapter 2, "Georges Bataille's Affectology," further pursues the philosophical divergence of laughter and humor through close analysis of a specific moment in intellectual history—André Breton's dramatic excommunication of Bataille from the Surrealist movement in 1929—and the subsequent work done by both men in the fields of humor and laughter. I offer an anatomy of Breton's theory of humour noir before embarking upon a sustained analysis of laughter as it appears in Georges Bataille's *Atheological Summa*. My argument is that Bataille's treatment of laughter reveals him to be one of our first affect theorists, and that the *Summa* is an object lesson in affectology. Reading Bataille in this light allows us to draw lessons from his work about how to compose affect in (and out of) language. With help from three of Bataille's sharpest interlocutors—Roland Barthes, Jean Paul Sartre, and Jacques Derrida—the chapter identifies four discrete affectological techniques that allow Bataille to intone language with the affect of a laugh. What he invents in the process is a new, post-Hegelian discourse that does away with agonistic thinking in favor of a hermeneutics of touch.

In Chapter 3, I turn to another major figure in the canon of twentieth-century laughter: Hélène Cixous. As with the previous chapter, I'm interested in reorienting our relationship to this "major laugh" by shelving for a moment the question of what it "means" to focus instead on its specific aesthetic form. Drawing on scholarship in sound studies, and particularly on Barthes's famous essay "The Grain of the Voice," I posit Cixousian laughter as a "sound affect" that poses a challenge to philosophical discourse because of its obstinate materiality. The bulk of the chapter is dedicated to a close reading of the affectological techniques practiced by Cixous in her 1983 novel *The Book of Promethea*, which takes the problem of writing laughter and other sound affects as its central theme. The final section notices a line of connection between Cixous's affectology and two other artistic depictions of laughter—*Hysteria* (1997), an eight-minute video artwork by the British artist Sam Taylor-Johnson (née Wood) and the block of 982 "Ha!"s with which Lorrie Moore begins her short story "Real Estate" (1998).

Buoyed by the previous chapter's ambulatory end, the final chapter moves easily between French theory and American black humor to proffer the "atomic laughter" of its title as the epitome of posthumorist laughter. Atomic laughter is a shattering strain of laughter that emerged across a wide array of texts in the wake of the Hiroshima and Nagasaki bombings. Taking two darkly comic works in which the nuclear bomb plays an explicit role—Kurt Vonnegut's *Cat's Cradle* (1963) and Stanley Kubrick's *Dr. Strangelove* (1964)—I argue that the explosion of atomic laughter obliterates humanist discourse to create a newly flattened philosophical terrain no longer riveted by the strictures of Enlightenment thought. The chapter concludes with a meditation on laughter as an affective embodiment of the planetary thought of Kostas Axelos and the nomadic poetics of Édouard Glissant.

The timeframe of this book, from roughly the beginning of the twentieth century to the late 1970s, begs the question of where posthumorism is today. In a brief coda, I follow its trail into the twenty-first century, where I find it languishing in the decentralized spaces of the Web as a laugh-loop GIF. I look at the online practice of making and sharing looped videos of laughter, and ask what the practice can tell us about how affects take shape in and move through digital space. If humor studies is invested in coding laughter as the sign of an inner emotion, what happens when laughter is literally coded as an object for viral sharing? My argument, finally, is that the laugh-loop video is one of the most daring experiments in creating a laughter without humor, and without humans. The shape of a laughter without us is precisely this: an infinite loop, a Möbius strip.

Notes

1   Robert Smithson, *Robert Smithson: The Collected Writings*, ed. Jack Flam (Berkeley and Los Angeles: University of California Press, 1996), 21.

2   Ibid., 23.
3   Ibid., 22.
4   Ibid., 21.
5   Ibid., 22.
6   Ibid., 59.
7   Ibid., 147.
8   Michel Foucault, *The Order of Things: An Archaeology of the Human Sciences* (New York: Vintage Books, 1994), xv.
9   Michel Foucault, "The Masked Philosopher," in *Ethics: Subjectivity and Truth*, ed. Paul Rabinow (New York: The New Press, 1997), 323.
10 Jack Halberstam and Tavia Nyong'o, "Introduction: Theory in the Wild," *The South Atlantic Quarterly* 117, no. 3 (2018): 454.
11 Ibid.
12 Friedrich Nietzsche, *Thus Spake Zarathustra*, trans. Graham Parkes (Oxford: Oxford University Press, 2005), 137.
13 Ibid., 138.
14 Ibid., 171.
15 Sianne Ngai, *Our Aesthetic Categories: Zany, Cute, Interesting* (Cambridge, MA: Harvard University Press, 2012).
16 Susan Friedman, *Planetary Modernisms: Provocations on Modernity across Time* (New York: Columbia University Press, 2018); Paul Saint-Amour, "Weak Theory, Weak Modernism," *Modernism/Modernity* 25, no. 3 (2018); Guy Stevenson, "Introduction," *Textual Practice* 34, no. 9 (2020): 1414; Aaron Jaffe, "Who's Afraid of the Inhuman Woolf?" *Modernism/Modernity* 23, no. 3 (2016).
17 Jaffe, "Who's Afraid of the Inhuman Woolf," 499.
18 Ibid., 497.
19 Alfred Jarry, *Exploits and Opinions of Dr. Faustroll, Paraphysician: A Neo-Scientific Novel*, trans. Roger Shattuck (Cambridge, MA: Exact Change, 1996) 21–2.
20 Ibid., 27.
21 Ibid., 103.
22 Ibid., 104.
23 Ibid., 27.
24 Ibid., 37, 38, 69, 85.
25 Ibid., 27.
26 Ibid., 75.
27 Ibid.
28 Christian Bok, *Pataphysics: The Poetics of an Imaginary Science* (Evanston, IL: Northwestern University Press, 2002), 42.
29 Rene Daumal, "Pataphysics and the Revelation of Laughter," in *Pataphysical Essays*, trans. Thomas Vosteen (Cambridge, MA: Wakefield Press, 2012), 3.

30 Ibid., 5, 4.
31 Ibid., 8.
32 Marcel Schwob, "Laughter," in *Evergreen Review Reader 1957-1966: A Ten-Year Anthology*, ed. Barney Rosset (New York: Grove Press, Inc., 1968), 299.
33 Walter Benjamin, *On Hashish*, trans. Howard Eiland and others (Cambridge, MA: Belknap Press of Harvard University Press, 2006), 21.
34 Ibid.
35 "One is very much struck by how long one's sentences are. This, too, connected with horizontal extension and (probably) with laughter. The arcade is also a phenomenon of long horizontal extension, perhaps combined with vistas receding into distant, fleeting, tiny perspectives. The element of the diminutive would serve to link the idea of the arcade to laughter," Benjamin, *On Hashish*, 20.
36 Walter Benjamin, *The Arcades Project*, trans. Howard Eiland and Kevin McLaughlin (Cambridge, MA: Harvard University Press, 1999), 325.
37 Cited in Peter Broome, *Henri Michaux* (London: Athlone Press, 1977), 104. Translation my own.
38 Take, for example, this passage from Michaux's second mescaline book: "There is a call of the infinite, enormous, all-invading. Why? How? As the wall closes in and recedes rhythmically, and your arm seems to lengthen periodically, there are also gales of unquenchable laughter, which mean nothing either," *Light through Darkness* (New York: The Orion Press, 1963), 6-7.
39 Henri Michaux, *The Major Ordeals of the Mind and the Countless Minor Ones* (New York: Harcourt Brace Jovanovich, Inc., 1974), 13.
40 William James, "On Some Hegelisms," in *The Will to Believe: And Other Essays in Popular Philosophy* (New York: Longmans, Green and Co.: 1896, 272).
41 Ibid., 295.
42 Ibid.
43 Ibid., 296.
44 Velimir Khlebnikov, "Incantation by Laughter," trans. Charles Bernstein in *The International Literary Quarterly* 10 (February, 2010) http://interlitq.org/issue10/velimir_khlebnikov/job.php; Djuna Barnes, *Nightwood* (New York: Harcourt, Brace, 1937), 210.
45 Anca Parvulescu, *Laughter: Notes on a Passion* (Cambridge; MA: MIT Press, 2010), 21.
46 Eve Kosofsky Sedgwick, *Touching Feeling: Affect, Pedagogy, Performance* (Durham, NC: Duke University Press, 2003), 17.
47 William James, *Varieties of Religious Experience* (New York: Cosimo Classics, 2007), 477.
48 Jaffe, "Who's Afraid of the Inhuman Woolf?" 497. Jaffe roughs out the perimeters of what he calls "critical inhumanism," which he envisions as a Venn diagram of four sets—ontology, matter, affect, and new media.

49 Ibid., 499.
50 Ibid., 498.
51 Foucault, *The Order of Things*, xvi.
52 Eve Kosofsky Sedgwick, *The Weather in Proust* (Durham, NC: Duke University Press, 2011), 79.
53 Donna Haraway, *Staying with the Trouble: Making Kin in the Chthulucene* (Durham, NC: Duke University Press, 2016), 31.
54 The phrase "dense, imploded zones" is lifted from Haraway's essay "A Game of Cat's Cradle," where she writes that "Technoscience provokes an interest in zones of implosion, more than in boundaries, crossed or not. The most interesting question is, What forms of life survive and flourish in those dense, imploded zones?" See Donna Haraway, "A Game of Cat's Cradle: Science Studies, Feminist Theory, Cultural Studies," *Configurations* 2, no. 1 (1994): 62.
55 Wyndham Lewis, *The Complete Wild Body* (Santa Barbara, CA: Black Sparrow Press, 1982), 237.
56 Ibid., 158.
57 Ibid., 151, 158, 158. "The Vorticist Manifesto," co-written by Wyndham Lewis, instructs the reader to "bring to the surface a laugh like a bomb." See, "Beyond Action and Reaction," in *Manifesto: A Century of Isms*, ed. Mary Ann Caws (Lincoln, NE: University of Nebraska Press, 2001), 341.
58 Gilles Deleuze and Félix Guattari, *What Is Philosophy?* trans. Hugh Tomlinson and Graham Burchell (New York: Columbia University Press, 1994), 176.
59 Ibid., 169.
60 Smithson, *The Collected Works*, 23.
61 Brian Massumi, *Parables for the Virtual: Movement, Affect, Sensation* (Durham, NC: Duke University Press, 2002), 28.
62 Ibid., 27, 13.
63 Raymond Williams, *Marxism and Literature* (Oxford: Oxford University Press, 1977), 133.
64 Donald L. Nathanson, *Shame and Pride: Affect, Sex, and the Birth of the Self* (New York; London: W. W. Norton & Company, 1992), 58.
65 Eve Kosofsky Sedgwick and Adam Frank, "Shame in the Cybernetic Fold: Reading Silvan Tomkins," *Critical Inquiry* 21, no. 2 (1995): 508. Emphasis my own.
66 Sedgwick, *Touching Feeling*, 19.
67 Sara Ahmed, *The Promise of Happiness* (Durham, NC: Duke University Press, 2010); *Loss: The Politics of Mourning*, ed. David L. Eng and David Kazanjian (Berkeley: University of California Press, 2003).
68 Lauren Berlant, *Cruel Optimism* (Durham, NC: Duke University Press, 2011), 81.
69 Eugenie Brinkema, *The Forms of the Affects* (Durham, NC: Duke University Press, 2014), xiii.

70 Williams, *Marxism and Literature*, 133.
71 Raymond Williams, "Literature and Sociology," in *Culture and Materialism: Selected Essays* (London: Verso Books, 2005), 27.
72 Sianne Ngai, *Ugly Feelings* (Cambridge, MA: Harvard University Press, 2005), 30.
73 This idea springs from a riff by Gilles Deleuze in his essay, "He Stuttered," in *Essays Critical and Clinical*, trans. Daniel W. Smith and Michael A. Greco (London; New York: Verso Books, 1998): 107–14.
74 Alexander R. Galloway and Eugene Thacker, *The Exploit: A Theory of Networks* (Minneapolis: University of Minnesota Press, 2007).
75 See, for example, Eugene Thacker, *In the Dust of This Planet* (Washington, USA; Winchester, UK: Zero Books, 2011); Graham Harman, *Weird Realism: Lovecraft and Philosophy* (Washington, USA; Winchester, UK: Zero Books, 2012).
76 See Timothy Morton, *The Ecological Thought* (Cambridge, MA: Harvard University Press, 2010), 15; Karen Barad, *Meeting the Universe Halfway: Quantum Physics and the Entanglement of Matter* (Durham, NC: Duke University Press, 2007).
77 Kathleen Stewart, *Ordinary Affects* (Durham, NC: Duke University Press, 2007), 4.
78 Ibid., 9–10.
79 Ibid., 9.
80 Ibid., 18.
81 Ibid.
82 Ibid., 19, 18.
83 Ibid., 19.
84 Kathleen Stewart, "Precarity's Forms," *Cultural Anthropology* 27, no. 3 (2012): 518.
85 The outlier here is Alfie Bown's recent book, *In the Event of Laughter: Psychoanalysis, Literature, and Comedy*, although even that, as one reviewer notes, "[leaps], somewhat vertiginously, between different traditions, genres and historical moments ... treating history as something of a sandbox for bricoleur theorization." See Max Maher, "Alfie Bown, *In the Event of Laughter: Psychoanalysis, Literature*," *Psychoanalysis and History* 21, no. 1 (2018): 116–17.
86 As we've already seen, William James's discussion of nitrous oxide laughter is found in an addendum to a previously published essay. In Chapter 2, too, we discover that André Breton's canonical definition of black humor is from his Foreword to an anthology, and Hegel's brief conceptualization of subjective and objective humor was a last-minute addition to his *Aesthetics*.
87 Jack Halberstam, "The Power of Unknowing," in *The Critical Pulse*, ed. Jeffrey Williams and Heather Steffen (New York: Columbia University Press, 2012), 266.
88 See Tyler Bradway on Sedgwick's prose style in "'Permeable We!': Affect and the Ethics of Intersubjectivity in Eve Sedgwick's *A Dialogue on Love*," *GLQ: A Journal of Lesbian and Gay Studies* 19, no. 1 (2013): 79–110. See also Stewart, *Ordinary Affects*.

89 Aristotle, *Parts of Animals* (Cambridge, MA: Harvard University Press, 1961), 281. The adage is repeated almost verbatim by William Hazlitt who writes in his "On Wit and Humour" that "Man is the only animal that laughs." For further reading, see *The Selected Writings of William Hazlitt*, ed. A. R. Waller and Arnold Glover (London: J. M. Dent & Co., 1903), 5.

90 The superiority theory is derived from a remark made by Thomas Hobbes in his *Human Nature* (1650) in which he describes laughter as the "sudden glory arising from some sudden conception of some eminency in ourselves, by comparison with the infirmity of others," quoted in Thomas Morreall, *The Philosophy of Laughter and Humor* (Albany: State University of New York Press, 1987), 20. The incongruity-resolution theory originated in a few sentences from *The Critique of Judgment* (1790), in which Immanuel Kant describes laughter as "an affection arising from the sudden transformation of a strained expectation into nothing," also quoted in Morreall, *The Philosophy of Laughter and Humor*, 47. The relief theory is in many ways a physiological and psychological counterpart to the incongruity-resolution theory. First articulated by Herbert Spencer and taken up later by Freud, it states that laughter arises in the overcoming of a moment of fear or aggravation, it is a therapeutic safety valve, relieving accumulated tensions.

91 Henri Bergson, *Laughter: An Essay on the Meaning of the Comic* (Scotts Valley, CA: CreateSpace Independent Publishing Platform, 2012), 1.

92 Ibid.

93 Ibid., 4, 31.

94 The phrase "jolly policeman" is borrowed from an essay by Wilson D. Wallis titled "Why Do We Laugh?" (1922) that explicitly invokes and extends Bergson's disciplinarian metaphor, "If scorn is the lash, laughter is the jolly policeman who keeps the social traffic going after the approved manner, whose power inheres not in itself, but lies in the tribal standard which it bodies forth," founds in Wallis, "Why Do We Laugh," *The Scientific Monthly* 15, no. 4 (1922): 344.

95 Bergson, *Laughter*, 69.

96 C. W. Kimmins, *The Springs of Laughter* (London: Methuen & Co., Ltd, 1928).

97 Salvatore Attardo dates the "idea of a field of humor research" to the mid-1970s, when "humor conferences" began springing up in Wales, America, Israel, and Ireland. See Salvatore Attardo, *Encyclopedia of Humor Studies* (Texas A&M University: Sage Publications, 2014), xxxi.

98 Robert Scruton, "Laughter" in *The Philosophy of Laughter and Humor*, ed. John Morreall (New York: State University of New York Press, 1987), 157.

99 Ibid., 170–1.

100 Cited by G. M. Wali, "'Fou rire prodromique' heralding a brainstem stroke," *Journal of Neurology, Neurosurgery, and Psychiatry* 56, no. 2 (1993): 210.

101 Donald Black, "Pathological Laughter: A Review of the Literature," *Journal of Nervous and Mental Disease* 170, no. 2 (1982): 67.
102 Bergson, *Laughter*, 60.
103 Georges Bataille, *The Unfinished System of Non-Knowledge* (Minneapolis: University of Minnesota Press, 2001), 135.
104 Speaking about his own work, Smithson explains that "the piece is there in the Museum, abstract, and it's there to look at, but you are thrown off it. You are sort of spun out to the fringes of the site." Smithson, *The Collected Works*, 178.
105 Édouard Glissant, *Poetics of Relation*, trans. Betsy Wing (Ann Arbor: The University of Michigan Press, 2010), 20.
106 Nathanael West, *Novels and Other Writings*, ed. Sacvan Bercovitch (New York: Literary Classics of the United States, 1997), 792.
107 Jean-Luc Nancy, *The Birth to Presence* (Stanford, CA: Stanford University Press, 1993), 370.
108 Erin Manning, *The Minor Gesture* (Durham, NC: Duke University Press, 2016), 1.
109 Ibid., 6.
110 See Siegfried Zielinski, *Deep Time of the Media: Toward an Archaeology of Hearing and Seeing by Technical Means*, trans. Gloria Custance (Cambridge, MA: MIT Press, 2006); Svetlana Boym, *The Off-Modern* (New York: Bloomsbury Academic, 2017).

1

Gestalt Looking: Nathanael West's "Ha Ha"

In 1928 the English poet and novelist Martin Armstrong published a philosophical inquiry into humor that represents an early attempt to figure laughter as an affect. The book opens with a short prelude in which an alien from the planet Canicula arrives on Earth with the mission of assembling a "neat thesis" regarding the human species.[1] Traversing the streets of London, the Caniculan is pleased to detect in mankind an "evolution, order struggling out of disorder, a will to tidiness working before his very eyes."[2] Charmed by this primitive will to order, the alien begins to pen a favorable review of Earth, but he promptly abandons his report after witnessing an outbreak of laughter in a restaurant:

> He turned his head to discover that a handsome, well-dressed woman, sharing a table with a very smart young man, was in the act of throwing back her head and opening her mouth. Then the young man opposite her did the same, and together they began to produce a series of incoherent and shocking noises. Other tables which were within sight of the catastrophe took up the cry—a strange, spasmodic barking, horrible and repulsive in the mouths of civilized creatures. The sound spread, increased; volley was added to volley; quackings, hoots, barkings, cluckings, swelled the chorus. Madness was filling the restaurant … The horrible truth burst upon him. The pursuit of order and reason which had so stirred his enthusiasm was no more than a thin veneer.[3]

The Caniculan registers the woman's laughter as a "catastrophe" for a couple of reasons. First, because he arrives late to the scene, he is unable to trace its source. The woman's head is already thrown back, her mouth already agape, and no pratfall or joke can account for the spreading sound. Second, the laughter that slips from the woman's mouth is contagious. It pulses through skin, muscle, and bone to make of the individual diners one, swollen chorus. Aghast, the alien flees the scene, "rushing with horror" back to his well-kempt home planet.[4]

In the introduction, I proposed that the co-emergence of humor studies and posthumorist laughter signaled a split in how we think about the nature, form, and direction of feeling. Like Armstrong's alien, humor studies has a vested interest in neatness and order, and so endeavors to read laughter as the rational response to a humorous stimulus that satisfies a particular human emotion such as joy, triumph, or relief. If a laugh cannot be slotted into our emotional schemas, it is stuffed into the asylum. We see this operation dramatized in the Caniculan's rattled response to the unfolding scene of laughter—after trying and failing to discern its humorous source, the alien pathologizes it as a sign of "madness" before beating a hasty retreat home. In contrast, posthumorists conceive of laughter not as the sign of an emotion that confirms the rationality of the subject (and the species) but as an affect that destroys the coherence of the same. In the spirit of radical alterity that animates the best science fiction, Armstrong's experiment provides the conditions of possibility for the reader to recognize laughter as an affect. The individual features of the woman and her companion are at their most well formed in the moment unto laughter. As it spreads, they and the rest of the restaurant's clientele recede from view, or at least are reduced to anonymous mouths hanging in thin air, a room full of Cheshire Cats. The commandeering of the narrative by the promiscuous movements of an unmanned laughter functions as a literary gestalt. We find ourselves paying attention to the dynamic spaces between characters, rather than the internal states of the characters themselves.

Armstrong's prelude is a parable. Confronted with laughter's inherent strangeness, we are faced with a choice. We can scrabble for the threads that once bound us, or we can tarry for a while amidst the disquietude of uncertainty, on the lookout for the arrival of something other, something new. I'm interested in how the second option might be parlayed into a style of literary criticism. How does a text read differently if we attune ourselves to affect instead of emotion? My suspicion is that, like the famous duck-rabbit illusion, there are literally two ways of reading a text. Rabbit: we train our eye on the individual and its associated structures of consciousness, personality, and subjectivity. If we notice any upsurges of feeling that do not accord with these structures, we map them back onto the psyches of the characters, or the author. Duck: we drag our gaze from the internal modulations of the individual to focus instead on the specific forms that affects take as they move through a text's surrounds. The duck-rabbit gestalt also informs how critics analyze laughter in literature. Rabbit: the critic passes a text's laughter through the endless mill of humor until it becomes legible as a sign of something else—a character's emotional state, a writer's sense of humor, or a text's comedic disposition, for example. Duck: the critic resists the urge to seal shut the zones of indeterminacy that laughter opens in a text and instead performs a close reading of these in-between spaces and states. It is with our eyes on the duck that we now proceed.

Slipping between All the Schools

This chapter takes as its case study Nathanael West's *The Day of the Locust*. Published in 1939, *Locust* explicitly stages the distinction between emotion and affect through two discrete forms of laughter. These two forms of laughter, and the ontologies they represent, push against one another to form the novel's tense core. The first is a self-reflexive laughter, an emotionally legible and mechanically reproducible "ha-ha" that camouflages the laugher among the crowds of caricatures that inhabit West's Hollywood. Self-reflexive laughter is a carefully crafted sound that characters deploy as part of a strategic effort to fix their subjectivity in a recognizable form. In its appeal to legibility, self-reflexive laughter conspires with humor studies to render feeling as a classifiable type, which is to say, as an emotion. The second strain of laughter is a grotesque laughter, an overspill of affect that creates pockets of ontological precarity in the novel.[5] Grotesque laughter dismantles human subjectivity into a series of unstable performances, the ontological bases of which are constantly on the move.

In its ability to cast its host beyond human forms and orders, West's grotesque laughter is an important prototype of posthumorist laughter. It has not been recognized as such, I think, because its strangeness threatens to capsize a literary criticism committed to achieving hermeneutic closure. As Armstrong's alien recoils from horror from the "catastrophe" of laughter, so West's critics have handled the strange scenes of laughter that pepper his novels gingerly, if at all. In a letter to Edmund Wilson that he wrote just a few weeks before *Locust* was published, West noticed a connection between his comic style and his marginal status in American letters. "Somehow or other, I seem to have slipped in between all the 'schools,'" he tells Wilson. "There must be something wrong with my kind of comic writing—no warm chuckles and no hearty guffaws, maybe, and distinctly 'bad-hat.'"[6] The punitive language—there *must* be something *wrong*—inflects West's statement with an air of confessional guilt. But what laws has he broken? West offers a tentative prognosis: there is, maybe, something peculiar about the laughter internal to and induced by his four slim novels. Twice, West asks us (asks Wilson) to imagine such laughter in terms of what it is not: it is a chuckle without warmth, a guffaw without heart. These negative definitions disarticulate the material burst of laughter—the chuckle and the guffaw—from the pleasure we ordinarily associate with humorful laughter, the hearty joy of getting the joke. West's novels are peppered with diegetic examples of such laughter, which erupt unprovoked as a series of spluttering coughs, painful wails, and monotone barks.

In the years following his death, critics worked tirelessly to reform West's "bad-hat" comedy by slotting his slippery oeuvre within established literary traditions. The first wave of West scholarship hit its peak around the mid-1970s and is mostly composed of a flurry of articles and essays that present West's work as epitomizing various comic traditions, from satire and the burlesque to black humor and the grotesque.[7] In the 1990s, critics returned to West, this time armed with Fredric Jameson's important codification of modernism and postmodernism.[8] West's odd comic affect was now explained as the effect of his teetering between modernist anxiety and postmodern playfulness, and *The Day of the Locust* was singled out in particular as a landmark in American literature's passage from modernism to postmodernism.[9] With Horkheimer and Adorno's rabid culture industry dog-eared as the villain of the piece, careful work went into detailing the deluge of copies, set-pieces, and simulations that constituted the consumerist fabric of *Locust's* Hollywood. Such postmodernist readings rendered *Locust* as a no-exit world populated by characters that are listless, politically passive, and as at least one critic has suggested, schizophrenic.[10] As the characters were pathologized, so too was their laughter. Postmodern analyses of West's final novel hear in its diegetic cries of laughter the death rattle of modernist interiority; a sonic echo of Jameson's own mournful announcement of the troubling "waning of affect in postmodern culture" that marked "the end of the autonomous bourgeois monad or ego or individual."[11]

Recently, though, affect theorists have queried Jameson's periodizing claim by arguing for a distinction between emotion and affect. When Jameson identified postmodernism as suffering from a "waning of affect," they argue, what he was actually referring to was a waning of *emotion*, where emotion is the discernible feeling belonging to that ego-centered, emotionally legible individual for which his essay is an elegy.[12] Affect, in contrast, is an impersonal force that does not originate in the individual, but rather passes through it as a tumultuous state of uncoded feeling. Equipped with these two discrete terms, critics started to reconsider how feeling functions in fiction, with particular interest being paid to those late modernist and postmodernist texts that have for too long remained pinioned under Jameson's theoretical framework. For while postmodernism may be subjectless it is most certainly not affectless, as Rei Terada observes, "poststructuralism is *directly* concerned with emotion. For this to be so, emotion would have to be non-subjective."[13] From the slant angle of affect, our critical assumptions about how modernism and postmodernism *feel* are undone, and the sharp distinction between the two begins to fade. Considering this, scholars are abandoning the category of postmodernism altogether to reperiodize twentieth-century literary study as "long modernism," to borrow Amy Hungerford's term.[14]

Like Woody Allen's ubiquitous Zelig, Nathanael West reappears amidst the rough and tumble of this paradigm shift, too. Two essays, one from 2004 and the other from 2006, use West as a case study to analyze the peculiar modern feelings to which affect studies tunes us. In "Nathanael West and the Mystery of Feeling" (2006), Jonathan Greenberg argues that West "explicitly thematizes the problem of feeling" by staging a confrontation between cool satire and hot sentiment.[15] "The push and pull of this ambivalence," he suggests, "constitutes the central dynamic of his fiction."[16] Although he is interested in the ambiguous affective terrain that West opens between the "private, ironic, aesthetic" mode of satire and the "public, sincere, and ethical-political" mode of sentiment, Greenberg ultimately locates the affirmative power of West's novels in what he takes to be their reinscription of feeling back onto the emotionally coherent individual. It is no coincidence, Greenberg observes, that "the artistic quests of virtually all West's protagonists can be seen as efforts to resolve the tension between the claims of satire and sentiment."[17] Published two years before Greenberg's essay, Justus Nieland's careful close reading of West's *Miss Lonelyhearts* moves in precisely the opposite direction. While Greenberg understands the artist-hero as a crucible in which the unruly affects of West's world might be contained and resolved, Nieland asks that we dwell more fully in, and ascribe value to, the novel's affective ambivalences. Nieland understands the "moments of emotional uncertainty, interruption, or incompletion" that animate West's earlier novel as subtle attacks against a model of community as "founded on identity and cemented by sympathy."[18] West's use of deadpan and slapstick radically depersonalizes feeling to reveal "an affect that eludes type" that is first and foremost *productive*—as Nieland argues, it holds the promise of inaugurating "the less coercive imperatives of a community yet to come."[19]

Minor theories of laughter and joking are built into Greenberg and Nieland's larger theses about the affective possibilities of West's novels. Writing specifically about *Locust,* Greenberg warns that "the joke, the laugh, or the 'involved comic rhetoric' runs the risk of trapping its user in a jaded, ironic role, shutting off the capacity for experience."[20] Nieland, who sees critical potential in the abjuration of the Cartesian individual, exercises a reversal of Greenberg's position. Laughter, he argues, does not create an affectless subject, but a subjectless experience of affect. For Nieland, West's work "is most radical when it rejects the notion that affect does the emotional work of self-preservation, generating laughter instead from the self's undoing and ungrounding."[21] In another essay, Nieland reinforces this supposition that laughter productively upends personal subjectivity: "*Some body is affected*: the face twitches and then splits as sound spews from the mouth. Later, this eruption will be registered as a titter or a chuckle, a cackle or a guffaw, but as laughter happens what matters most is its impingement on the body, the somatic fact of being moved."[22] Here, Nieland uses laughter to disclose the work we do in translating affects into emotions. This process is first and foremost an aesthetic one: we arrest an affect in the bonds of a word.

Greenberg and Nieland's differing accounts of the form and function of West's laughter are useful companions to the two strains of laughter that I see comprising the action of *The Day of the Locust*. Self-reflexive laughter, and its related notion of stillness, shares traits with Greenberg's model. Like Greenberg, I understand self-reflexive laughter as trapping the subject in a clichéd role and so cordoning off their ability to engage with and experience the world. However, while Greenberg sees such activity as an anathema to the protagonist's artistic endeavors, I associate the two. Both are invested and involved in the stilling of ontological precarity as a generalized style, caricatured expression, or reproducible artwork. Grotesque laughter, which corresponds with a desire for motion, shares traits with Nieland's model. It is radically impersonal and works to disarticulate the subject from its ontological moorings. It inherits its name from Mikhail Bakhtin, whose model of the grotesque body functions similarly according to a logic of excess, process, and mutation; as Bakhtin notes, the grotesque body "is not a closed completed unit; it is unfinished, outgrows itself, transgresses its own limits."[23] As other critics have noted, the material flow that characterizes Bakhtin's grotesque body dovetails with an ontology of becoming as articulated by Deleuze and others.[24] Drawing directly from Deleuze and Guattari's political philosophy, I understand West's grotesque laughter as signposting an alternative mode of being that eschews the individual—that scion of psychoanalytic depth and Enlightenment rationality—in favor of an affective materiality that reconstitutes the social as an dynamic space of temporary attachments and encounters.

Self-Reflexive Laughter

The desire for stillness is most clearly associated with Tod Hackett, our protagonist and Ivy-League transplant into the mutable streets of Hollywood. Tod, we learn, is an artist who seeks to capture the churning violence of the Los Angeles scene as oil on canvas. The earliest descriptions of Tod mark him as an advocate of stillness. Watching from his office window, he waits for the commotion of the film crew below to pass before he leaves for the day. He opts for a streetcar home because "he was lazy and didn't like to walk."[25] Upon his return home, he immediately "lays down on the bed."[26] Throughout the novel he is pulled from scene to scene by various external forces: a talent scout had brought him, passive and slab-like, to LA; he wants to move apartments but is struck by an "inertia" that is broken only by his accidental meeting of the dwarf Abe Kusich, under the duress of whom Tod finally goes to new quarters. Tod always rides in the passenger seat of cars and is "pulled along" by women at parties.[27]

Tod's physical passivity is juxtaposed with his fetishistic fascination with the frantic tempo of LA and its residents. He is infatuated with and produces multiple paintings of Faye Greener, an aspiring actress who has perfected a highly kinetic mode of seduction that is purely gestural. Her father, Harry Greener, captures Tod's imagination with his slapstick salesman routine: "The old man was a clown and Tod had all the painter's usual love of clowns."[28] And in Homer Simpson, Tod excitedly finds the "exact model for the kind of person who comes to California to die," the people that Tod has come to Hollywood to paint.[29] With his "unruly hands and fever eyes," Homer is a passive conduit for the vibratory waves of violent tension that pulse through LA.[30] From these brief sketches alone, it is clear that Tod's fascination with movement is connected to his artistic sensibilities. When confronted with movement—whether it is Faye's seductive gestures, Harry's pratfalls, or Homer's shuddering hands—Tod's first inclination is to petrify it in paint and ink. Movement is arrested in a variety of art objects in the novel: the deeply engraved lines of "The Dancers," a lithograph Tod has produced depicting the Greeners and Abe; the frozen frame of the photographic still of Faye that he hoards in his apartment; and the dry paint of Tod's ongoing masterpiece, the grotesque tableaux of an LA riot titled "The Burning of Los Angeles."

Tod's desire to aesthetically arrest movement finds a corollary in a particular strain of laughter which, following Tyrus Miller, I call self-reflexive laughter. For

Miller, the mirthless laughter that peppers late modernist literature "stiffens" the subject in a "zero degree of subjectivity" that allows for a minimal trace of the self to remain: "I laugh, therefore I (still) am."[31] In this way, self-reflexive laughter marks "the minimal spatial difference between conscious life and the pure extensivity of dead nature: a difference that preserves the subject, however diminished, in situations of adversity."[32] West's self-reflexive laughter shares several of these qualities as identified by Miller. It is a mirthless attempt to still subjectivity and so protect a person from the contagious copying that composes modern life. There is one important difference, however. For Miller, the minimal self that is caught in the amber of self-reflexive laughter is the last bastion of authenticity left afloat amid an increasingly virulent culture of simulation. Miller's formulation assumes that an authentic subject is not only still available (albeit in a reduced form), but that such a model of subjectivity is desirable and to be fought for. In West's Hollywood, however, the possibility of both authenticity and subjectivity has been revoked. There is nothing singular or self-contained about Faye Greener the hypersexualized femme fatale, Earle Shoop the handsome romantic foil, Harry Greener the ex-vaudeville clown, Abe Kusich the bad-tempered dwarf, or Homer Simpson the domesticated cuckold. *Locust's* characters are all generalized types, a feature that has long been the hallmark of comedy. Crucially, though, the parameters that confine them to stock roles are not the literary conventions of comedy, but the culture of simulation that structures their surroundings. Buckling under the weight of images, the individual gives way to the caricature. The self-reflexive laughter that issues forth from the mouths of West's characters does indeed rigidify them into a reduced form. However, this reduction marks not the preservation of individual difference, but the final, fatal abbreviation into generality.

Within *Locust's* Hollywood, then, the comic has fused with the commodity to limit the subject to the aesthetic confines of reproducible stock characters. In their famous essay, "The Culture Industry: Enlightenment as Mass Deception," Horkheimer and Adorno warn of this cooption of comedy and laughter by mass culture. Laughter, which used to correspond to the rich state of "happiness," has been hollowed out and recruited by the culture industry to signal "fun," which the authors depict with rancor as the simulated shadow of happiness, a "medicinal bath" that submerges and suffocates the subject under its somatic surface.[33] This type of laughter is "a sickness infecting happiness and drawing it into society's worthless totality."[34] *Locust's* self-reflexive laughter is the sound of an individual's final capitulation to these generalizing forces of commodification as his or her singularities are dissolved into a "worthless totality." The first example of self-reflexive laughter in the novel belongs to Abe Kusich, the pugnacious dwarf bookie whom Tod meets in the hallways of his apartment complex:

> He was on the way to his room late one night when he saw what he supposed was a pile of soiled laundry lying in front of the door across the hall from his own. Just as he was passing it, the bundle moved and made a peculiar noise. He struck a match, thinking it might be a dog wrapped in a blanket. When the light flared up, he saw it was a tiny man. The match went out and he hastily lit another. It was a male dwarf rolled up in a woman's bathrobe.[35]

This initial encounter with Abe further solidifies our impression of Tod as preoccupied with stillness, which here has ontological dimensions. He burns through two matches in his desperation to *see* Abe, that is, to illuminate, observe, and subsequently fix Abe's uncertain status. Tod's reliance on vision, the sense historically associated with Enlightenment ideals of scientific observation and the self-contained subject, confirms his desire for fixity and particularization. We see Teresa Brennan's claim that "sight is the sense that renders us discrete, while transmission breaches individual boundaries" dramatized here, as Tod beams his gaze down the corridor in an effort to render Abe discrete.[36]

Abe's weird proliferations, from discarded object, to animal, to unidentified form, to human of uncertain gender and unlikely stature, are an example of the indeterminacy that charges West's novel. The culture industry spits out sameness at a manic rate and marks difference as deviant. However, this mass move toward generality can subdue but not entirely eradicate the disavowed affects, desires, movements, and sensations that bubble to the surface in these interstitial moments. The culture industry therefore produces both the self-protective impulse to freeze into a caricatured type, and the field of precarity of which Abe is momentarily a part. West's novel is complicit in creating dark passageways in which such precarity is able to gestate, away from the bright lights of mass culture. The dim corridor stands in stark opposition to the SunGold Market that Homer Simpson frequents, which is described as a "large, brilliantly lit place" where products are bathed in a carefully choreographed light show that "heightens the natural hues of the different foods. The oranges were bathed in red, the lemons in yellow, the fish in pale green, the steaks in rose, and the eggs in ivory."[37] Here, things are not only what they seem, but more so, thanks to the aesthetic intervention of management.

Tod, our very own aesthete, first registers Abe's ontological precarity as movement—the bundle, it *moves*. Even after identifying him as human, Tod cannot relax until Abe has met the aesthetic requirements of his type. In this case, it is a stylish hat that successfully "fixes" Abe: "When the dwarf came out wearing his hat, Tod felt better. The little man's hat fixed almost everything."[38] As his choice in headwear suggests, Abe is complicit in his own generalization. He paints himself in broad, aesthetic strokes that are lifted from the fashionable products of mass culture. "That year, Tylorean hats were being worn a great deal along Hollywood Boulevard," Tod remarks.[39] Abe's language is riddled with mobster clichés that he poaches from various hard-boiled film noirs of the era: "So you're a wise guy, hah, a know-it-all," he admonishes Tod.[40] Indeed, Abe has fashioned himself as a comedic hybrid by borrowing from two of the most recognizable comedy acts of the 1930s: the Tyrolean hat is Chico Marx's trademark, and the "wise-guy-eh" is one of Moe Howard's most beloved catchphrases. By trafficking in the signs of popular culture, Abe exaggerates his "dwarf bookie" characteristics into comic generalities.

Given Abe's predilection for self-caricature, it is not surprising that he is the first character to deploy self-reflexive laughter. Standing with Tod outside his lover's apartment, Abe cracks a misogynistic joke at the expense of the resident, whom he describes as "a lollapalooza—all slut and a yard wide" before laughing at his own joke.[41] But the subject of Abe's joke and the direction of his laughter become ambiguous when, a few pages later, Tod reveals that "when he got to know him better, he discovered that Abe's pugnacity is often a joke."[42] We have been misled—when Abe "laughed at his own joke," he was laughing at himself-in-general, not the woman-in-particular. If the joke is the red herring of the scene, let us turn our attention to Abe's laughter: "He laughed at his own joke, using a high-pitched cackle more dwarflike than anything that had come from him so far, then struggled to his feet and arranged the voluminous robe so that he could walk without tripping."[43] As a sound engineer would choose a particular laugh track to engineer an emotional response in his audience, Abe selects and "uses" a high-pitched cackle that strategically produces the effect of dwarfishness. Abe's self-reflexive laughter heralds his exit from the realm of precarity—the bundled formlessness of his garment is rearranged to become recognizable as a robe, and the interstitial corridor is left behind as Tod, finally reassured by Abe's newly stable status as "dwarf," invites him into his rooms. To fix Abe as a type, West suggests, is to neutralize the threat of tripping—on the formless garment and in the dimly lit hallway. The possibility of a sudden stumble into the unknown has been assuaged.

A little later in the novel, Abe once again uses self-reflexive laughter to make of himself a stock figure. Arriving at Homer's house to attend a cockfight, Tod hears from the surrounding darkness a disembodied laugh, "Someone laughed, using only twin notes, ha-ha and ha-ha, over and over again."[44] We later learn that this laugh belongs to Abe who, significantly enough, is referred to here not by name but as generalized type: "The four short sounds, ha-ha and again ha-ha, distinct musical notes, were made by the dwarf."[45] "Made" by Abe, the "ha-ha" is repetition without a difference, it signals his brutal reduction of laughter into a manufactured and so infinitely reproducible score. But the "ha-ha" belongs to West too. In his hands, the literary shorthand for laughter becomes violent and strange. He shears it of context and repeats it too often, and we become aware, suddenly, of the stark difference between writing "ha-ha" and the event of laughter, which never makes it on the page. The ha-ha bores a hole in the novel through which the reader catches a glimpse of West at his typewriter, hammering the two keys one after another, over and over. In this way, West repeats Abe's self-reflexive laugh at a meta-level, punching out the pre-crafted "ha-ha" to show the paucity of habitual language in fixing the affect of laughter in language.

The pinioning of laughter under the frame of the linguistic formulation "ha-ha" mirrors Tod's encasement of movement within the frames of his artworks. For example, Tod makes Abe the subject of a lithograph titled "The Dancers" in which he transforms Abe's ontological precarity—his shifting status as bundle-dog-woman-dwarf—into the aesthetic imitation of movement. "The Dancers" depicts an audience whose pinioning stare drives "Abe and the others to spin crazily and leap into the air with twisted backs like hooked trout."[46] Abe's slippage into possible dog form in the corridor is weakly simulated here as simile—Abe is not becoming-trout but is frozen in an image that is *like* a trout. And of course, Tod's Abe is not spinning or leaping or twisting. He is as static as they come: a planographic surface rendered in wax and stone. Further damning is the fact that the lithograph is an art form designed specifically to allow for the mass printing of identical images. The dancing Abe can be reproduced at will. Tod's unfinished masterpiece, a grotesque tableau tentatively titled "The Burning of Los Angeles," is a more grandiose attempt to still movement, and specifically the movement of affect, within an artistic frame. However, in this case the subject matter simply refuses to be contained. Tod can only seem to produce an ever-proliferating "series of cartoons," and the novel ends with the painting unfinished.[47] Instead of being arrested on canvas, the violent mob scene that Tod imagines is realized in the novel's culminating scene of violence—a film premiere turned bloodbath. As we shall see, Tod's absorption in the mutative body of the roiling crowd signals the end of the possibility of art to represent and so contain the unchecked flows of affect that traverse West's Hollywood.

Grotesque Laughter

The similitude between Tod's incomplete "The Burning of Los Angeles" and the novel's final scene acts as one of the few narrative portals between the two states that motivate *Locust*'s action. I've loosely defined the first state as a desire for stillness and the second as a desire for motion, or perhaps desires in motion. The desire for stillness is authored and authorized by the culture industry, which strives for a neat, closed system in which each and every citizen is a fixed, unchanging type with fixed, unchanging tastes. As we have already seen, this cultural imperative to *be still* is strongly tied to aesthetic practice: Abe designs a self-reflexive laugh to stop his ontological slippage, Tod creates lithographs and cartoons and paintings in an effort to arrest the feverish buzz of LA and its residents, and West himself stiffens the material overspill of laughter beneath a rigid "ha-ha" that is the literary version of canned laughter, itself a powerful henchman of the culture industry's demand for conformity. In West's novel, though, the indeterminate throb of life refuses to remain stopped. As the aesthetic surface of Tod's canvas gives way to the unpredictable, teeming body of the crowd, so the caricatured type explodes, through grotesque laughter, into an uncontrollable display of unmanned feeling that we today recognize as affect.

The chief conduit for this transformation is Harry Greener, the ex-vaudeville performer who has repurposed his slapstick routine into a salesman technique. Cannier than Abe, Harry knows that comedic caricature and self-reflexive laughter are a means of survival. He considers his clowning to be "his sole method of defense" because "most people, he had discovered, won't go out of their way to punish a clown."[48] Sensitive to the cultural consciousness of the Depression era, Harry's self-chosen caricature is a crude rendering of the destitute banker. As with his "unconvincing" banker costume, Harry's comic routine has been carefully designed to clearly demarcate the difference between real suffering and a comic aestheticization of pain. A review of a past performance praises Harry's "gloriously funny" show of agony that would be "unbearable if it were not obviously make-believe."[49] Tod recognizes the comedic appeal of this hamming of emotion, "[Harry let out] a second-act curtain groan, so phony that Tod had to hide a smile."[50] Even hapless "dope" Homer Simpson recognizes Harry's jerking slapstick-salesman routine as comedy: "Homer understood that this was to amuse, so he laughed."[51]

Harry's brand of clowning works because it adheres to the cardinal rule of comedy as articulated by Aristotle in his *Poetics* (c. 330 BC): the comic must render himself as a generalized aesthetic object rather than as an experiencing subject, otherwise his show of agony would be, as Harry's reviewer notes, unbearable. Aristotle argued that comedy converts tragic material—horror, pain, and grief—into risible fodder by diffusing the specificity of events and characters and offering only the aesthetics of pain with its particularities removed. For Aristotle, then, comedy "consists of some defect or ugliness which is not painful or destructive."[52] Aesthetics replaces feeling, ugliness replaces suffering. Bergson's *Laughter* corroborates this formulation, claiming that "comedy gives us general types [and] is the ONLY one of all the arts that aims at the general."[53] More than any other character in *Locust*, Harry has labored to reduce his expressive palate to its most general, caricatured dimensions in an effort to turn himself into a consumable comic object. As Tod observes,

> [Harry] had very little back or top to his head. It was almost all face, like a mask, with deep furrows between the eyes, across the forehead and on either side of the nose and mouth, plowed there by years of broad grinning and heavy frowning. Because of them, he could never express anything either subtly or exactly. They wouldn't permit degrees of feeling, only the furthest degree.[54]

Harry's years of clowning have disabled his ability to express anything besides the broadly signified and easily identified emotions of "happy" or "sad." Tod describes this disablement as a dispossession: Harry's head is an eerily detached "it" that refuses to admit other minor feelings to break across and disturb its caricatured surface.

In describing Harry's transformation from feeling subject to aesthetic object, Tod uses two telling descriptors that recall two historical modes of codifying affect as emotion: "all face" and "mask." *Mask* summons to mind the exaggerated emotions depicted by the Melpomene and Thalia masks of ancient Greek theater. *All face* recalls a more modern understanding of the physiognomy or "look" of feeling. This codification has its roots in Charles Darwin's *The Expression of the Emotions in Man and Animals* (1872), which was famous for including Guillaume Duchenne de Boulogne's photographs of faces as evidence for Darwin's larger claims as to the evolutionary origins of emotions. What is not widely known is that Darwin cropped the original photographs to render invisible the electrodes that Duchenne used to galvanize the face into a rigid expression long enough for a long-exposure photograph to be taken. Christopher Turner describes this medical practice: "Using his electrical devices, Duchenne could 'fake' emotions in his subject, activating and fixing expressions without inflicting torture, as though he were, as he puts it, 'working with a still irritable cadaver.'"[55] Duchenne's disturbing description of his subject as an "irritable cadaver" whose facial muscles are spasmed not by feeling but by electricity is a gothic-tinged update of the generalizing comedy of caricature. Fused with modern technology, the "painless defect" that Aristotle identified as the germ of comedy becomes the benumbed grimace that allows Darwin to categorize with broad strokes a whole range of human emotions, from happiness to disgust. It's worth pointing out that Darwin's book is an important text for humor studies, which routinely cites his claim that laughter "primarily expresses mere happiness or joy" as proof that laughter is the sign of an emotion and nothing more.[56]

The similarities between Darwin and Tod's projects are striking—both take stillness as their method and goal, and both recognize the image as a powerful resource in identifying (and so giving name to) those movements that are, as Darwin himself acknowledges, "often extremely slight, and of a fleeting nature."[57] In Darwin's case, the face is twice frozen as a readable image: first by way of electroshock, and then again under the flash of a camera. In his introduction, Darwin explains the aesthetic dimensions of his project, and in particular the role the visual arts had to play in his research:

> I had hoped to derive much aid from the great masters in painting and sculpture, who are such close observers. Accordingly, I have looked at photographs and engravings of many well-known works; but, with a few exceptions, have not thus profited. The reason no doubt is, that in works of art, beauty is the chief object; and strongly contracted facial muscles destroy beauty.[58]

Darwin ultimately found his models not in the art gallery but in the asylum, a historical fact that suggests he was not familiar with the paintings of Francisco Goya, whose grotesques pay close attention to the strongly contorted facial muscles of the madman, and so would have provided a useful resource (and a shortcut) for anyone interested in the same.[59] Goya, of course, is one of Tod Hackett's favorite artists and, I think, his Dr. Duchenne. As Darwin used Duchenne's photographs of madmen to capture the fleeting expressions of human emotion, so Hackett planned to use Goya's aesthetic model of the grotesque to capture the unruly waves of affect that course through Homer's hands and Hollywood's crowds both.

Reading Darwin's study of human expression and Hackett's study of Los Angeles bifocally allows us to see *Locust* as thematizing the larger modern project of apprehending feeling. There is one crucial difference between the two, though, one that helps us glimpse West's own stake in the skirmish between affect and emotion. Tod's painting, unlike Darwin's book, is never completed—something goes wrong and *affect escapes*. We find a precursor to this failure in a scene with Harry Greener, the clown whose wind-up routines and frozen facial expressions initially appear to fulfill the requirements of the aesthetic comic object. A little under a third of the way through the novel, though, as he is performing his slapstick salesman routine in Homer Simpson's living room, his aestheticization of emotions gives way to actual suffering, thus breaching the basic Aristotelean prerequisite for comedy:

> Suddenly, like a mechanical toy that had been overwound, something snapped inside of him and he began to spin through his entire repertoire. The effort was purely muscular, like the dance of a paralytic. He jigged, juggled his hat, made believe he had been kicked, tripped, and shook hands with himself. He went through it all in one dizzy spasm, then reeled to the couch and collapsed.[60]

Harry's comic skill—the transparency of his acting feeling—has been revoked. This "snapping" is not as sudden as the previously quoted section suggests. Earlier in Harry's routine he stumbles where he did not intend to stumble; "a momentary indisposition," he murmurs distractedly as he retreats to the couch.[61] This slipup opens a zone of indeterminacy in Harry's routine; he no longer knows "whether he is acting or sick."[62] In this moment of stumbling distraction the comedic act also loses its footing, and Homer's laughter evaporates.

The disappearance of Homer's laughter registers the disintegration of the comic spirit as it is formulated by Bergson. Bergson argued that the strategies of mimesis that constitute Aristotelian comedy—stereotyping, stock characters, caricature, repetition—have permeated modern life in the repetitive labor of industrial capitalism and the reproducibility of its commodity products. Modern comedy imitates the rigidity of automatism to make visible this troubling "deflection of life towards the mechanical," and laughter serves as the all-important social corrective to this absentminded inelasticity; it is a "social gesture that singles out and represses a special kind of absentmindedness in men and in events."[63] For Bergson, versions of comic rigidity—the tic, the stumble, the stutter—are troubling symptoms of "separatist tendencies, that inclines to swerve from the common centre round which society gravitates: in short, it is the sign of an eccentricity."[64] Without a universalizing laughter available to deliver the separatist individual back into the elastic field of humanity, we are left with undesirable "eccentricities" that threaten the very fabric of society. Harry's thoughtless, laughless stumble is Bergson's nightmare: an absentminded human fatally exiting the social without any hope of return.

Of course, this is only a nightmare if you *want* to return, both to the social and to the subject. Bergson's repeated positing of laughter as a corrective cast a punitive air over his model of comedy, the logic of which only holds if we agree that modern life is fundamentally *good*, minus an eccentric or two. From a more disenchanted vantage point, though, we may understand Harry's stumble not as a threatening eccentricity to be corrected by a socially minded laughter, but as a certain plasticity that productively disturbs both the self-contained individual and any society that takes such an individual as its basic unit. Viewed in this light, Bergson's examples of eccentricity—a clown becoming a ball, a sentence becoming a stutter, a walk becoming a stumble—become readable as blueprints for an alternate model of society based in difference rather than identity. In such a society, as Deleuze and Guattari explain in *Anti-Oedipus*, the individual would be freed from the rigid confines of the ego to become instead "a transpositional subject moving full circle, passing through all the states."[65]

In a later work, Deleuze explains this model of emergence in terms of a stumble. With the best dancers, he says, there often comes a moment in which their dance steps give way to involuntary motor steps that hold the capacity to produce difference. By way of example, Deleuze turns to the musical comedy stylings of Fred Astaire and Gene Kelly:

> What counts is the way in which the dancer's individual genius, his subjectivity, moves from a personal motivity to a supra-personal element, to a movement of world that the dance will outline. This is the moment of truth where the dancer is still going, but already a sleepwalker, who will be taken over by the movement which seems to summon him: this can be seen with Astaire in the walk which imperceptibly becomes dance (Minelli's *Band Wagon*) as well as with Kelly in the dance which seems to have its origin in the unevenness of the pavement (Donen's *Singing in the Rain*). Between the motor step and the dance step there is sometimes what Alain Masson calls a "degree zero," like a hesitation, a discrepancy, a making late, a series of preparatory blunders ... or on the contrary a sudden birth.[66]

When Astaire and Kelly trip into dance, they are not showcasing but abdicating from their training to become pure, impersonal movement. Another way of saying this is that in falling out of step with themselves (their "personal motivity") they fall in step with the dynamic drift of affects and sensations that constitute their surrounds, that which Deleuze calls the "movement of world." Crucially, the passage from dance- to motor-step (or from emotion to affect) is made possible by a *stumble* in time or space: "a hesitation, a discrepancy, a making late, a series of preparatory blunders." In Deleuze's account, to lose one's footing is to enter an indeterminate zone that requires the improvisation of new styles of motion and relation—it is an opening up, not a falling down.

Harry's stumble is one such impersonal movement that sees him shudder across the line that separates comic acting-as-object from tragic suffering-as subject. Beyond subject and object, there opens an affectively charged space in which each new movement creates a new state of being. A "gallant smile" gives Harry the aura of a stately gentleman; almost immediately he is rendered inanimate, as a "whistling sigh" escapes him "like air escaping from a toy balloon"; next, a mouth wipe transforms him into a cliché of satiated masculinity, a "man with a big mustache who had just drunk a glass of foamy beer."[67] Imperceptibly, Harry's actions exceed his command as he becomes enmeshed in a series of transformations: becoming-gallant, becoming-balloon, becoming-satiated. Harry's comic step finally gives way to motor step in the abrupt gushing forth of grotesque laughter:

> Harry had his man where he wanted him. He began to practice a variety of laughs, all of them theatrical, like a musician tuning up before a concert. He finally found the right one and let himself go. It was a victim's laugh.
> "Please stop," Homer said.
> But Harry couldn't stop. He was really sick. The last block that held him poised over the runway of self-pity had been knocked away and he was sliding down the chute, gaining momentum all the time. He jumped to his feet and began doing Harry Greener, poor Harry, honest Harry, well-meaning, humble, deserving, a good husband, a model father, a faithful Christian, a loyal friend.[68]

As with Kelly and Astaire's dancing, Harry's laughter begins as the virtuoso performance of the highly trained craftsman. He proves himself to be a master of self-reflexive laughter, with access to a "variety" of laughs that represent different stock types, one of which is the "victim." However, Harry's aesthetic use of self-reflexive laughter reels out of control to become grotesque laughter. Concurrently, his subjectivity becomes unfixed and then is evacuated altogether: he has "let himself go."

The ontological potential of Harry's grotesque laughter is revealed by the non-specificity of West's language. We are told that "Harry couldn't stop," which we take to mean that he cannot curb his laughter. However, the transition between performing a type of laughter and occupying types of self is left unmarked. When we picture the scene—Harry's subjectivity manically unspooling into a series of subject-positions—we must add a sonic dimension in our minds, even though the laughter refuses to subsist as a textual representation on the page. Crucially, how Harry "does" variations of himself is not disclosed. We are told he "jumps up," but this is the only action verb provided. It is very possible that there is zero space between Harry's laughter and his ontological slippage. Harry's self-repetition with a difference—poor Harry, honest Harry, well-meaning Harry, humble Harry, deserving Harry—may literally be being enacted by way of the shifting sonic configurations of his laughter.

Either way, Harry's grotesque laughter registers and incites his ontological instability. This is an inversion of the incongruity resolution theory of humor that informs Bergson's model of the comic: laughter does not resolve but *produces* ontological uncertainty. However, Harry does not experience his laughter as a positive liberation from subjectivity. Instead, it registers as the painful, perhaps fatal, restriction of his breathing as he begins "clutching his throat" and "gasp[ing] painfully for breath."[69] After his initial laughing fit leaves him pallid and exhausted, Harry asks for his daughter, Faye. A lifelong costar in Harry's bits and tricks, Faye assumes that he is aping suffering and dons the "tragic" expression of doting daughter. Enraged and truly sick, Harry again bursts into laughter: "He didn't want to laugh, but a short bark escaped before he could stop it. He waited anxiously to see what would happen. When it didn't hurt, he laughed again. He kept on, timidly at first, then with growing assurance. He laughed with his eyes closed and the sweat pouring down his brow."[70] This outburst is more clearly involuntary. The laughter takes on a physicality of its own: it is not that Harry cannot stop himself from laughing, but rather that he cannot stop the *it* of laughter. Laughter registers on the page as a material flow that passes through Harry's body first as pouring sweat and then as pouring noise: "Harry couldn't stop laughing now, He pressed his belly with his hands, but the noise poured out of him. It had begun to hurt again."[71]

Three times Harry is overwhelmed by grotesque laughter, and three times he suffers a painful ontological mutation. The first dismantles his subjectivity into various types; the second is an accidental bark that signals a twist into animality; and the third absorbs its affective coordinates to become unbridled "noise," which N. Katherine Hayles in a different context has defined as the creative stumble of an informational pattern into randomness. For Hayles, the randomness of noise should be viewed "not simply as the lack of pattern but as the creative ground from which pattern can emerge."[72] In this way, Harry's laughter—or, more precisely, the laughter that passes through Harry—moves in degrees away from the self-contained subject and toward expression as an impersonal affect. The three stages of Harry's laughter combine into a final grotesque laugh:

> But Harry was only gathering strength for a final effort. He began again. This new laugh was not critical; it was horrible. When [Faye] was a child, he used to punish her with it. It was his masterpiece. There was a director who always called on him to give it when he was shooting a scene in an insane asylum or a haunted castle. It began with a sharp, metallic crackle, like burning sticks, then

gradually increased in volume until it became a rapid bark, then fell away again to an obscene chuckle. After a slight pause, it climbed until it was the nicker of a horse, then still higher to become a machinelike screech.[73]

At first, Harry's laughter is described as an artistic "masterpiece" designed for the purposes of mass entertainment. However, as the scene unfolds, the artistic "I" disappears beneath the elastic "it" of laughter, which develops in a series of mutative stages so rapid it gives the impression of time-lapse footage. The laugh starts as a "sharp metallic crackle" that recalls the static interference of a radio signal. West swiftly bends this machine noise into the elemental sound of "burning sticks," which again suggests a shift in forms, this time from stick to ash. This sound grows louder until it once again becomes animal (a "rapid bark"), then salaciously human (an "obscene chuckle"), then animal (a "nicker of a horse"), then a "machine-like screech." In all, the laugh undergoes six transformations: machine, wood, dog, human, horse, machine. It breaches the borders of the individual also, spilling out of Harry and passing through Faye, who "laughed, not willingly" in response to her father's fit.[74]

Although Harry initiates the stock laugh to damage his relationship with Faye, this general laugh bursts out of type to become an engine of difference: it is a jostling force that breaches ontological and bodily borders both. In her book about the psychopathology of humor, Mikita Brottman argues that Harry's grotesque laughter is symptomatic of his barrenness; it is "empty and apocalyptic and exposes the essential sterility of his consciousness."[75] But after close inspection it is difficult to argue that the laughter is "empty," rather, it seems overfull. What Brottman must mean, I think, is that the laughter has emptied itself of *Harry*, the personal identity of whom has been eclipsed by the machine-wood-dog-human-horse-machine *thing*. If self-reflexive laughter colludes with photography in its fixing of the emotional subject as a readable object, then grotesque laughter colludes with cinema in its insistence on perpetual movement. It is telling that Harry's grotesque laughter was originally conceived for cinema as a stock laugh. Finally identifiable only as pure noise, Harry's laughter is precisely that polyamorous "affect that eludes type" that Nieland positions at the heart of his reading of *Miss Lonelyhearts*.[76]

The Crowd That Roils

The connection between affect, cinema and movement, and the painful folding out of the subject's limits is consolidated in the mob scene with which West closes his novel. On the streets of Hollywood, a recalcitrant crowd forms to witness the world premiere of an unnamed film. Penned in by police, the crowd stand "facing the theater with their backs toward the gutter."[77] All eyes are fixed on the bright lights of Hollywood's dream machine. Tod, ever the aesthete, attempts to "kill some time by looking at the crowd," but this time the crowd looks back, simultaneously deflecting and refracting his painterly gaze: "People shouted, commented on his hat, his carriage, and his clothing."[78] Frightened, Tod scrutinizes the crowd with a renewed vigor: "There was a continuous roar of catcalls, laughter and yells, pierced occasionally by a scream. The scream was usually followed by a sudden movement in the dense mass and part of it would surge forward wherever the police line was the weakest. As soon as that part was rammed back, the bulge would pop out somewhere else."[79] Tod's strategy of aesthetically stilling movement requires that he understand the crowd *in general*, its basic coordinates and broad dimensions. To this end, he awards the crowd its own discrete pronoun: "it" is a "dense mass," a singular entity that emits one brutish "roar." Even in these early stages of Tod's process though, the crowd's multitudinous energies refuse to be reduced or contained. Tod cannot disguise the various sonic modalities of laughter, yells, catcalls, and screams that constitute the crowd's roar, nor can he deny the crowd's bulging will to extension and emergence.

As the passage wears on, West uses multiple metaphors of movement to portray the crowd as a dynamic topography engaged in perpetual autopoiesis. First, it is a body of water with a "hacking cross-surf" that carries Tod as human flotsam; second, it is a rotating industrial machine that grinds its contents into a fine dust "like a grain between millstones"; finally, it is a convulsive organism that scuttles about on "churning legs and feet" and is riven by biological "spasms."[80] As Harry's grotesque laughter pushes him through various temporary ontological configurations, so here the crowd is forever mutating: it is a tidal current, a pulverizing machine, a spasmodic body. This capacity for difference on a macro scale is repeated on the micro scale of the individual. Caught amid the crowd's emergent movements, individuals are concertinaed together to form not a single mass, but new, partial assemblages. Tod finds himself momentarily conjoined to a "very skinny boy, wearing a Western Union cap [who] had his back wedged against his shoulder," then to a girl whose legs become entangled with his own so she "moved with him every time he moved."[81]

This reading of *Locust's* crowd as holding a powerful capacity for ontological disarray and bodily heterogeneity invites comparisons to Mikhail Bakhtin's conceptualization of the carnivalesque, and his related notion of the grotesque body. In *Rabelais and His World* (1965), Bakhtin suggests that the carnival-grotesque form finds its apogee in the spirited carnival crowd, which in its joyful will to variation and difference provides us with the chance to "enter a completely new order of things."[82] Bakhtin treats the crowd as a blueprint for an alternate type of sociality that would resemble "a body in the act of becoming. It is never finished, never completed; it is continually built, created, and builds and creates another body."[83] Bakhtin's throbbing crowd is bound together by the "positive regenerating power" of laughter, which in its contagious transmissibility serves to erode the fastidiously policed borders of the Enlightenment individual and return to us the material possibilities of the body.[84]

The utopian tenor of Bakhtin's regenerative laughter and carnival crowd is missing from West's novel, where neither Harry's grotesque laughter nor the crowd's grotesque body is given the space to survive. Harry experiences the loosening of his subjectivity with mortal terror, and rightly so, for the grotesque laughter that overwhelms his body is the first symptom of a nameless sickness that will ultimately claim his life. The crowd, too, is endowed with the capacity to unshackle the individual from rigid structures of subjectivity, but its expansive energies are literally barricaded in on all sides. Its constitutive flows cannot extend or emerge into difference; every time a surging "part was rammed back, the bulge would pop out somewhere else."[85] West permits only one thing to "pop out" from the crowd: Tod Hackett. The final scene of the novel, which narrates Tod's exit from the crowd and his subsequent fit of self-reflexive laughter, is the pallid, emptied-out version of Harry's grotesque laughter. In a desperate attempt to avoid becoming part of (and partial among) the jostling masses, Tod clings to a rail and relinquishes his hold only when he is secured from the other side by police officers, at which point "he let go of the rail and they hauled him up and over it."[86]

We remember that Harry "let himself go" amid a promiscuous laughter that demanded ontological transpositionality. In contrast, Tod's letting go is the apposite terminus of his novel-long will to stillness—authorities lift and carry his body to the back of the police car as a dead weight. Now, lying prone in the vehicle, Tod breaks into an equally prone laughter that alters neither pitch nor tempo. "The siren began to scream and at first he thought he was making the noise himself. He felt his lips with his hands. They were clamped tight. He knew then it was the siren. For some reason this made him laugh and he began to imitate the siren as loudly as he could."[87] Although Tod is unable to pinpoint the "reason" for his laughter, it adheres to the Bergsonian logic of the incongruity-resolution theory of humor. Tod laughs in the moment he successfully distinguishes between his own voice and the wail of the siren; it is his triumphant identification and intellectual fixing of the difference between man and machine. Tod's self-reflexive laughter is the enduring sound of *Locust*. Beyond the car's metal shell, the grotesque crowd continues to riot and roil, but Tod's aesthetic ambitions are by now much reduced. Instead of attempting to aesthetically mimic and so fix the crowd on canvas, he copies the flat sonic pitch of the lone siren. Taken together, then, Tod's laughter and the siren shriek register through negation his inability to aesthetically represent the grotesque crowd and grotesque laughter.

Of course, such laughter *is* given aesthetic form, by West in his novel. To read its specific forms and ontology, the reader must discard theories of humor that can only recognize laughter as corresponding to an individual's emotional state, whether it be joy, triumph, or relief, and instead consider laughter as an affect. This twist in critical perspective—from personal emotion to impersonal affect— amounts to a gestalt shift: instead of peering into a character's psyche to ascertain why they laugh, we pay attention instead to how the incommensurable *what* of laughter disturbs and reconfigures the very ground on which subjectivities are constructed. Viewed as an affect, *Locust's* laughter cannot tell us how Tod and Harry *feel* as modern or postmodern subjects living under the conditions of late capitalism. Instead, it creates pockets of ontological precarity that allow West to test out the affordances and limitations of an alternate mode of being based in difference rather than identity. The appearance of posthumorist laughter in a text always signals that text's complicity with and participation in the philosophical project of poststructuralism. To recognize West's work as in conversation with such theories, we must learn to resist the critical impulse to tag, classify, and otherwise "fix" laughter as the effect of humor, and instead examine the specific ways in which it moves through texts as a form of affect.

Notes

1   Martin Armstrong, *Laughing: An Essay* (New York: Harper and Brothers, 1928), 3.
2   Ibid., 3
3   Ibid., 5–6.
4   Ibid., 6.
5   The term *ontological precarity* is used mostly by a group of writers interested in how neglected populations are made vulnerable under the logic of late capitalism. Judith Butler's *Precarious Life* discusses how post-9/11 modes of censorship worked not

only to silence dissenting voices, but also to establish "whose lives can be marked as lives, and whose deaths will count as deaths" in Judith Butler, *Precarious Life: The Powers of Mourning and Violence* (London: Verso, 2009), xx–xxi. Elsewhere, Butler notes the elasticity of the concept: "Lives are by definition precarious: they can be expunged at will or by accident; their persistence is in no sense guaranteed. In some sense, this is a feature of all life, and there is no thinking of life that is not precarious" in Butler, *Frames of War: When Is Life Grievable?* (New York: Verso, 2009), 25. Closest to my definition of the term is Jasbir Puar's formulation of precarity as "the ever-shifting 'foldings' into and out of life and death that are bio-political population constructs, but also ontological assemblages of bodily debility and capacity, coming and going, rising and receding" in Puar, "Precarity Talk: A Virtual Roundtable with Lauren Berlant, Judith Butler, Bojana Cvejic, Isabell Lorey, Jasbir Puar, and Ana Vujanovic," *The Drama Review* 56, no. 4 (2012): 164.

6   West, *Novels and Other Writings*, 792, 793.
7   For critical work on West's comic stylings see, for example, Norman Podhoretz, "Nathanael West: A Particular Type of Joking," in *Nathanael West: A Collection of Critical Essays*, ed. Jay Martin (New Jersey: Prentice-Hall, Inc., 1971): 154–60; James F. Light, "Varieties of Satire in the Art of Nathanael West," *Studies in American Humor* 2, no. 1 (1975): 46–60; Jay Martin, "Nathanael West's Burlesque Comedy," *Studies in American Jewish Literature (1975-1979)* 2, no. 1 (1976): 6–14.
8   See, for example, Ulrike Weisserborn, *Just Making Pictures: Hollywood Writers, the Frankfurt School, and Film Theory* (Tübingen: G. Narr, 1993); Jonathan Raban, "A Surfeit of Commodities: The Novels of Nathanael West," in *The American Novel and the Nineteen Twenties*, ed. Malcolm Bradbury (London: Edward Arnold, 1971): 215–32.
9   The critical consensus was that while West's depiction of Hollywood as a culturally arid space overrun by simulation marks the landscape of *Locust* as postmodern, the filtering of events through the organizing consciousness of painter and protagonist Tod Hackett proved the continued (albeit depleted) existence of the modernist individual. See, for example, Dieter Meindl, *American Fiction and the Metaphysics of the Grotesque* (Columbia, MO: University of Missouri Press, 1996), in which he writes that "what keeps *The Day of the Locust* from becoming indistinguishable from a postmodern text is its awareness, anchored by the point-of-view character Tod, of a lost existential alternative to Faye Greener's mode of being as lexical playground," 184.
10 See Diane Hoeveler, "'This Cosmic Pawnshop We Call Life; Nathanael West, Bergson, Capitalism, and Schizophrenia," *Studies in Short Fiction* 33, no. 3 (1996): 411–22.
11 Fredric Jameson, *Postmodernism, or, the Cultural Logic of Late Capitalism* (New York: Verso, 1993), 10, 15.

12 In *Parables for the Virtual*, Brian Massumi rejects Jameson's thesis in a brisk aside, "Fredric Jameson notwithstanding, belief has waned for many, but not affect," which, as he explains in a footnote, "has become pervasive rather than having waned," 27, 260n.
13 Rei Terada, *Feeling in Theory: Emotion after the Subject* (Cambridge, MA: Harvard University Press, 2001), 3.
14 Amy Hungerford, "On the Period Formerly Known as Contemporary," *American Literary History* 20, no. 1 and 2 (2008): 410–9.
15 Jonathan Greenberg, "Nathanael West and the Mystery of Feeling," *Modern Fiction Studies* 52, no. 3 (2006): 590.
16 Ibid.
17 Ibid.
18 Justus Nieland, "West's Deadpan: Affect, Slapstick, and Publicity in *Miss Lonelyhearts*," *Novel: A Forum on Fiction* 38, no. 1 (2004): 74, 80.
19 Ibid., 78, 80.
20 Greenberg, "Nathanael West," 599.
21 Nieland, "West's Deadpan," 74.
22 Justus Nieland, "Editor's Introduction: Modernism's Laughter," *Modernist Cultures* 2, no. 2 (2006): 82.
23 Mikhail Bakhtin *Rabelais and His World*, trans. Hélène Iswolsky (Indiana: Indiana University Press, 1984), 26.
24 See Simon J. Williams, "Bodily Dys-Order: Desire, Excess and the Transgression of Corporeal Boundaries," *Body & Society* 4, no. 2 (1998): 59–82; Sara Cohen Shabot, "The Grotesque Body: Fleshing Out of the Subject," in *The Shock of the Other: Situating Alterities*, ed. Silke Horstkotte and Esther Peeren (New York: Rodopi, 2007), 57–68.
25 Nathanael West, *The Day of the Locust* (New York: Bantham Books, 1975), 1.
26 Ibid., 4.
27 Ibid., 1, 5, 9, 13.
28 Ibid., 20.
29 Ibid., 22.
30 Ibid.
31 Tyrus Miller, *Late Modernism: Politics, Fiction, and the Arts between the World Wars* (Berkeley and Los Angeles: University of California Press, 1999), 5. Miller's two key examples are the laughs of Wyndham Lewis and Samuel Beckett.
32 West, *Locust*, 51.
33 Max Horkheimer and Theodor Adorno, *Dialectic of Enlightenment: Philosophical Fragments*, trans. Edmund Jephcott (Stanford, CA: Stanford University Press, 2002), 112.
34 West, *Locust*, 112.

35 Ibid., 5.
36 Teresa Brennan, *The Transmission of Affect* (Ithaca, NY: Cornell University Press, 2004), 17.
37 West, *Locust*, 32.
38 Ibid., 6.
39 Ibid., 8.
40 Ibid.
41 Ibid., 6.
42 Ibid., 9.
43 Ibid., 6.
44 Ibid., 100.
45 Ibid.
46 Ibid., 4.
47 Ibid., 65.
48 Ibid., 20.
49 Ibid., 21.
50 Ibid., 119.
51 Ibid., 35.
52 Aristotle, *Poetics of Aristotle*, trans. S. H. Butcher (New York: MacMillan, 1902), 21.
53 Bergson, *Laughter*, 52.
54 Ibid., 67.
55 Christopher Turner, "Tears of Laughter," *Cabinet: A Quarterly of Art and Culture* 17 (Spring 2005): 70.
56 Charles Darwin, *The Expression of the Emotions in Man and Animals* (New York: D. Appleton and Company, 1897), 197.
57 Ibid., 12.
58 Ibid., 14.
59 Indeed, the subject of Goya's portrait "The Madman" shares a striking resemblance to the "sensitive old man" that appears in several of Duchenne's plates.
60 West, *Locust*, 37.
61 Ibid., 35.
62 Ibid.
63 Bergson, *Laughter*, 31.
64 Ibid., 7.
65 Gilles Deleuze and Félix Guattari, *Anti-Oedipus: Capitalism and Schizophrenia*, trans. Robert Hurley, Mark Seem, and Helen R. Lane (New York: Continuum Books, 2004), 97.
66 Gilles Deleuze, *Cinema II: The Time Image*, trans. Hugh Tomlinson and Robert Caleta (New York: Continuum Books, 2005), 58.
67 West, *Locust*, 35.

68 Ibid.
69 Ibid.
70 Ibid., 41.
71 Ibid., 42.
72 N. Katherine Hayles, *How We Became Posthuman: Virtual Bodies in Cybernetics, Literature, and Informatics* (Chicago: University of Chicago Press, 1999), 286.
73 West, *Locust*, 42.
74 Ibid.
75 Mikita Brottman, *Funny Peculiar: Gershon Legman and the Psychopathology of Humor* (New York: Routledge, 2012), 70.
76 Nieland, "West's Deadpan," 77.
77 West, *Locust*, 129.
78 Ibid.
79 Ibid.
80 Ibid., 135.
81 Ibid., 136.
82 Bakhtin *Rabelais,* 34.
83 Ibid., 317.
84 Ibid., 45.
85 West, *Locust*, 130.
86 Ibid., 139.
87 Ibid., 140.

2

George Bataille's Affectology

In the previous chapter I proposed Nathanael West's fourth and final book, *The Day of the Locust*, as a chrysalis in which two divergent strains of laughter are quietly gestating: the first, a self-reflexive laughter that holds an interest in self-identity and self-preservation; the second, a grotesque laughter that defenestrates the subject into a zone of indeterminacy that is charged with affect. West's novel is important because it recognizes the philosophical freight that each laugh can bear: the battle between self-reflexive laughter and grotesque laughter is a battle too between emotion and affect, identity and difference, aesthetic fixity and the creative stumble, and more generally, between the rationalizing logic of humor and the material event of laughter. This chapter makes a fold in time and space—from New York, 1939 to Paris, 1929—to recover another primal scene in the philosophical divergence of laughter from humor. Its players are André Breton and Georges Bataille, and its site of action Surrealism, which by March 1929 could no longer stretch to house both Breton's intransigent idealism and Bataille's gleefully heterogeneous materialism. In the wake of the split, Breton developed a theory of "humour noir," which he posited as the unsmiling triumph of the ego against the harsh buffetings of external reality.[1] Meanwhile, Bataille solicited the contagious paroxysm of laughter to construct a new philosophical discourse that is, I argue, the first affectology.

The first part of this chapter adds much-needed flesh to the concept of humour noir by connecting Breton's brief but suggestive notes on the subject to the texts he was reading—specifically, Hegel's discussion of subjective and objective humor from his *Aesthetics* and Freud's meditation on gallows humor from his 1927 essay "On Humour." This radial reading resolves in a deep-focus portrait of humour noir. Like West's self-reflexive laughter, the purpose of humour noir is to protect the subject from the unruly surges of affects that constitute the social field, and its protocols for doing so are aesthetic in nature. Perhaps the most famous example of humour noir, penned by Freud and reiterated by Breton, is the occasion of the criminal who at his own execution quips, "Well, this is a good beginning to the week."[2] Confronted with the brute reality of his own death, the criminal coolly crafts a laconic witticism, and in so doing is transported high above the scene. Humour noir, in other words, is a fantasy of wit as transcendence; Breton famously called it "a superior revolt of the mind," where what the mind is revolting against is the material reality of life itself.[3]

It is precisely Breton's desire to fix the dynamic processes of life within well-defined aesthetic forms that so enraged Bataille. "It is regrettable," Bataille writes, "that nothing can enter into M. Breton's confused head except in poetic form. All of existence, conceived as purely literary by M. Breton, diverts him from the shabby, sinister, or inspired events occurring all around him, from what constitutes the real decomposition of an immense world."[4] In place of Breton's "servile idealism," Bataille proposed a philosophy of base materialism that was structured around his notion of the *l'informe* (the formless).[5] The paradigmatic figure of the formless in Bataille's thought was laughter. Reading laterally across his oeuvre, it appears again and again as a radical excess that overruns the Hegelian dialectic and floods its gears. In his early erotic fiction, it leaks from mouths with an orgasmic materiality. The most famous of these, *The Story of the Eye* (1928), contains an orgy scene in which laughter mixes with vomit, semen, urine, and blood in a festival of poly-directional desire: "A young girl was throwing up, and all of us had exploded in such wild fits of laughter at some point or other that we had wet our clothes, an armchair, or the floor."[6] In his later sociological formulation of a general economy that operates according to overflow and expenditure rather than lack and accumulation, Bataille proffers laughter as a powerful demonstration of pure sovereignty because it "does not serve anything—and no purpose—other than itself."[7] In laughter, we thoughtlessly spend calories without return.

The second part of this chapter offers a close-reading of laughter as it appears across three of Bataille's works—*Inner Experience* (1943), *Guilty* (1944), and *On Nietzsche* (1945)—to which Bataille gave the collective title *The Atheological Summa*. My purpose is not to explicate the philosophical tenets of Battaillean laughter—I agree with just about everyone else that its major function is to detonate the Negativity that lies at the heart of Hegelian philosophy, and that its minor function is to undermine the ontology of lack that grounds, through psychoanalysis and capitalism, modern life.[8] To detonate and undermine: in Bataille's hands the developmental dialectic, the bounded individual, and philosophical discourse itself are all put under extreme pressure. But Bataille's contribution to philosophy is not only defined by these negative gestures—he builds as many forms as he demolishes. The bulk of this chapter is dedicated to delineating those positive forms. The first such form is posthumorist laughter. For while Nietzsche might have been the first to commit it to paper, it is from Bataille that it gets its philosophy and its politics; he is its most formidable architect. The second form for which Bataille is responsible is a particular style of philosophical discourse that in the terms of this book I am calling an *affectology*. Like his interlocutor Roland Barthes, Bataille was perpetually on the lookout for how discourse might be rigged to transmit the raw stuff of affect, still living, from author to reader. My wager here is that the *Atheological Summa* is one such "rigged" discourse, and my task as it unfolds over the next several pages is to identify the formal operators that Bataille uses to achieve this effect.

André Breton's Humour Noir

Before he began developing his affectology, and one month after his expulsion from the Surrealist movement, Georges Bataille published the anti-Breton pamphlet *Un Cadavre*, which featured as its frontispiece a death portrait of Breton. Its epilogue, penned by Bataille, implored readers "to spit … in the face of André Breton, at the clown with closed eyes."[9] Bataille's rendering of Breton as a cadaverous clown gestured toward a major casualty in the development of Breton's Surrealism, a casualty that Bataille, given his commitment to bodily delirium, was the first to identify: its ousting of laughter. Laughter had held a privileged place in the first "Manifesto of Surrealism" (1924), where it appeared in connection with the Surrealist image, those strikingly emotive, oddly impersonal phrases that arrive in the writer's conscious mind like an insistent stranger "knocking at the window."[10] For Breton in 1924, the "greatest virtue" of the Surrealist image is "the one that is arbitrary to the highest degree, the one that takes the longest time to translate into practical language."[11] Feinting from language, the Surrealist image is recognizable for its "strong comical effect" and its capacity to "provoke laughter."[12]

Six years later, though, we find Breton summoning laughter for very different purposes. In *The Second Surrealist Manifesto* (1930), he marshaled abstraction to transfigure the unruly burst of laughter into a bullwhip. "I am thirty-four years old," he declared, "and more than ever I am of the opinion that my thought it capable of lashing like a burst of laughter those who never had a thought in the first place and those who, having once had one, have sold it."[13] For those who had subscribed to the experimental principles of the first Manifesto, the hardening of Surrealism's laughter into a derisive mode of thought that is "like" laughter registered as a troubling detour. Anaïs Nin wrote that Breton "betrayed what I suspected in Surrealism, the part of it that is conscious, premeditated, and an intellectual technique."[14] Her partner, the American author Henry Miller, confirmed that "the Surrealists are too conscious of what they are doing," and worried that their "desire to posit an ism, to isolate the germ and cultivate it, is a bad sign."[15] Critics agreed. In his introduction to Maurice Nadeau's *The History of Surrealism* (1944), Roger Shattuck accused Breton of stripping the "love and laughter" from Surrealism, writing that "it is the massive, stentorian style of Breton that has deflected attention from the delight [Surrealists] took in the bizarre inconsistencies of life."[16] Elsewhere, Clifford Browder has attested to Breton's unsmiling stoicism by demarcating the difference between laughter and humor, "while not unsusceptible to humor, Breton was too much the mage to laugh readily or seek to provoke laughter in others."[17]

As Nin et al. suspected, the mutation in Breton's laughter signaled an important shift in the aims of his Surrealism. While the first Manifesto courted the arbitrary and the absurd, the Second Manifesto placed the "control of ideas" at the center of Surrealism's aesthetic project; its goal was nothing less than the absolute synthesis of reality by the poetic mind.[18] In perhaps his most famous formulation of Surrealism's revised aims, Breton explains:

> Everything tends to make us believe that there exists a certain point of the mind at which life and death, the real and the imagined, past and future, the communicable and the incommunicable, high and low, cease to be perceived as contradictions. Now, search as one may one will never find any other motivating force in the activities of the Surrealists than the hope of finding and fixing this point.[19]

The expulsion of laughter and its playmates from Surrealism, those "bizarre inconsistencies" and "immediate absurdities," corresponded with Breton's growing interest in theorizing a particular strain of laughless humor that he detected in writings by Hegel and Freud. This strain, which Breton would later dub "humour noir," upheld the principles of aesthetic fixity, dialectical resolution, and intellectual mastery that now sat at the heart of his Surrealism.

***

On March 29, 1935, Breton delivered a lecture in Prague in which he identified Hegel's concept of objective humor as a valuable tool in achieving the "final resolution" of "interior reality and exterior reality" that was the "supreme aim of Surrealism."²⁰ Paraphrasing Hegel, Breton described the dialectic as "the force that made the accidents of the outer world a matter of interest on the one hand, and on the other hand the force that made the caprices of personality a matter of interest."²¹ This struggle between outer and inner "ends in the triumph of objective humor, which is their dialectical resolution."²² Five years later, Breton would again invoke Hegel's objective humor in his preface to *Anthologie de L'Humour Noir* (1940), an anthology of forty-five darkly comic fragments that marked his first sustained attempt to conceive of humour noir as a philosophical concept and literary genre. There, Breton commended Hegel for "raising" humor from the base level of the body to the clean intellectual plains of the mind. Breton writes, "We can credit Hegel with having made humor take a giant step forward into the domain of knowledge when he raised it to the concept of objective humor."²³

Hegel's brief and somewhat cryptic conceptualization of objective humor was a last-minute addition to his discussion of Romantic art in the *Aesthetics*. Hegel finds an example of objective humor in *West-Eastern Divan*, a collection of lyric poems by Goethe:

> Here love is transferred wholly into the imagination, its movement, happiness, and bliss. In general, in similar productions of this kind we have before us no subjective longing, no being in love, no desire, but *a pure delight in the topics*, an inexhaustible self-yielding of imagination, a harmless play, a freedom in toying alike with rhyme and ingenious meters—and with all this a depth of feeling and cheerfulness of the inwardly self-moving heart which through the serenity of the outward shape *lift the soul high above all painful entanglement* in the restrictions of the real world.²⁴

Laughter has no place in the practice of objective humor. This is a purely intellectual endeavor—a triumph of the imagination that lifts the individual "high above" the surges of sentiment that constitute reality. Elsewhere, Hegel presented laughter as a bodily aberration that belonged to anthropology not philosophy. It was only when the "vulgar peals of side-splitting laughter of an empty-headed or uneducated person [evolved] into the gentle smile of the noble soul" that we can consider it as "something originating in the will" and therefore open to philosophical debate.²⁵ Hegel's objective humor, then, performs a double function: it achieves the dialectical interpenetration of subjectivity and objectivity while protecting the humorist from the vulgar bodily buffetings of laughter.

The same language of intellectual triumph, anti-sentimentalism, and self-preservation is present, too, in Freud's work on humor. In 1905, Freud published *The Joke and Its Relation to the Unconscious,* in which he analyzed a vast series of jokes to conclude that "the processes of condensation (with or without substitute-formation), displacement, representation by absurdity or by the opposite, indirect representation, etc., which we have found taking part in the creation of jokes, all show a far-reaching agreement with the processes of the 'dream-work.'"[26] Freud used these similarities to argue that both dreams and jokes serve the same basic psychical purpose: they dress up our repressed, unconscious desires in non-threatening forms—a dream, a joke—which can then be expelled without anxiety. As Hegel imbued objective humor with the ability to save the subject from sentiment, so Freud argued that the key function of humor was to preserve our emotional energies, observing that "humorous pleasure [comes] from savings in expenditure on feeling."[27] Laughter in Freud's account is not an unreasonable bodily gesture, but an emission of psychic energy that makes good economic sense.

Freud's humor, like Hegel's objective humor and Breton's humour noir, works to waylay an imminent eruption of affect by transmuting it into an aesthetic form—a lewd pun, a felicitous witticism, or a poetic image, for example. In a later essay titled "On Humour," which he wrote in Vienna in the Summer of 1927 as in France Breton's Surrealism was beginning to fracture and fail, Freud presented humor as an antidote to, or blocker or, affect. Humor is produced when an onlooker might "anticipate that the victim will show signs of some affect; he will get angry, complain, manifest pain, fear, horror, possibly even despair ... but his anticipations are deceived; the other man does not display any affect—he makes a joke."[28] It is in this essay, too, that we find Freud's seminal example of gallows humor, discussed at the beginning of this chapter, in which a criminal waylays his fear of execution by transmuting it into a witticism. For Freud, such refusal of sentiment results in a sublime invulnerability:

> Humour has in it a *liberating* element. But it has also *something fine and elevating,* which is lacking in the other two ways of deriving pleasure from intellectual activity. Obviously, what is fine about it is the triumph of narcissism, the ego's victorious assertion of its own invulnerability. It refuses to be hurt by the arrows of reality or to be compelled to suffer. It insists that it is impervious to wounds dealt by the outside world, in fact, that these are merely occasions for affording it pleasure.[29]

Breton cites this section in full in his preface before famously defining humour noir as a "superior revolt of the mind" that is the "mortal enemy of sentimentality."[30] For Hegel, Freud, and Breton, then, humor is both a carapace and a pinnacle that protects the subject from, and situates him high above, the teeming mess of reality.

Georges Bataille's Affectology

As surely as Breton's humour noir is an ode to Hegelianism, Bataille's laughter is an absolute refutation of it. There are many useful explications of how Batallean laughter disconcerts Hegelian discourse, but the first and best is a 1967 essay by Jacques Derrida entitled "From Restricted to General Economy: A Hegelianism without Reserve."[31] There, Derrida figures Hegelianism as a massive vortex that sucks all objects and ideas into its cavity of influence; all objects and ideas, that it, except the laughter of Georges Bataille. In Bataille, writes Derrida, "a certain burst of laughter exceeds [Hegelianism] and destroys its sense, or signals, in any event, the extreme point of experience which makes Hegelian discourse dislocate *itself*."[32] Designed as a means of shoring up meaning under the sign of Lordship, the system of the dialectic cannot bear the profligacy of laughter's burst; indeed, the sheer fact of laughter's escape is enough to put a dent in Hegelian discourse, which retains its power over philosophy through its claims of universalism. Bataille's laughter, then, holds the promise of rousing us from a deep sleep in which we had dreamed the dream that Hegelianism was the whole world, was *philosophy itself*. As Derrida puts it, "To laugh at philosophy (at Hegelianism)— such, in effect, is the form of the awakening."[33]

As a radical excess that dislocates the dialectic, Bataillean laughter can be recognized today under another name: affect. Although he did not use the term, I still find the dearth of scholarship connecting Bataille to affect curious. In their editor's introduction to *The Affect Reader*, Melissa Gregg and Gregory Seigworth offer a definition of affect that chimes with Bataille's project: affect, they write, is a "bloom-space" the "vibrant incoherence" of which "makes easy compartmentalisms give way to thresholds and tensions, blends and blurs."[34] Anticipating this contemporary definition of affect as an uncoded wave of feeling that temporarily casts the individual into a desubjectivized realm of pure movement and sensation, Bataille described the torrential rush of laughter as an "(impersonal) external joy" that diffuses its hosts into one "happy contagion of warmth and light."[35] Of great interest to Bataille is how laughter's weird exteriority might be used to storm the gates of classical humanism. To be caught in the spell of laughter, he writes in *Guilty*, is to experience new models of being and becoming that take entanglement, rather than separation, as their structural seed. As in Gregg and Seigworth's formulation of affect as proof of a body's "infinitely connectable, impersonal, and contagious belongings," Bataille's laughter "reduces" the laugher "to the impersonal state of a living substance: he escapes himself and thereby opens himself to the other."[36]

To further cement Bataille's status as a proto-affect theorist, we might compare his experiments in laughter with a contemporary adventure in affect. Consider, for example, this famous passage that appears in his *Summa* not once but twice, first in *Inner Experience* and then in *On Nietzsche*:

> The enduring vortex that composes you throws itself toward similar vortices with which it forms a vast figure, animated by a measured agitation. Now to live signifies for you not only the flux and the fleeting play of light that unifies itself in you, but the passages of warmth and light from one being to another, from you to your fellow being or from your fellow being to you (even in the moment when you read me, the contagion of my fever reaches you): words, books, monuments, symbols, laughter are only so many paths of this contagion, of these passages.[37]

Like the contrast dye that doctors use to visualize the branching pathways of the circulatory system, Bataillean laughter agitates and animates the intricate networks "of warmth and light" that exist between individual subjects. This reticular miasma is the central character, too, of Brian Massumi's account of affect as it appears in *Parables for the Virtual*. Like Bataille's "enduring vortex," Massumi understands affect as escorting us beyond ourselves to an "in-between space composed of accumulated movements," a pre-personal field of sensation in which individuals flow into one another as so many streams.[38]

If Bataille's laughter is an affect, then his philosophy is an affect theory. The benefit in reading him in this way is that Bataille, back in the 1930s and 1940s, was tackling head-on a question that still plagues affect theory; namely, if affect skirts philosophical discourse, indeed, signals the absolute end of discursivity, then how may it be thought and expressed? How can it communicate (itself)? Derrida proposes an answer. What Bataille must do, and *does* do, is invent new compositional forms that use the excessive burst of laughter, rather than Hegel's dialectic, as their structural basis:

> How, after having exhausted the discourse of philosophy, can one inscribe in the lexicon and syntax of a language, our language, which was also the language of philosophy, that which nevertheless exceeds the oppositions of concepts governed by this communal logic? Necessary and impossible, this excess had to fold discourse into strange shapes.[39]

What Bataille offers across his entire body of work, but especially in his *Summa*, is something like an origami manual for a post-Hegelian discourse. His idiosyncratic style contorts language into "strange shapes" that open up a line of affect between reader, text, and world; as Joanne Faulkner has observed, his prose is identifiable in a line up for its "helter-skelter movement that registers different intensities and moods according to the affect that the reader undergoes in relation to the text."[40]

Suspicious of representational language even at the best of times, Bataille was particularly sensitive to its insufficiency in accounting for affect. In the presence of those "vague inner movements" that for him constituted affect, language "is dispossessed, cannot say anything, limits itself to stealing these states away from attention (profiting from their lack of precision, it draws attention elsewhere right away)."[41] Bataille's solution to the problem of writing affect was characteristically violent. "If we live without contestation under the law of language, these [affective] states are in us as if they did not exist," he writes. "We [must] throw ourselves against this law."[42] This confrontational approach stands in marked contrast to contemporary work in affect, which cultivates a much more placid (some would argue, sentimental) disposition. Seigworth and Gregg, for example, invite us to marvel at all the different ways in which affect can take form. Affect, they write, can be figured

> as excess, as autonomous, as impersonal, as the ineffable, as the ongoingness of process, as pedagogico-aesthetic, as virtual, as shareable (mimetic), as sticky, as collective, as contingency, as threshold or conversion point, as immanence of potential (futurity), as the open, as a vibrant incoherence that circulates about zones of cliché and convention, as a gathering place of accumulative dispositions.[43]

While this catalogue of descriptors is intended to show the reader how expansive affect is, both as a critical object and as a field of study, it also suggests that affect can only be glimpsed through an ever-expanding constellation of proximate terms. Bataille takes a different approach. Rather than trying to refine language so that it gets closer to affect, he seeks to inject affects into his writing's very form. Although this affectological process is necessarily violent, its endgame is not to obliterate but to rewrite the linguistic code so that language can become a carrier and conductor of affect.

In what follows, I identify four affectological techniques used by Bataille: the mixing of subjective and objective codes, the *mot glissant* or "slipping word," hypersubstitution, and the temporality of the instant. Because these tactics share the common goal of overthrowing language's laws, they are not always clearly distinct from one another. Each exists in relation to a particular quality of affect—its excessive, autonomous, contagious, and nonlinear characteristics respectively. To help me in this work, I recruit three of Bataille's most astute interlocutors—Jean Paul Sartre, Jacques Derrida, and Roland Barthes—all of whom seek to account for the affects that power and are produced by Bataille's writing. Not surprisingly given the central role of feeling and sensation in his own work, it is Barthes who is at the fore of such discussions. In *Roland Barthes by Roland Barthes*, a work of auto-theory the experimental organizational structure of which was inspired by Bataille's *Encyclopedia Acephalica*, Barthes describes being won over by Bataille's writerly style:

> Bataille, after all, affects me little enough: what have I to do with laughter, devotion, poetry, violence? What have I to say about "the sacred," about "the impossible"? Yet no sooner do I make all this (alien) language coincide with that disturbance in myself which I call *fear* than Bataille conquers me all over again: then everything he *inscribes describes* me: it sticks.[44]

To make Bataille's books work, Barthes suggests, the reader must consent to an exchange of discourses—the personal language of emotion (that "which I call *fear*") must be swapped out for an "alien" language that corresponds with those unnamed feelings or "disturbances" that we have here identified as affects. It is only by forfeiting the naming game of representational language that the reader opens herself to the text: it is only then that everything *sticks*.

The material "stickiness" that Barthes admires in Bataille's prose is the very same quality that so offended Jean Paul Sartre, whose scathing review of *Inner Experience* was published in 1943. Titled "The New Mystic," Sartre's essay compulsively returns to the "powerful affective potential" of Bataille's language, a quality that repulses and attracts him in equal measure.[45] And yet, despite his objection to what he calls the "fleshly closeness" of Bataille's prose, Sartre cannot help but emulate it.[46] Consider, for example, his appeal to touch and sensation when discussing the discursive possibilities of Bataille's philosophy: "We can *sense* that this plastic, molten substance, with its sudden solidifications that liquefy again as soon as we *touch* them, needs to be rendered in a special form and can never be at home with an all-purpose language."[47] In the same essay, Sartre identifies a key formal feature of this "special" style, and in so doing prepares the ground for our investigation of the first technique of Bataille's affectology:

> At times the style is close to choking or drowning in its efforts to render the gasping suffocations of ecstasy or anguish [...]; at others, it is broken up with

little bursts of laughter; at yet others, it sprawls out into the balanced periods of reasoning. The sentence of intuitive rapture, condensed into a single instant, is found side by side, in *Inner Experience*, with the leisurely discursive mode.[48]

Here, Sartre scolds Bataille for mixing up two different philosophical modes: the objective rigor of "balanced" analytic reasoning and the phenomenologist's account of subjective experience. Sartre understands this inconsistency as an unfortunate side effect of Bataille's "formless and flabby" ideas.[49] But what if we took this discursive hybridity as a deliberate affectological strategy deployed by Bataille? How might this alter our understanding of its purpose and effect?

Practice 1: An Operation of Mixing

Like any other scholarly field, affect studies houses several competing definitions of its critical object. Perhaps the one aspect upon which there is universal agreement is that affects are neither properly subjective nor objective but belong instead to "intersubjective and interobjective systems of social desiring."[50] Because subjects and objects are the main building blocks of human language, affects' in-between status poses a problem to their narratability. As Kathleen Stewart writes in her *Ordinary Affects*, "affects don't lend themselves to a perfect, three-tiered parallelism between analytic subject, concept, and world"; instead, they present themselves as "a tangle of potential connections."[51] To perform this entanglement in language, affect scholars often call upon different types of paradox—tautologies, oxymorons, irony—to mix up the long-held dichotomies that structure our perception of the world. Early on in her affectology, for example, Stewart uses a paradoxical both/and/but construction to define affect as "both flighty and hardwired, shifty and unsteady but palpable too."[52] At once flighty and hardwired, unsteady and palpable, affects are in excess of categories, and they demand that language become excessive too.

Bataille's mixing of subjective and objective codes is an affectological technique that does similar work. It registers how affects explode, or more properly, *fuse* subject and object in complex patterns of arrangement. In *Guilty*, Bataille meditates on how such a technique would allow us to imagine different types of relations between subject and object beyond the simple binary opposition that has been handed down to us ad infinitum. "Is it possible to look at the world as the fusion of a subject and an object, in which the subject, the object, and their fusion would not cease to change such that between the subject and the object several forms of identity would exist … ?"[53] In practice, Bataille's code-mixing firms up as three distinct formal techniques: (1) the fusion of objective language and subjective language; (2) the slippage between first and third person; and (3) the development of a narrative "I" that is simultaneously autobiographical and unmanned.

To see these strategies in action, let's turn to a famous scene from *Inner Experience* in which Bataille describes a burst of laughter that overwhelmed him late one evening in 1928. We'll use this sample as a case study for investigating Bataille's other affectological techniques, and so it is worth citing here in full:

> Fifteen years ago (perhaps a bit more), I returned from I don't know where, late in the night. The rue de Rennes was deserted. Coming from Saint Germain, I crossed the rue de Four (the post office side). I held in my hand an open umbrella, and I believe it wasn't raining. (But I hadn't been drinking: I say it, I'm sure.) I had this umbrella open without needing it (if not for what I will speak about later). I was very young then, chaotic and full of empty drunkenness: a round of indecent, dizzying ideas, but already full of anxieties, rigor, and crucifying, running their course … In this shipwreck of reason, anguish, solitary degradation, baseless, worthlessness came due: a little later the festivity started again. What is certain is that this ease, simultaneously a collision with the "impossible," burst in my head. A space constellated with laughter opened its dark abyss before me. Crossing the rue du Four, I became in this unknown "nothingness," suddenly … I negated these gray walls that enclosed me, I rushed into a kind of rapture. I laughed divinely: the umbrella came down on my head covering me (I covered myself expressly with this black shroud). I laughed as perhaps one had never laughed: the final depth of each thing opened itself up—laid bare, as if I were dead.
>
> I don't know if I stopped, in the middle of the street, masking my delirium under an umbrella. Perhaps I jumped (no doubt it's illusory): I was convulsively illuminated; I laughed, I imagine, while running.[54]

Perhaps because it is so extravagantly riddled with "I"s, this passage appears at first glance to be a straightforward example of episodic memory. And yet, something is not quite right. Precise details, such as the street names, are offset by a vagueness that throws the spatial-temporal coordinates of the anecdote into question. The episode occurred fifteen years ago *or perhaps a bit more*, when Bataille was on his way back from *I don't know where*. These demonstrations of incompleteness dare the reader to question the veracity of the event. Did this happen? Is it true? How do we know? Bataille addresses these questions by mixing up two modalities of truth: surety and belief. He is "sure" he hadn't been drinking; he "believes" it wasn't raining. To add to the confusion, Bataille uses *belief*, the heady diction of religious faith, to describe self-evident meteorological facts, and *surety*, a word that in its resoluteness suggests objective truth, to describe his perceived state of intoxication.

This uneasy balance that had been struck between our pair of terms—the objective surety of a subjective sensation, and a subjective belief about an observable object—is further offset by Bataille's invocation of a third term, *illusion*, which does not align clearly with either objectivity or subjectivity. "Perhaps I jumped (no doubt its illusory)," he recalls. Roland Barthes, in a 1972 essay about Bataille called "Outcomes of the Text," uses the example of noble/ignoble/low to explain how Bataille's introduction of a "third term" disturbs the structure of opposites that we ordinarily use to interpret the world:

> Bataille's heterology consists in this: there is a contradiction, a simple, canonical paradigm between the first two terms: *noble* and *ignoble* ("the fundamental division of the classes of men into noble and ignoble"); *but* the third term is not regular: *low* is not the neutral term (neither noble nor ignoble), nor is it the mixed term (noble and ignoble). It is an independent term, concrete, eccentric, irreducible: the term of seduction *outside the* (structural) *law*.[55]

In his mixing up of subjective and objective codes, Bataille is not absenting himself from epistemology in order to roil in the passions of the body, rather, his burlesque discourse is making a claim about the need for and value of knowledge games that aren't structured by the dialectic. To participate in such games, we need to do more than simply mix up subjective and objective codes. The necessary second move is the introduction of a third term that throws the binary form off-kilter once and for all.

Bataille's other two techniques of code-mixing are intimately related; they work together to unsettle the form and function of the narrative "I." Returning to the long passage printed above, we remember that the hyper-repetition of the "I" at first suggested that we were caught in the throes of personal memory. In reading the passage, though, this proliferation produces the opposite effect: its overuse exhausts the word of its content. We'll consider this weird detachment of signifier ("I") and signified (an agential being) in the next section, but for now it bears stating explicitly that Bataille's over-use of the first-person pronoun throws the speaker's identity into question. Other readers testify to this same sensation. Stuart Kendall, who recently translated Bataille's *Summa* for SUNY Press, has observed that one of the major challenges in translating Bataille is that his "language and syntax leave distinct doubt as to the identity of the individual in question in a given sentence."[56] Like his hero Friedrich Nietzsche, for Bataille "every word is a mask, a hideout," including and most especially the word "I."[57]

Elsewhere, Amy Hollywood has persuasively argued that the "uneasy proximity" between "emotion and subjectivity" and "the language of philosophical and scientific objectivity" in Bataille's work, combined with his tendency to fictionalize his own biography, gives us "reasons to distrust the transparency of [his] autobiographical gestures and to read them as strategic."[58]

There is another problem with the "I" that ricochets through the Rue de Four episode. In all his voluminous writings on ecstatic experience, Bataille repeatedly insists that it is impossible for the subject to persist during an encounter with the "impossible" as it is described above. The "I" is the entry price to the darkened realm of laughter. In her prolonged reading of the scene, Anca Parvulescu gestures to precisely this problem: "Bataille makes it clear that the experience never becomes the object of memory, because in that it would become linked to an author, it would become an event in a biography, and lose its connection to the unknown."[59] Indeed, Bataille makes no appeal to memory in his narrative—as Parvulescu points out, the story is not presented to us as an "impression" or "reminiscence," but instead as a strange combination of subjective facts, objective beliefs, and convulsive illusions. To drive her argument home, Parvulscu draws our attention to a tiny but telling detail: "The 'I' that tells the story was not quite there when his laughter burst," she writes, before adding in parentheses, "(Bataille later refers to this 'I' in the third person [as] 'the man with the umbrella')."[60] Bataille uses this slippage between first and third person to slip in and out of his skin, suggesting that there is a way of becoming external to oneself, or rather, external to a Self. In this way, he can testify to how affect moves between subject and object—the protagonist of the scene, finally, is the unmanned laughter that blusters through and destabilizes the fragile "I."

Practice 2: An Operation of Slipping

The slipperiness of the first person in the Rue de Four episode helps introduce the second major technique of Bataille's affectology: his use of "slipping words." Bataille coined this term, *mot glissant*, to refer to words that, if handled in a particular way, work as little engines of defamiliarization that reveal the gap that exists between language and the world. While his comments on slipping words are cryptic and slight, in *Inner Experience* he does provide us with an example. "I will only give one example of a slipping *word* ... the word *silence*," he writes. "As a word it is already, as I have said, the abolition of a sound that is a word;

among all words it is the most perverse, or the most poetic: it is itself proof of its own death."⁶¹ A slipping word doesn't mean a signified so much as it mutilates it, and it is this inherent violence toward meaning that establishes it as "perverse." And yet, as Bataille suggests above, the slipping word has a second, "poetic" function. As Leslie Anne Boldt-Irons explains, to deploy a slipping word is to unleash a productive energy that is usually held in reserve: "The words *silence* and *God* are slipping words, whose reverberating signifiers rupture the limits of their signifieds, in order that their energy be released."⁶²

The linguistic operation of slipping rends signifiers from their signifieds so that they might remember their other abilities, specifically, their capacity to carry a charge, an intensity, an affect. Sartre offers a description of this procedure: "When inserted into M. Bataille's texts, words that had precise meanings in the works of Hegel or Heidegger lend it a semblance of rigorous thought. But as soon as you attempt to grasp that thought, it melts like snow. The emotion alone remains, that is to say, a powerful inner disturbance in respect of vague objects."⁶³ Sartre's commentary allows us to recognize slipping as a technique whereby words are slowly drained of their meanings (denotative, connotative) and their purpose (communicating thought, carrying meaning) to become amulets that emit a pulse of affect, where affect is a "powerful inner disturbance" that is not reducible to the objects between which it passes. Submitted to this slipping movement, discourse becomes autonomous in the sense that it is released from its practical obligation to grasp and take hold of the world of objects in linguistic form. In *Guilty*, Bataille proposes this rupture between word and world as heralding a promising transition from "narrow communication," which "has as its object a concern for things," to "full communication," which is "comparable to flames, to the electrical discharge of lightening." His example of full communication? A mother making faces and strange sounds to provoke her child's laughter, which he describes as a "disequilibrium of the senses."⁶⁴

Practice 3: An Operation of Hypersubstitution

The above image of the intoxicating channel of energy that laughter opens between mother and child is a reminder that for Bataille one of laughter's most important qualities is its transmissibility. In *Eroticism*, Bataille writes that the "contagious nature" of laughter "rules out the possibility of dispassionate observation" by drawing us into a "disturbed state of mind,"

> Seeing and hearing a man laugh I participate in his emotion from inside myself. This sensation felt inside myself communicates itself to me and that is what makes me laugh: we have an immediate knowledge of the other person's laughter when we laugh ourselves or of excitement when we share it. That is why laughter or excitement or even yawning are not things: we cannot usually feel part of stone or board but we do feel part of the nakedness of the woman in our arms.[65]

Why does Bataille laugh? His laughter has nothing to do with humor. He does not see the same pratfall or hear the same joke as the laughing man; he is witness only to the biological disorder that is laughter. But Bataille's model of contagion is more complicated than the simple one-to-one formula of a laugh for a laugh. It contains a crucial interim step. In the interval between witnessing laughter and joining in laughing, a space opens "inside" oneself in which one can share wholly in the unnamed "sensations" and "emotions" of another. What you experience, in other words, is empathy without reserve. The man's laughter disturbs and recalibrates Bataille's insides (a site that is so much vaster than the "brain" or the "mind") so that he can pick up a new frequency that is tuned to affects rather than worldly things—those stones, those boards.

In *Inner Experience*, Bataille's meditation on laughter as contagion becomes a meditation about the boundaries of the body, both individual and social. The "flashes and reboundings" of contagious laughter reveals to us our own radical permeability and invites us to imagine a community that would be built on collective compenetration rather than our "fixed isolation," to borrow Bataille's terminology. "For those who laugh together become like waves in the sea," he writes, "as long as the laughter lasts there is no longer a partition between them, they are no more separated than two waves, but their unity is also undefined, as precarious as that of the agitation of the waters."[66] In affect studies as in Bataille's *Summa*, an affect's contagiousness is often expressed by way of a liquescent imagery of waves, streams, and flows. Consider, for example, Cynthia Willett and Julie Willett's essay on xenophobia and affect in which they argue that "affects can also spread like a physical contagion across thousands of miles via waves of energy transmission. Whole epidemics of panic, fear, and even laughter can unfurl through these imperceptible waves."[67] Here, though, what I'm interested in is how laughter's contagiousness is baked into Bataille's prose not at the level of content—the metaphor of the wave—but at the level of form, in the way that his key terms bash against and begin to resemble one another. I call this process *hypersubstitution*.

We know that a contagion has spread successfully because bodies will begin to copy one another, they all will burst into boils or laughter, depending. The same effect is achieved by Bataille through hypersubstitution, which bashes and clumps keywords together until they begin to behave similarly. After reading the *Summa*, it is impossible to hear the word "laughter" without hearing strains too of sacrifice, eroticism, ecstasy, anguish, and inner experience. How, then, does hypersubstitution work? First, to ensure a rampancy of movement between and across terms, there can be no limit set on the number of keywords in play. Late in *Inner Experience*, Bataille acknowledges his tendency to amass keywords:

> Previously I designated the sovereign operation under the names of *inner experience* and the *extremity of the possible*. Now I also designate it under the name of *meditation*. Changing the word signifies the problem of using whatever word it might be (*sovereign operation* is of all the names the most fastidious; *comical operation* in a sense would be less misleading). I like meditation better but it has a pious appearance.⁶⁸

Bataille does not throw out old terms in favor of new ones; he piles synonyms upon synonyms. Here, for example, he introduces "meditation" in addition to "the names of inner experience and the extremity of the possible." In *On Nietzsche*, he declares that "I no longer want to speak of *inner* (or mystical) *experience* but of *impalement*," but no sooner has he announced this hard transition from one term to another than he throws another synonym of the pile: "You might similarly say Zen."⁶⁹ Bataille's refusal to retire older terms causes keywords to gravitate toward one another and clump together. There are dozens of examples of such clumping in the *Summa*. In *Guilty*, Bataille mostly sticks to list of threes or fours, for example: "eroticism, mad laughter, ecstasy," "a kind of a-religious sacrifice, laughter, poetry, ecstasy," and "sacrifice, laughter, and eroticism."⁷⁰

Armed now with a host of examples, we can see that Bataille's keywords are not synonyms but analogues of one another; they don't mean the same thing so much as they share a structural similarity that allows them to *do* the same thing in and to the text. Bataille says it plainly in this permutation from *Inner Experience*, where he refers to "knowledge found in *laughter, anguish, or any other analogous experience*."⁷¹ Roland Barthes identifies a similar operation in *The Story of the Eye* whereby the novel's dominant images of egg, eye, and sun

> endlessly exchange meanings and usages in such a way that breaking eggs in a bath tub, swallowing or peeling eggs (soft-boiled), cutting up or putting out an eye or using one in sex play, associating a saucer of milk with a cunt or a beam of light with a jet of urine, biting the bull's testicle like an egg or inserting it in the body—all these associations are at the same time identical and other.⁷²

Barthes recognizes this process of endless exchange as a "kind of general contagion of qualities and actions" that enacts the book's eroticism.[73] Here, as in the *Summa*, keywords bind together to form a circuit through which a set of "qualities and actions" can travel. And again, the emphasis on action is key: we are reminded that for Bataille words have an operational existence, they are performative not descriptive. Bataille's eroticism develops not only out of an exchange of meanings (synonymy) but out of an exchange of usages and behaviors (analogy) in which an egg might roll like an eye, or an eye shine like the sun.

Sartre both noticed and distrusted the idiosyncratic way in which Bataille deployed what he calls "argument words," observing that "he will slip into his argument words that are merely suggestive, such as 'laughter,' 'torment,' 'agony,' 'rending,' 'poetry,' etc., which he diverts from their original meaning to confer on them gradually a magical evocative power."[74] Sartre's language of slippage highlights the proximity of hypersubstitution with the slipping operation that we've already analyzed above. Both trouble the relationship between signifier and signified so that we can no longer depend on words to refer directly to their sign objects. However, there are important differences. Slipping is the name we give when a word is simultaneously overinvested and exhausted of meaning, so that it detaches from any single meaning. As Derrida has said, to make a word slip "is to make the entire discourse slide."[75] Hypersubstitution is the name we give when keywords are swapped out and stuck together with such frequency that they begin to share in each other's signifying power.

The result of this technique too is different. While slipping causes discourse to tremble, hypersubstitution causes discourse to gel. The logic here is simple: for qualities to pass back and forth between keywords, they must be connected. The *Summa* is most often noted for its aesthetics of fragmentation, mixing together as it does heterogeneous genres, forms, and styles of writing. The method of hypersubstitution, though, suggests that Bataille understands the three books that comprise the *Summa* as sharing a circulatory system. Carrying the analogy further, we might think of the keyword clumps as fatty lumps that clog the *Summa*'s arteries and veins, and in so doing make us conceive of the three books as a single entity. Barthes reaches a similar conclusion in his analysis of *The Story of the Eye*, arguing that the rampant exchange that takes place between Bataille's key motifs gives the novel the impression of completeness, an egg-like self-sufficiency. Bataille, he writes, "leaves us with no alternative but to regard *Story of the Eye* as a perfectly spherical metaphor: each of its terms is always the significant of another term (no term being a simple thing signified) without it being possible ever to break the chain."[76] The image of unity through connectivity is instructive. We are told that in modernity the center cannot hold, and yet, there are other ways of holding people and things together—here, reticular lines of communication. Bataille's affectology suggests that is through contagion, not an appeal to the center, that we might be able to experience a "unity [that is] undefined, as precarious as that of the agitation of the waters."[77] The technique of hypersubstitution plays out this promise of affective contagion in language by signaling, through the clumping and cross-contamination of various keywords, the *Summa*'s status as an interconnected whole.

Practice 4: The Temporality of the Instant

Hypersubstitution speaks to how affects space themselves between and across bodies (textual and otherwise). The final section of this chapter examines how Bataille's affectology represents affect's temporality. Before we get there, though, it behooves us to ask: What is the time of an affect? Can we "time" affect—does it have duration? When does an affect happen? These questions continue to animate affect studies, in part because of the emphasis that field-defining work by Brian Massumi and Eve Sedgwick put on the time and timing of affects. Ruth Leys reminds us of the importance temporality played for scholars seeking to establish affect as a viable critical object:

> What [Massumi] and other affect theorists share with Tomkins and Ekman— hence also with Sedgwick and Smail—is a commitment to the idea that there is a disjunction or gap between the subject's affective processes and his or her cognition or knowledge of the objects that caused them. The result is that the body not only "senses" and performs a kind of "thinking" below the threshold of conscious recognition and meaning but—as we shall see in a moment— because of the speed with which the autonomic, affective processes are said to occur, it does all this before the mind has time to intervene.[78]

The larger stakes in establishing this gap are not lost on Leys. The temporal delay between sensing and thinking is what allows Massumi and others to argue for the field-forming distinction between affect and emotion, where affect is posited as existing prior to all human systems of perception and action, and emotion is understood as the remainder that is left after affect has been processed by such systems. Affect is always "pre" something—prelinguistic, preconscious, precognitive. In contrast, "emotion is the intensest (most contracted) expression of that capture [of affect by perception]."[79]

In Massumi's model, the time of an affect is best described as a radical priorness, an *always already before*. Affects' beforeness is so extreme that it applies to linear time itself. Affect, Massumi writes, is "associated with non-linear processes—resonation and feedback that momentarily suspend the linear progress of the narrative present from past to future."[80] The non-decomposability of this temporal model makes it very difficult to recount how or why a thing or event came into being, a difficulty that finds its motif in the famous "missing half-second" between stimulus and cognition that Massumi marks as the *when* of affect. Affect, he writes, is "a state of suspense, potentially of disruption. It is like a temporal sink, a hole in time, as we conceive of it and narrativize it."[81] In *Guilty*, we find Bataille using a very similar set of terms to figure laughter as "a leap that cannot be defined by its conditions. The laughter is suspended; it leaves the one who laughs in suspense."[82] So then, we must ask: In what grammatical tense do we write a sinkhole in time? How can language be made to register the lively state of indeterminacy that bristles in the moment right before something (perceptible) happens?

To find a foothold in Bataille's treatment of affects' temporality, let us return to the Rue de Four and to that burst of laughter that carries him past the extreme limit of sense and self. Paying attention now to tense and time, we see that the laughter on the Rue de Four simultaneously heralds an inner experience ("A space constellated with laughter opened"), embodies inner experience ("I laughed as perhaps one had never laughed: the final depth of each thing opened itself up"), and registers that an inner experience is happening ("I laughed divinely"). Bataille takes up this triple folding of time again in a later essay called "Nonknowledge, Laughter, and Tears," where he abuses linear causality to characterize laughter as both the cause and result of inner experience. On the same page of the essay, Bataille submits these two sentences: "*When we laugh* we pass from the sphere of the known, from the anticipated sphere, to the sphere of the unknown and of the unforeseeable," and "In sum, *it makes us laugh* to pass very abruptly, all of a sudden, from a world in which each thing is well qualified, in which each thing is given in its stability, generally in a stable order, to a world in which our assurance is suddenly overthrown."[83] Laughter is both the precipitator of inner experience and a corporeal effect of the same.

We are confronted, then, with a laughter that takes place simultaneously before, during, and after inner experience. With linear time tied in a knot and classical causality befuddled, Bataille's affectology proposes an alternate form of time—the radiant flash of the instant. In his essay on Bataille, Derrida argues for the instant as the "temporal mode of the sovereign operation":

And the *instant*—the temporal mode of the sovereign operation—is not a point of full and unpenetrated presence: it slides and eludes us between two presences; it is difference as the affirmative elusion of presence. It does not give itself but is stolen, carries itself off in a movement which is simultaneously one of violent effraction and of vanishing flight [84]

Cut loose from chronological time, the instant does not submit or subordinate to anything—not to past, present, or future, and most definitely not to the knowing, cognizing subject.[85] The fugitivity that Derrida recognizes as a quality of the instant is due to its radical independence from these systems; according to Bataille, "nothing in the instant is knowable" because "in the instant there is no longer an ego possessing consciousness ... the instant immediately kills the ego!"[86] In Bataille's philosophy, the death of the ego is the liberation of life itself, as he writes, "the seizure of the instant—in which the will is relinquished at the same time—certainly has decisive value" in its unleashing of what he calls "free existence."[87]

Bataille's description of the instant as a seizure suggests that the instant is an embodied unit of time, or perhaps that the instant is the time of embodiment. Other scholars have noticed the correlation between the spasming body and the "excessive gleam of the instant" to which Bataille's prose keeps step.[88] Jenn Joy, for example, observes that "in this strange temporality of laughter and of non-knowledge, pasts and presents collide in convulsive breath, awkward silences, gasps, groans, spasms."[89] Catherine Clément gives us another name for the bodily spasm that boosts us out of durational time: the syncope. Etymologically related to syncopation, the syncope is a moment of physical suspension—of breathing, movement, thought, self, or consciousness—that provokes "a sudden flight into nonexistent time."[90] Examples include a swoon, an asthma attack, a hallucinatory apparition, a yogi retention of breath, an orgasm, and, of course, a laugh. Name-checking Bataille as the "essential laugher," Clement is careful to back only the kind of excessive laughter that puts the ego to death: "Laughter, but only as long as it is in bursts, unrelenting, an insatiable fire, until consciousness is extinguished. Uncontrollable laughter exhausts consciousness and makes it more tractable, more open to entering other landscapes."[91]

Bataille's temporality of the instant is the time of affect. In the instant, cognition and continuity are put on pause (or in Clement's bombastic account, put to death) so that affect might come rushing in as "a sort of rapture."[92] Bataille achieves this effect through two affectological techniques. First, he upsets classical notions of linear causality by combining past, present, and future into one overstimulating ensemble. The Rue de Four laughter cannot be properly situated on a timeline: it has happened, is happening, and will happen. Second, he uses suspension points to hitch the narrative flow of his prose. The scene is riddled with hyphens, dashes, and ellipses that rend literal holes in his report. It's impossible for anyone who has read Bataille to conceive of these gaps as empty—the zero-point of his philosophy (his affect theory) is that the point of suspension is the point where communication happens. Consider this assertion from *Inner Experience*, "[In ecstasy] there is no longer subject=object, but 'gapping breach' between one and the other and, in the breach, subject and object are dissolved, there is a passage, communication."[93] Taken in the context of Bataille's philosophy, the suspension points that score the Rue de Four report are concrete iterations of the missing half second in which Massumi locates affect. Like Massumi's "hole in time," the suspension points are not empty but overfull—they hold the sensation of affect itself.

Like Derrida's *pharmakon*, the word "suspension" is a composite of at least two contrasting meanings. It is both a verb meaning to call off or arrest (to suspend time or a bank account) and a noun meaning a heterogeneous chemical mixture that contains solid particles. Taken together, these two definitions help us recognize the function Bataille ascribes to writing, which in *Literature and Evil* he memorably describes as a "solidified instant."[94] "Literary communication—which is such in so far as it is poetic—" he writes, "is the *sovereign* process that allows *communication* to exist, like a solidified instant, or series of instants."[95] The *Summa*, in other words, is both a sovereign suspension from temporalized activity and a suspension mixture that holds dispersed within it heterogeneous particles and codes (Barthes would say, the operations of a "burlesque, heteroclite" knowledge). It is simultaneously a hitch in breath and a "solid" presence overfull with affect.

In *The Disavowed Community*, Jean-Luc Nancy writes beautifully about the world-building that can happen in the instant. The instant, he observes "is the infinitesimal suspension of time where gazes—voices, silence—are exchanged and bodies touch. In this suspension, something appears—one might say, a world—and doesn't disappear."[96] Nancy's appeal to touch directs us back toward Bataille, and specifically to his meditation on communication as "not only the flux and the fleeting play of light that unifies itself in you, but the passages of warmth and light from one being to another."[97] I like this sentence for the tenderness with which it imagines separate beings cleaving together, through "passages of warmth and light" that I'm interpreting here as passages of laughter, of affect. We might rotate this claim out to think of the *Summa* as depending not only upon the fleeting play of affects and sensations that unify it, but on the transmission of these affects from text to reader. The goal of Bataille's affectology, finally, is to imbricate language with the affective structure of a laugh—its scale (radical excess), its gesture (sliding), its materiality (contagion), and its time (the instant)—to ensure that what is passing back and forth between reader and text is not a joke but the whole world.

Notes

1. I retain the French "humour noir" to distinguish Breton's unique conceptualization of humor from the literary genre of American black humor, which is the object of Chapter 4's critical attention.
2. Sigmund Freud, "Humour," *The International Journal of Psychoanalysis* 9 (January 1928): 1.
3. André Breton, "Lightning Rod," in *Anthology of Black Humor*, ed. Mark Polizotti (San Francisco: City Lights Books, 1997), xvi.
4. Georges Bataille, "The 'Old Mole' and the Prefix Sur in the Words Surhomme [Superman] and Surrealist," in *Visions of Excess: Selected Writings, 1927–1939*, ed. Allan Stoekl (Minneapolis: University of Minnesota Press, 2013), 41.
5. Ibid.
6. Georges Bataille, *Story of the Eye by Lord Auche*, trans. Joachim Neugroschel (San Francisco: City Lights Books, 1987), 15.
7. Mikkel Borsch-Jacobson, "The Laughter of Being," *MLN* 102, no. 4 (1987): 745.
8. See Borsch-Jacobson, also Lisa Trahair, *The Comedy of Philosophy: Sense and Nonsense in Early Cinematic Slapstick* (Albany, NY: SUNY Press, 2007), and Parveluscu, *Laughter*.
9. Michel Surya, *Georges Bataille: An Intellectual Biography* (New York: Verso, 2002), 135.
10. André Breton, *Manifestoes of Surrealism*, trans. Richard Seaver and Helen R. Lane (Ann Arbor: Ann Arbor Paperbacks, 1972), 21.
11. Ibid., 38.
12. Breton, *Manifestoes*, 23, 38.
13. Ibid., 137.
14. Mark Polizzotti, *Revolution of the Mind: The Life of André Breton* (New York: Farrar, Straus and Giroux, 1995), 447.
15. Henry Miller, "An Open Letter to Surrealists Everywhere," in *The Cosmological Eye* (New York: New Directions Press, 1961), 181.
16. Roger Shattuck, "Introduction: Love and Laughter: Surrealism Reappraised," in *The History of Surrealism*, ed. Maurice Nadeau (Cambridge, MA: The Belknap Press of Harvard University, 1989), 26.

17 Clifford Browder, *André Breton: Arbiter of Surrealism* (Geneva: Librairie Droz, 1967), 153.
18 Breton, *Manifestoes*, 144.
19 Ibid., 123–4.
20 André Breton, "What Is Surrealism?" in *What Is Surrealism? Selected Writings*, ed. Franklin Rosemont (New York: Monad, 1978), 156.
21 Breton, *Manifestoes*, 266.
22 Ibid.
23 Breton, "Lightning Rod," xvi.
24 Ibid., 611. Emphases my own.
25 Benjamin Rutter, *Hegel on the Modern Arts* (Cambridge: Cambridge University Press, 2010), 77, n33.
26 Sigmund Freud, *The Joke and Its Relation to the Unconscious* (New York: Penguin Classics, 2003), 154.
27 Ibid., 226.
28 Freud, "Humour," 2.
29 Freud as cited by André Breton in "Lightning Rod," xviii. Emphases my own.
30 Ibid., xvi.
31 See Borsch-Jacobson, "The Laughter of Being"; Parvulescu, *Laughter*.
32 Jacques Derrida, "From Restricted to General Economy," in *Writing and Difference*, trans. Alan Bass (Chicago: The University of Chicago Press, 1978), 319.
33 Ibid.
34 Melissa Gregg and Gregory J. Seigworth, "An Inventory of Shimmers," in *The Affect Theory Reader*, ed. Gregg and Seigworth (Durham, NC: Duke University Press, 2010), 9.
35 Georges Bataille, *Guilty*, trans. Stuart Kendall (Albany, NY: SUNY Press, 2011), 30; Georges Bataille, *Inner Experience*, trans. Stuart Kendall (Albany, NY: SUNY Press, 2014), 95.
36 Gregg and Seigworth, "Inventory," 4; Bataille, *Guilty*, 130.
37 Bataille, *Inner Experience*, 97 and repeated in part in Georges Bataille, *On Nietzsche*, trans. Stuart Kendall (Albany, NY: SUNY Press, 2015), 39.
38 Ibid., 57.
39 Ibid.
40 Joanne Faulkner, *Dead Letters to Nietzsche, or, the Necromantic Art of Reading Philosophy* (Athens, OH: Ohio University Press, 2010), 106.
41 Bataille, *Inner Experience*, 21–2.
42 Ibid., 22.
43 Gregg and Seigworth, "Inventory of Shimmers," 9.
44 Roland Barthes, *Roland Barthes by Roland Barthes*, trans. Richard Howard (New York: Hill and Wang, 2010), 144.

45 Jean Paul Sartre, "The New Mystic," in *Critical Essays (Situations 1)*, trans. Chris Turner (Calcutta: Seagull Books, 2010), 223.
46 Ibid., 222.
47 Ibid., 223–4. Emphases my own.
48 Ibid., 224.
49 Ibid., 262.
50 Gregg and Seigworth, "Inventory of Shimmers," 7.
51 Ibid., 4.
52 Stewart, *Ordinary Affects*, 3.
53 Bataille, *Guilty*, 37.
54 Bataille, *Inner Experience*, 40.
55 Roland Barthes, "Outcomes of the Text," in *The Rustle of Language*, trans. Richard Howard (Berkeley and Los Angeles, CA: University of California Press, 1989), 246.
56 Stuart Kendall, "Translator's Introduction: The Wanderer and His Shadow," in *On Nietzsche*, xx.
57 Ibid.
58 Amy Hollywood, *Sensible Ecstasy: Mysticism, Sexual Difference, and the Demands of History* (Chicago: University of Chicago Press, 2002), 41.
59 Parvulescu, *Laughter*, 85.
60 Ibid., 84–5.
61 Bataille, *Inner Experience*, 23.
62 Leslie Anne Boldt-Irons, "Sacrifice and Violence in Bataille's Erotic Fiction: Reflections From/Upon the *Mise en Abime*," in *Bataille: Writing the Sacred*, ed. Carolyn Bailey Gill (London and New York: Routledge 1995), 98.
63 Sartre, "The New Mystic," 239.
64 Bataille, *Guilty*, 129.
65 Georges Bataille, *Eroticism: Death and Sensuality*, trans. Mary Dalwood (San Francisco, CA: City Lights Books, 1986), 153.
66 Bataille, *Inner Experience*, 98.
67 Cynthia Willett and Julie Willett, "Going to Bed White and Waking Up Arab: On Xenophobia, Affect Theories of Laughter, and the Social Contagion of the Comic Stage," *Critical Philosophy of Race* 2, no. 1 (2014): 84–105.
68 Bataille, *Inner Experience*, 194.
69 Bataille, *On Nietzsche*, 71.
70 Bataille, *Guilty*, 97, 125.
71 Ibid., 45. Emphasis my own.
72 Roland Barthes, "The Metaphor of the Eye" in *Roland Barthes, Critical Essays*, trans. Richard Howard (Evanston: Northwestern University Press, 1972), 245.
73 Ibid.
74 Sartre, "The New Mystic," 228.

75 Derrida, "From Restricted to General Economy," 333.
76 Barthes, "Metaphor of the Eye," 245.
77 Bataille, *Inner Experience*, 98.
78 Ruth Leys, "The Turn to Affect: A Critique," *Critical Inquiry* 37, no. 3 (Spring 2011): 457.
79 Massumi, *Parables*, 14.
80 Ibid., 26.
81 Ibid.
82 Bataille, *Guilty*, 90.
83 Bataille, *The Unfinished Business of Non-Knowledge*, 135. Emphases my own.
84 Derrida, "From Restricted to General Economy," 333.
85 Ibid., 333. Georges Bataille, "Surrealism and How It Differs from Exceptionalism," in *The Absence of Myth: Writings on Surrealism*, trans. Michael Richardson (London; New York: Verso Books, 1994), 66.
86 Bataille, *The Unfinished Business of Non-Knowledge*, 204.
87 Bataille, "Surrealism and How It Differs," 66.
88 Ibid., 149.
89 Jenn Joy, *The Choreographic* (Cambridge, MA: MIT Press, 2004), 98.
90 Catherine Clement, *Syncope: The Philosophy of Rapture*, trans. Deirdre M. Mahoney and Sally O'Driscoll (Minneapolis: University of Minnesota Press, 1994), 27.
91 Ibid., 8, 7.
92 Bataille, "Surrealism and How It Differs," 66.
93 Bataille, *Inner Experience*, 64.
94 Georges Bataille, *Literature and Evil*, trans. Alastair Hamilton (London: Penguin Books, 2012), 161.
95 Ibid.
96 Jean-Luc Nancy, *The Disavowed Community*, trans. Philip Armstrong (New York: Fordham University Press, 2016), 71–2.
97 Bataille, *Inner Experience*, 97.

3

The Grain of Hélène Cixous's Laugh

The first lesson in laughter is a lesson in looking. In 2000, Hélène Cixous looked at the word *écrire* and saw squatting within in it another: *rire*. While others might consider this a coincidence, after all, *écrire* holds no etymological connection to *rire*, Cixous took it as compelling evidence that the gesture of writing and the gesture of laughing were intimately bound to one another. "I write knowing that the verb laugh, *rire*, is in cahoots with the verb write, *écrire*."[1] A decade or so later, Cixous noticed another word at the heart of *écrire*: *cri*. To write, she observed, is to translate "the sharp and short cries of reality. Literature is for yelling at length, pushing cries all the way to music".[2] Seen through Cixous's eyes, the word *écrire* appears as a triptych: a three paneled diorama of writing, laughter, and those other sounds that lie below the threshold of phonetic speech. In this chapter, I propose these as the three main elements of Cixous's affectology, which turns on her ability to translate the raw stuff of nonlinguistic sound—laughter, cries, and music—into written language.

***

The second lesson in laughter is longer, and it is a lesson in listening. In a footnote to "The Laugh of the Medusa," Cixous namechecks the prolific French writer and filmmaker Marguerite Duras as one of the few practitioners of écriture féminine, but in the interest of maintaining momentum she does not elaborate.[3] "I'll just point out some examples," she tells the reader, "one would have to give them full readings to bring out what is pervasively feminine in their significance. Which I shall do elsewhere."[4] Five months later, Cixous sat down with her friend Michel Foucault to discuss Duras's work. Cixous's commentary on Duras is valuable because of the attention it brings to the specific operations of écriture féminine. Yes, Duras's writing enacts a "certain outpouring that almost goes beyond the text," but how did it get to be this way?[5] What literary techniques does Duras use to achieve this effect? Cixous's close reading of Duras's 1969 novel *Destroy, She Said* offers an answer: écriture féminine advances through the author's manipulation of sounds and affects, which work together to make of the text a material "sound body."[6] To build her case, Cixous focuses in particular on the polyphonic twist of music, laughter, and speech with which Duras's novel ends:

> A kind of gaiety that emanates— a gaiety that emerges against a background of violence, of course—from those three strange beings, the trinity represented by Stein, Thor, and Alissa, who keep themselves apart from the others. They remain active while the others are passive or overwhelmed. There's *something* that constantly communicates and circulates, and which triumphs. There's laughter ending with the phrase "she said." It all ends with laughter and music.[7]

Foucault suggests that the laughter that circulates between Stein, Thor, and Alissa might be a sign that "something amusing" is happening in the scene, but Cixous disagrees. "I don't see anything amusing in what happens between these people, between what remains of these people," she says. "I see something that isn't closed; I see a kind of infinite generosity."[8] Cixous's interpretation of Duras's laughter depends upon her attunement to the novel's dense sonic texture. To "see" what Cixous sees, we must hear what she hears. What are the aural dimensions of *Destroy, She Said*? What are its tunings, its acoustics, its rhythms?

The scene in question takes place in a quiet, dark room with our three main characters; Stein and Thor are speaking in low voices so as not to disturb Alissa, who is sleeping. Their idle chat is interrupted by a faraway noise that slowly becomes discernible as music. The unmanned melody holds a strange autonomy that is suggestive of an absolute outside, an absolute Other; Duras writes, "With infinite pain the music stops, begins again, stops, repeats, starts again. Stops." The whole scene is an exercise in close listening—first, Thor and Stein attempt to ascertain *what* the noise is ("a sort of crack in the air?" one of them ventures), then they seek to identify its source ("Is it coming from the forest?"), and finally they register the affects that it carries ("What pain. What immense pain," murmurs Stein).[9] In the performance notes appended to the novel, Duras listed the music as Bach's "The Art of the Fugue," an experimental work that is famous for taking the permutational form of the fugue to its limit. Duras's choice of this particular fugue, in which Bach exhausts the recombinant possibilities of four themes, suggests the varied, intricate ways in which different voices can enter into relation with one another. The fugue swells "majestically loud" and, as if in answer, Alissa's "mouth widens in pure laughter." The "theme" of her laughter is then picked up and imitated by Stein and Thor in contrapuntal fashion: they "laugh to see her laugh." It is not clear whether Alissa is waking or asleep when she utters the novel's enigmatic last line, "'Music to the name of Stein,' she says."[10]

Cixous's analysis of this scene as an example of écriture féminine depends upon two critical gestures. First, she refuses to decant laughter from the novel's other sounds. It is only by listening to Stein, Thor, and Alissa's laughter in concert with the drifting fugue that Cixous can hear it not as the gatekeeping cry of an exclusive community (as Foucault is wont to do), but as a willingness to become involved in and entangled with that which is outside, that which is other. Remembering that the fugue is in this final sequence the carrier of an "immense pain," Cixous observes that "what remains between these characters [in this final sequence] isn't closed off, it opens on to the infinite, but to an infinity of pain."[11]

The intimate tie that exists in the novel between Bach's fugue and the throb of affect (that infinite, subjectless pain) is Cixous's second concern. She is fascinated by the fact that, in Duras's novel, there is a zero degree of difference between sound and affect. The fugue *is* pain, and the laughter *is* a feeling that Cixous haltingly describes as "a kind of gaiety."[12] What we are left with in these final moments, then, is a block of sound affects—a laugh-gaiety-music-pain that moves through the novel's diegetic world, but also breaches the bounds of the text to be "transmitted like lightening through the body and skin" of the reader.[13] It is this porosity that qualifies Duras's novel as a feminine text, as per Ian Blyth's observation that "for there to be an écriture féminine, in the widest possible understanding of the term, the writer must be able to bring the outside world, the truly 'other' into her writing."[14] In her closing remarks on Duras, Cixous reinforces this connection between sound and the figure of the outside: "[Duras] has a good ear even if her gaze is cut short; she has a good ear, and that's what makes up for it, that's *where the outside comes back in*."[15]

***

The conversation between Cixous and Foucault about Duras was published in 1975, the same year as Cixous's Medusa essay, which remains one of the most anthologized expressions of twentieth-century feminism. That essay, together with its unofficial partner piece "Castration or Decapitation?" (1976), contains some of Cixous's most famous comments on laughter and écriture féminine, and it is to these two essays that people flock when they wish to speak on the subject. Galvanized by Cixous's bombastic invitation "to smash everything, to shatter the framework of institutions, to blow up the law, to break up the 'truth' with laughter," feminist scholars quickly glossed "Medusan laughter" as a subversive style of female, and feminist, humor. In 1978, for example, B. Ruby Rich coined the term "Medusan film" to refer to films that "offer an explosive humor coupled with sexuality to discomfort patriarchal society."[16] For Rich (and many others, including Frances Gray, Kathleen Rowe, and Domnica Radulescu), the concept of "Medusan laughter" is enabling because it provides a model for recognizing the political significance of female laughter, female humor, and female comedy.[17] While these projects are commendable for how they extend Cixous's ideas in new contexts, they are not really *about* Cixous, nor are they about the laughter that ricochets through her oeuvre; as Anca Parvulescu has persuasively argued, the critical use-value of Cixous has mostly depended upon a "reduction of [her] complex and nuanced laughing textual choreography to an argument about the 'subversiveness' of women's humor."[18]

In a 1999 interview, Cixous expressed her exasperation at having her writings glossed and miniaturized by Anglo-American feminists. She, like the mortal Gorgon Medusa, has also suffered a decapitation—scholars have cleaved her theoretical "head" from the vast bodily territories of her fiction. For, as she reminds the interviewer, the ideas that animate her theoretical manifestos have long been present in her creative works. "I, myself, did not feel like writing [the theoretical essays]," she says, "because I thought that I had written them a long time ago. I had written everything I wanted to write ten years before I started writing those."[19] We might take Cixous's imaginative rewriting of the Medusa myth—itself an object lesson in écriture féminine—as a blueprint for reversing this violence. Criticizing Freud (and Perseus before him) for casting their gaze only on "Medusa's head," Cixous dilates her gaze and tips her ear to return to Medusa her body and her voice.[20] "You only have to look at the Medusa straight on to see her. And she's not deadly. She's beautiful and she's laughing."[21]

This same double gesture—step back and listen—is at work in Cixous's reading of Duras, which attends to the intricate ways in which laughter becomes involved with the novel's other sounds and affects. In this chapter, then, I model my treatment of Cixous on her treatments of Duras and Medusa. Rather than extracting a strain of laughter from her theoretical essays and glossing it as a synonym for feminist subversion, I listen to the delicate ways in which laughter communes with other sounds and affects across her theoretical and poetic work, and particularly in the 1983 novel *The Book of Promethea*, which plays out the problems of writing sound affects in language as its central theme. One effect of reading Cixousian laughter as belonging to a larger aural economy is that it allows us to recognize the affiliation between Cixous and a cadre of artists and writers interested in representing sound affects through experimental techniques. In lieu of an ending, this chapter follows one such line of connection to examine two contemporary artworks that successfully present laughter as a material sound affect: Sam Taylor-Johnson's short film *Hysteria* (1997) and Lorrie Moore's short story "Real Estate" (1998).

Écriture féminine, I wager, is an adventure in affectology; it is, after all, an inventive writerly practice that aims to resculpt language so that it might better carry and conduct what Cixous calls, with appropriately diluvial flair, "the flood of fine and subtle affects that take our body as a place for manifestation."[22] And, as with Georges Bataille, a fellow soldier in the war against lack, Cixous's affectology finds its most powerful leitmotif in a laughter that overflows without reserve. My purpose in this chapter is to chase down a precise understanding of how laughter relates to and propels Cixous's project of écriture féminine. While this might seem like well-worn ground, there has been little curiosity among scholars about how écriture féminine and laughter work on one another. Contra this lack of interest, Parvulescu forwards the idea that "écriture féminine, of which too much and too little has been said, offers the promise of a laughing text."[23] The answer to the question of *how* precisely this "laughing text" is brought into being must deal, I wager, with the very particular ways in which Cixous conceives of and choreographs sounds and affects in her work. Through an appeal to sound studies, and specifically to Roland Barthes's brief but suggestive comments on "writing aloud," I argue that écriture féminine is a materialist project that weaves together laughter and other nonphonetic sounds to make of the text an open field through which both sounds and affects can pass.

Cixous and Sound Studies

Although this was not the case in 1975 when Cixous was discussing Duras with Foucault, the intersection between sound and affect is today a busy one. In the past decade or so, the structural similarities between the two have prompted several critics to agree that sound quite literally *is* affect. As Walter Gershon has explained, "sounds are a form of resonance and can therefore be understood as a kind of vibrational affect."[24] Working in a similar vein, other scholars have argued for an analogous relationship between sound and touch. As Ryan Bishop explains, we are not touched by sound so much as "sound *is* touch":

> Though we often refer to touch primarily as resident in the fingers, touch, however, operates in a disseminated manner, literally covering the remainder of the body, as well as the head. Touch is dispersed, enveloping and encompassing.

When airwaves touch the ear, we call the effects 'hearing' or 'sound,' and the disseminated, expansive operation of touch makes it more pervasive than the other senses and structurally supportive of them.[25]

Simultaneously "expansive" and "pervasive," Bishop's description of how sound touches on and in the body recalls Eve Sedgwick's description of tactility in *Touching Feeling*. There, Sedgwick speaks beautifully about how a haptic criticism, one based in touch not sight, might force the relentless binaries that structure Western thought into remission: "The sense of touch makes nonsense out of any dualistic understanding of agency and passivity; to touch is always already to reach out, to fondle, to heft, to tap, or to enfold, and always also to understand other people or natural forces as having effectually done so before oneself."[26]

Before this clutch of scholars had made a compost pile of touching, feeling, and sounding out, Cixous was there, handling similar ideas with a similar eye. Consider, for example, this passage from "Castration" in which Cixous describes the feminine text as a delicate crosshatching of touch, sound, and affect:

> there's something in [feminine texts] that's freely given, perhaps because they don't rush into meaning, but are straightway at the threshold of feeling. There's tactility in the feminine text, there's touch, and this touch passes through the ear. Writing in the feminine is passing on what is cut out by the Symbolic, the voice of the mother, passing on what is most archaic. The most archaic force that touches a body is one that enters by the ear and reaches the most intimate point. This innermost touch always echoes in a woman-text. So the movement, the movement of the text, doesn't trace a straight line. I see it as an *outpouring* ...[27]

Cixous's readers have long understood her thick descriptions of the female voice as symbolic: historically, women have been silenced, and now their voices must be heard. What I'm suggesting though, is that we take Cixous's descriptions of sound—how it touches on, moves through, and engrains itself in bodies—literally. I'm bolstered in these efforts by the emphasis on materiality in affect and sound studies, in which sound quite literally *is* touch which quite literally *is* affect, and also by Cixous's treatment of Duras, in which she seeks to answer the question "How does Duras's work touch me?" by tipping her ear to the page.

In what follows, I'm particularly interested in how Cixous puts the sonic modalities of music and laughter to work in her work. In a 1984 interview with Verena Conley, she explains the value of music specifically:

> When the name of the apple begins to thicken and replace the apple, we all know that moment, the linguists as well as the psychoanalysts. In women's

daily life, this is a big question. The ideal, or the dream would be to arrive at a language that heals as much as it separates. Could one imagine a language sufficiently transparent, sufficiently supple, intense, faithful, so that there would be reparation and not only separation? I am attempting to write in that direction. I try to write on the side of a language as musical as possible.[28]

Here, Cixous invests a "musical" language—where "music" refers to both composed music and the sonorous material that contours the world in which we live—with the potential to recover the direct relation between word and world. Extending this idea, Cixous goes on to develop an image of the author as a recording instrument through whom the "music of the world" passes. In what is perhaps the most reproduced passage of any of Cixous's interviews, she says,

> I always privilege the ear over the eye. I am always trying to write with my eyes closed. What is going to write itself comes from long before me, *me* [*moi*] being nothing but the bodily medium which formalizes and transcribes that which is dictated to me, that which expresses itself, that which vibrates in almost musical fashion in me and which I annotate with what is not the musical note, which would of course be the ideal.[29]

Contrary to accounts of the feminine text that peg it as a rampant deluge of female self-expression, Cixous here imagines écriture féminine as a kind of mediumship in which the author allows herself to be touched by the "vibrations" of her surrounds. Through incredible concentration and control, the author might invent a musical language in which signs do not stand in for but materially summon forth their sign object.

Laughter, too, gains special prominence in Cixous's work because of its rampant materiality; it is a vibration of sound and feeling that streams in the spaces between world and word, inside and outside. This liminal quality marks Cixous's earliest theoretical and fictional depictions of laughter. In her Medusa essay, Cixous famously describes the feminine text as "the rhythm that laughs you."[30] The same year, she repeats the same line but with a difference; it appears in her "Sorties" essay as "the rhyth-me that laughs you."[31] The first iteration suggests that laughter is exterior to the subject—it is a rhythmic event that "touches you" from the outside. The second, from "Sorties," cracks open *rythme* (the French word for rhythm) to reveal an insouciant, English-speaking other; in this version, it is an elusive "me" (not "moi") that laughs "you." Playing at the edge of French and English, Cixousian laughter designs for itself a third space that is in excess of the subject-object relation.

We see Cixous experimenting with this third space in her claustrophobic first novel, *Angst* (1977). Having spent the entirety of the book trapped in her own perspective, the narrator is suddenly able to see herself through the eyes of another; as Ian Blyth has argued, the scene bears witness to "a new way of relating to both the "I" and that which is "outside":

> Yes, I saw! I saw myself too. Through the eyes of the mad god. That vision at point blank range. Laughter tore me apart. I sat down on the top step, absolutely alone, I was escaping, anguish pouring out of my throat, I am losing, letting myself go, it was a new kind of anguish, a keen joy, I was casting off my body; I must have laughed for hours, ruinous laughter ravaging my flesh. I began to spit blood. I spewed up my story from the very first moment. That joyous laughter is clearing me out, wiping my heart clean.[32]

It's hard not to pick up the scent of Duras: here, as in the final scene of *Destroy, She Said*, laughter is both the methods and the means by which one enters into risky, intimate relation with the shifting figure of the outside. It's no mistake, I think, that Duras places her leaky sound affect at the novel's very end, a strategy that Cixous will emulate in her own work—laughter is the final sound not only of *Angst*, but of several of her texts, both theoretical ("Castration or Decapitation?") and poetic (*La (The Feminine)*). To end on laughter, Cixous submits, is not to end at all.

The Grain of a Laugh

In her translator's introduction to *The Book of Promethea*, the novel by Cixous to which we soon will turn, Betsy Wing says that Cixous's laughter poses a challenge to discourse not because of its connection with a subversive sense of humor, but because of its obstinate materiality. "Laughter, communifying and healing, like voice, is a bodily effect," she writes. "And it is in terms of the body and its rhythms that translation must work."[33] In search of a principle of translation for Cixous's laughter, Wing alights upon Roland Barthes's speculative notion of "writing aloud," the aim of which Barthes recounts in a passage from *The Pleasure of the Text* (1973) that Wing cites almost in full:

> writing aloud is not phonological but phonetic; its aim is not the clarity of messages, the theater of emotions; what it searches for (in the perspective of bliss) are the pulsional incidents, the language lined with flesh, a text where we can hear the grain of the throat, the patina of consonants, the voluptuousness of

vowels, a whole carnal stereophony; the articulation of the body, of the tongue, not that of meaning, of language.[34]

To write aloud would be to invent a language that was all materiality and no meaning, or to invoke Kaja Silverman, "all cry and no word."[35] "A tall order!" Wing exclaims, and a tall order it is indeed—Barthes himself admits that such writing is yet to come.[36] Nevertheless, he cannot help cajoling his reader, "Let us talk about it *as though it* existed."[37]

Because of the relations it spins among sound, affect, and language, Barthes's concept of "writing aloud" serves as a generative counterpoint to Cixous's écriture féminine. It is bound to another Barthesian concept—the grain of the voice. In a 1972 essay, he theorizes the "grain" as the sound the human voice makes as it is molded by a specific body—it holds the trace of the darting tongue and the folding glottis that produced it. Although grain stands outside of semantic signification, to say that it is non-signifying and nonlinguistic would be to miss that, for Barthes, the grain taps into older forms of signifying play that belong to what Rebecca Lentjes has usefully described as "the language of sound."[38] Like Cixous's "musical language," the language of sound remembers a time when "sound-signifiers" held direct relationships with body and world. Barthes explains, "The 'grain' is that: the materiality of the body speaking its mother tongue; perhaps the letter, almost certainly *signifiance*."[39] Initially proposed by Kristeva, Barthes understands signifiance as a third level of meaning-making that "by contrast to the first two levels, communication and signification ... refer[s] to the field of the signifier."[40] The elusive third meaning that is generated by the materiality of the body is steeped in affect and sensation—as Barthes puts it, signifiance "is meaning, in so far as it is *sensually produced*."[41]

Like Cixous's Medusan laughter, Barthes's grain has been taken up widely by critics. The associated notion of writing aloud, though, has received comparatively little attention. There are a couple of reasons for this. Like Sartre reading Bataille or American feminists reading Cixous (Toril Moi, Rita Felski, Susan Sellers), there is a certain squeamishness among scholars in handling what they take to be its overly subjective, erotic, and excessive elements, which Barthes described as an "aesthetics of musical pleasure."[42] This is compounded, I think, with Barthes's own uncertainty as to what writing aloud actually looks like. Like Massumi writing about affect, Barthes expends a lot of energy talking about what writing aloud is *not*. His "Grain" essay opens with a diatribe against "poetic, emotive predicates" that swamp the voice in adjectives and heightened imagery.⁴³ Unlike a voice's timbre, its grain is "theoretically locatable but not describable," and so Barthes sets about the task of pinpointing its topographical coordinates.⁴⁴ Take, for example, this passage, in which Barthes discusses the voice of a Russian bass:

> something is there, manifest and stubborn (one hears *that*) beyond (or before) the meaning of the words, their form (the litany), the melisma, and even the style of execution: something which is directly the cantor's body, brought to your ears in one and the same movement from deep down in the cavities, the muscles, the membranes, the cartilages, and from deep down in the Slavonic language, as though a single skin lined the inner flesh of the performer and the music he sings.⁴⁵

To locate the grain of the voice in language, Barthes deploys that same unsteady placeholder that Cixous uses to refer to Duras's sound affects. "*Something* is there," *some* resolutely material *thing*, "manifest and stubborn," that moves out to touch the outer edge of the reader-listener's ear. Barthes tells us that this relation of touch is "direct," which is to say, is material: the *something* that is being brought to our ears "is directly the cantor's body."

We know that in Duras's *Destroy, She Said*, music and laughter open the borders of bodies to their constitutive outside. So too in Barthes account, where the voice's grain lays open a field of relation that is traversed by affects. Having urged us to leave language to its task of "reducing [pleasure] to a known, coded emotion," Barthes redirects our attention to the peculiar forms of attachment that spring from the voice's grain:

> I am determined to listen to my relation with the body of the man or woman singing or playing and that relation is erotic—but in no way 'subjective' (it is not the psychological subject in me who is listening; the climactic pleasure hoped for is not going to reinforce—to express—that subject but, on the contrary, to lose it.)⁴⁶

Barthes' theory of listening is also a theory of writing: what he is "determined" to do is discover a method of attesting to modes of erotic feeling that lie beyond the bounds of the psychological subject. This same project animates Cixous's *The Book of Promethea*. Hailed by several Cixous scholars as an exemplary work in écriture féminine, *Promethea* is a valuable supplement to materialist theories of sound and voice. In what follows, I use the book as a bridge to connect Cixous's écriture féminine (which is taken up in literary criticism but rarely in sound studies) and Barthes's writing aloud (which is taken up in sound studies but rarely in literary criticism) to develop a working theory of an affectology that takes sound as its primary method of inscription.

Writing Promethea Aloud

"Very well then. I am going to try and do the introduction. Since no one wants to do it for me. Neither of the two who really made this book can bring herself to do it."[47] So begins *The Book of Promethea*, a novel by Cixous that was published in French in 1983 and in English translation in 1991. Like language to affect, we arrive at *Promethea* already too late: the book has already been "made" and its two author-protagonists departed; as the narrator notes, "the book took off by itself."[48] The absentee book tells of the passionate love affair between H and Promethea, where H is to Hélène what K is to Kafka. And yet H, a professor who is the "author of numerous book beginnings," is unable to find traction with her own story. Her language, "so pretty, so agile, and so theoretical," cannot contain Promethea, who holds all the "grand, continental dimensions" of the feminine as Cixous limns it in her theoretical work.[49] H. herself has tried to commit Promethea to the page, but, as the narrator tells us,

> her efforts so far have produced nothing written other than convulsions, trancelike humming, and a hypnotizing/hypnotized state; for a week she has been tormented, she burns to write something, gentle warmth emanates from her whole body, but still nothing comes of it. Besides, at the same time she is also busy burning old books, manuals, professional papers, theoretical volumes—because they keep her from doing the one thing that now seems urgent and right to her: shouting the loud hymn of ecstatic pleasure, breaching the hide of the old tongue's hard blare.
>
> —She no longer knows where to begin: singing, burning, abolishing, liquidating, flowing, gushing; so she does it almost all at once in moist, glowing disarray.[50]

We recognize this flowing, glowing disarray as the mark of écriture féminine, but something isn't right here—H.s exposure to Promethea (to the feminine) has been too sudden and too violent, and she is unable to translate her experience into language. With H.'s tongue refusing to tie itself to language, our narrator steps in. A self-proclaimed "minor character," the narrator is a version of H, she verges on H.[51] The difference between the "I" and H is slight, but the narrator nevertheless tries to parse it for us: "I could say that H is my night person. She is more willing to be submerged than I. She lets herself become a little impersonal, whereas I am afraid of getting lost. I prefer being on the mare's back than in the cave she came from, where the earliest music echoes."[52]

The Book of Promethea is not so much about Promethea as it is about the narrator's efforts to *write* Promethea, as she admits early in the novel,

"Promethea is my heroine. But the question of writing is my adversary."[53] The novel's fragmentary form is a sign of the difficulty of the task in hand. It moves fitfully back and forth between two modes—the narrator's metacommentary on the challenge of committing Promethea to the page, and her (mostly) faithful transcription of two notebooks kept by H detailing her love affair with Promethea. Because we only encounter Promethea through the narrator's literary efforts, the whole book takes on the impression of scaffolding. It never really gets started, or it is a series of starts, as per the narrator's admission that "the whole book is composed of first pages."[54]

***

In a 2010 seminar, Cixous "talked about the pregnant Medusa as the most feminine being that could be imagined. When her head is cut off by Perseus, she gives birth through her throat to Pegasus, symbol of poetic inspiration."[55] In another version of the Medusa myth, Pegasus and his brother Chrysaor are born in the moment that droplets of Medusa's blood fall into the ocean. With this in mind, let's cut to the first physical appearance of Promethea in the novel:

> I need to open the window and call her with my voice … I open my notebook, I open the window, I call, and my heroine is there, really. I am overwhelmed.
>
> I warn her: "I am writing on you, Promethea, run away, escape. I am afraid to write you, I am going to hurt you!"
>
> But rather than run away, she comes at a gallop. Through the window she comes, breathing hard, and alive as can be, she flings herself into the book, and there are bursts of laughter and splashes of water everywhere, on my notebook, on the table, on my hands, on our bodies.[56]

The similarities between Pegasus and Promethea are strong enough, I think, for us to interpret her as Medusa's hot-tempered offspring, and to therefore read *The Book of Promethea* as something like a sequel to "The Laugh of the Medusa." Like Pegasus, Promethea is the symbol and source of poetic inspiration in the novel—inventing a way to write her in language is the book's substrate and goal. And, also like Pegasus, Promethea is figured as a mare in flight, "she comes at a gallop." Finally, the way that Promethea materializes on the page as "bursts of laughter and splashes of water" recalls Pegasus's violent origin story—her body contains traces of a laughing mother and rough ocean waters. Promethea is not laughing, not does she embody the spirit of laughter. Rather, she *is* laughter, a material emission that hits books and bodies at high speeds.

Cixous strengthens the Pegasus triptych of horse, laughter, and liquid throughout the novel, always in the context of the narrator's attempt to write Promethea. In one fragment, Cixous uses these three images to forge an image of Promethea as a fitful and impassioned body that careens through the sentence, disturbing its form. "You who cry you who laugh the way you cry you who spout you who snort and quiver, who stamp and shake your great silver mane, you who warble, you who spill your liquids and sweat honey!"[57] A little later, the narrator "watches, enchanted" as Promethea tries on "a thousand faces," but the cumulative effect of Promethea's rapid transfigurations is overwhelming, and the narrator demands that she stop. Promethea, disobedient and willful, transforms one last time into a figure that consecrates the intimacy between laughter and water, she becomes "a child crawling out of the river on all fours and shaking with laughter."[58] In each case, Promethea's laughter is simultaneously an incitement and impediment to poetic creation, as per the narrator's formulation: "everything unsayable: laughter."[59] The same uneasy coupling of "unsayability" and laughter marks another passage in which the narrator fantasizes about a mode of writing that would be pure vocal effect: "Suppose there were no paper! I am afraid it muffles our laughter a bit, I hope our cry will tear it."[60]

But a paperless writing is possible. Promethea has made of her voice an inscription device that can write affects directly on (or in) the listener's body. The narrator recognizes the "lively musical pains" that wrack her body as "Promethea writing at this moment directly on my heart," in part because she has felt these sensations before.[61] Disturbed by Promethea's vocal ability to cut to her heart, the narrator struggles to develop an art of listening that would be able to make the "crackle" of her voice signify as language. "I slow down to listen to the words crackling in my heart," she says, "I want to understand its tongue, I want to grasp its words, I want to put them in my mouth, suck on them and pronounce them."[62] Promethea's method of vocal inscription resonates strongly with Barthes's writing aloud, which he, too, imagines as a "crackle" that reverberates in the listener's body as an erotic charge. In *The Pleasure of the Text*, he notes that writing aloud "[throws] the anonymous body of the actor into my ear: it granulates, it crackles, it caresses, it cuts, it comes: that is bliss."[63]

Promethea is Barthes's grain incarnate. Consider the following passage, one of two long meditations on her vocal effects:

> Promethea's speech is very simple and high and very pointed like a mountain. She uses few words because there are few at that altitude but they are sparkling and transparent like glaciers at the very top. Her vocabulary comes always

from the guts, hers or the earth's. It comes out smoking and violent, with roots still permeated with blood, with earth, with salt, with oil. But she also uses gentler forms, ancient recitations that ripple out along the road, in airy notes, in rainbowed bubbles of sound, leaving silver traces in the air. Generally, her languages are ancient and fresh and lightly limned as the paintings at Lascaux. They are all clairvoyant. She speaks in evocations and eruptions more than in metaphors. Whereas I, I drill, I dig, I sink in, I plow even the sea, I want to turn it over. No, we do not speak at all the same languages. Things she lets bubble up in a shower of sparks, I would like to collect and bind. She burns and I want to write out the fire!⁶⁴

Promethea's voice is directly shaped by her body (it "comes away from the guts") and doesn't hold much linguistic content (she "uses few words"). What is perhaps most striking about her language, though, is the direct, sensory attachment it holds to the world. Her voice literally *writes on* the world, "leaving silver traces in the air," and it is suggested by Cixous that the "freshness" of Promethea's language is due to it not depicting or representing but rather *presenting* its sign object. Can we say that Promethea *is* a fire, as she is a laugh? Cixous explains this quality of Promethea's voice in terms that again recalls the "carnal stereophony" of Barthes's grain:

> Watch out for words with her! Because Promethea is the person who has not cut the cord binding words to her body. Everything she says is absolutely fresh. Comes straight from the flesh of her lungs, the fibers of her heart. She doesn't know any other way of speaking. That's why her words are few and fiery. And all her sentences are strong and young and incandescent, because they are caused by a convulsion of her whole earthly body.⁶⁵

When Cixous describes a "way of speaking" that "comes straight" from the lungs, what she means is a language that does not take a detour through signification before it spasms mouth and air. We've seen this language before in that early description of H.'s ability to write "convulsions."⁶⁶ While the narrator takes this to be a sign of H.'s writer's block, we might recognize it instead as the early developmental stages of writing aloud. H.'s convulsions are test runs as she learns to write directly from her "whole earthly body," a process that Barthes has already warned us requires the loosening, perhaps even the loss, of the self.

For both Barthes and Cixous, the relinquishing of one's grip on the psychological subject is experienced as an unfolding outward, a blooming forth into the open spaces that lie between self and other. As I've already suggested, both writing aloud and écriture féminine are practices of mediumship: the author consents to be touched by and vows to transmit the sound affects that surround her. Promethea embodies this practice—her voice traverses an interim zone that is between here and there, between you and me. Promethea's words, we are told, "are all clairvoyant. She speaks in evocations and eruptions."[67] *Eruption* and *evocation* both suggest the summoning forth of an interior, whether that be one's bloody innards or a memory from childhood. However, the "clairvoyance" of Promethea speech invokes the second definition of the term *evocation* to mean the rousing of something external to the self, a deity or the dead. Promethea's speech is therefore positioned by Cixous on the fault line of Self and Other, of inside and outside—her "gut vocabulary" can limn her own eruptions, yes, but also the Earth's; her languages might sing blood or soil, depending.

Against Metaphor

My argument about how sound affects work in Cixous's novel depends upon my taking her descriptions of Promethea, and Promethea's voice, literally. What if the "bursts of laughter" that announce Promethea's presence really *do* soak into the pages of the narrator's notebook? How might we recognize their stain? This is all to say: what would happen if we took écriture féminine to mean the direct inscription of the sound affects of music and laughter in language—a form of writing aloud? The ongoing material turn in the humanities and social sciences, to which sound and affect studies belong, has depended on scholars taking seriously the material vitality of that which had previously been taken to be abstract and inert. Questions that a previous generation of scholars would have taken for riddles, such as "What is the emotion of an electron?" or "What is the shape of a feeling?" are now viable research questions.[68] The opening line of Teresa Brennan's *The Transmission of Affect*, "Is there anyone who has not, at least once, walked into a room and "felt the atmosphere?" is a neat example of such a gesture.[69] Brennan refuses to take the dead metaphor "feeling the atmosphere" as figurative, and instead uses it as a vantage point from which to rethink how affects, as energetic phenomena, literally fill up and move through social space.

The Book of Promethea invites this kind of materialist reading, or at least aspires to it. We know that representational language cannot render Promethea; her untranslatability is the book's dramatic core. The narrator reserves special ire, though, for the limitations of figurative language, and specifically metaphor, in capturing Promethea's qualities. Throughout the novel, Cixous develops a tension between metaphor and Promethea's style of writing aloud. In an early passage, we witness an attempt by H. to describe the love she shares with Promethea:

> It makes me drool (H moans), the minute I open my mouth I dribble metaphors, "forest," "narrative," "woman-fish," it is all pretend. [...] in short, all I want to say, very quickly, before the metaphors swoop straight down on my heart to steal its blood, is that I have found the entrance to a life so rich in personal events, one so stirred up, so potent and nascent, a life that never stops bursting into lives, into shouts of life, into tears of life, into laughs of life, into songs of life, into terrors of life.[70]

If sound affects—shouts, tears, laughs, songs, terrors—are the bursting forms of life itself, then metaphor is here figured as their natural predator. They eke out of H.'s mouth as a "dribble"—a faltering stream that in its slowness and thinness is the opposite of the "singing, burning, abolishing, liquidating, flowing, gushing" gait of H.'s language post-Promethea, or the "evocations and eruptions" of Promethea herself. To speak in metaphors is to grind signifiance, to borrow Kristeva's term, through the mill of signification, a process of translation that will always effect a loss. Cixous's narrator knows this. Having used metaphor to describe Promethea as an arrow, she quickly renounces the rhetorical device as simultaneously insufficient and dangerous. "I am dropping the arrow now," she tells the reader. "It is only a metaphor. I wish I could lay all weapons down."[71]

Cixous's suspicion of metaphor in *The Book of Promethea* is surprising because, as several of her best critics have pointed out, metaphor has long held a privileged place in her writing. In the late 1990s, Mireille Calle-Gruber nominated metaphor as "Cixous's favorite means of transportation ... since this trope draws, spins, and threads its way across page [sic] more easily than any other."[72] Cixous is drawn to metaphor because its logic of substitution and transference animates the connective tissue of her text. For example, taken as a metaphor, "the text is a rhythm that laughs you" sets in place a feedback loop between text and rhythm through which different qualities of each term can flow.[73] It is with a similar appeal to movement and sensation that Deleuze characterizes Cixous's writing as a "writing in strobe, where the story comes alive, different themes connect up, and words form various figures according to the precipitous speeds of reading and association."[74] Deleuze's suggestive comments have produced some compelling accounts of Cixous's fiction; I'm thinking here in particular of Michael Nass's "Flicker" essays, which pose Cixous's stroboscopy as a kind of synesthetic translation of the cinematic or photographic function. "Cixous's art of writing is ... photographic or cinematic through and through—with its lighting, its speed, its 'clicks,' as we shall soon see, its" Naas argues, it is a "high-speed art of replacement or substitution."[75]

This art of replacement and substitution that we associate with metaphor plays out too in the complex phonetic texture of Cixous's prose. In his foreword to *The Cixous Reader*, Jacques Derrida observed that "Hélène has a genius for making the language speak ... She knows how to make it say what it keeps in reserve, which in the process also makes it come out of its reserve."[76] To illustrate his argument, Derrida performs a close reading of three words written by Cixous, "tous les deux": "All two of them: '*tous les deux*' is one of the most singular works of French grammar," he explains, because it "can always be heard as *all* the 'twos,' all the couples, the duos, the differences, the dyads in the world."[77] So long as it remains read and not heard, which is to say, on the page and not in the mouth, "tous les deux" is able to hide its secrets from the reader, it is able to keep itself in reserve. Speak it aloud, though, and we can hear its multiplicity—to stress a different phoneme is to call forth a different meaning. Derrida's example is by no means an anomaly: Cixous's prose is marked by its recombinant phonetic texture. As Laurent Milesi explains in his translator's introduction to *Tomb(e)*, "Cixous' narrative is an infinite orchestration of ever-recombining motifs, often working at the most resistant idiomatic core of the French language, across polysemy, homonym, and homophony."[78]

It's clear that both Derrida and Miseni understand Cixous's "infinite orchestration" of the sounds of the French language as a prolonged gesture of deconstruction. Through puns, homonyms, and other forms of sound play, Cixous slips along the chain of signifiers to access the reserves of language, which Derrida calls "the place where [language] seems to be crawling with secrets."[79] There is much fun to be had in discerning the secrets that bustle beneath Cixous's language, and it is this task that critics mostly set themselves when attending to her writing's sonic texture. Take, for example, Geert Lernout's analysis of "Fort-Sein," the title Cixous gave her editor's introduction to a special volume of *Poetique* from 1976. Lernout applauds Cixous for choosing a title that "opens up an infinite series of echoes," and then carefully traces its reverberations out to form a genealogy of intertexts, "First the Freudian/Lacanian *fort/da*, then the Derridean *seing* of *Glas* (1974) with its Hegelian and Heideggerian connotations (*Sein*, *Dasein*, *Seyn*), and then the French *sein*, *signe*, *fort*, *for*, *fors*, etc."[80] Like Bataille's techniques of *mot glissant* and hypersubstitution, Cixous's use of metaphor and sound play opens words to a recombinant field of multiplicity and variation: she, too, makes discourse slide.

So, écriture féminine advances in part through metaphor and complex phonetic play. But there is another way in which language and sound work in and through Cixous's writing. As she herself has noted, at the heart of l'écriture féminine is a cry (l'é-*CRI*-ture), and at its end a laugh (ec-*RIRE*). A cry, a laugh, a song, a sob: these types of vocalizations are not involved in the infinite play of signification. They do not carry symbolic meaning; they carry instead the material pulse of affect. In their case, there is no longer any gap between the word and the world; the sound does not represent the affect, it *is* the affect, and vice versa. If Cixous's first use of sound marks écriture féminine as a deconstructive gesture, her second hints at a project that is affectological in nature—it is an attempt on Cixous's part to summon forth a totally material language that would neither translate an emotion nor represent a signified but would behave like, would literally *be*, the affects they announce.

While *Promethea* contains both kinds of sound play, it lists dramatically toward the second, the sound affect. It is therefore no surprise that the book sees Cixous pulling away from metaphor, that dazzling art of substitution and replacement that Cixous, in conversation with Calle-Gruber (and, remotely, with Lacan), linked to the inner workings of the psyche. "For me, the origin of the metaphor is the unconscious," she explains.[81] The exhaustion of metaphor in *Promethea* signals an attempt on Cixous's part to move from the deep reserves of the Self (and of language) to experiment instead with developing a sound writing that would be able to commune with that which lies outside the psychoanalytic subject and semiotic signification. By 1983, the opening gambit of the "Medusa" essay that "Woman must write her self" is due a revision; *Promethea*'s Cixous says instead, "Woman must write the brink of self and Other."[82] Several critics before me have viewed *Promethea* as marking a shift in Cixous's preoccupations, away from representing the self's psychic and emotional interiors (see, for example, *Angst*) and toward the direct presentation of the (female) Other, a task that Susan Sellers calls "writing with the voice of the Other."[83] The ambiguity of Sellers's preposition "with" helps us recognize a central dilemma of *Promethea*—what writerly method would permit the narrator to write *with* (alongside) Promethea's voice instead of writing *with* (using) Promethea's voice? How, in other words, does one get close to the voice of the Other without commandeering it?

Developing the Sound Image

In this chapter I've argued that Promethea is a blend of sound affects that move in the spaces between Self and Other, and that the novel's central theme is the task of rendering the grain of Promethea's voice in writing. If it seems at this point that the question of how to write the sound affect in language has been hopelessly deferred, this is because both Cixous and Barthes dedicate more time circling the question than they do answering it. Both begin their separate inquiries with a negative gesture: Barthes's "Grain" essay is predicated on his rejection of descriptive language ("Are we condemned to the adjective?"), and Cixous's *Promethea* opens with the narrator's dismissal of academic discourse. H.'s theoretical language is an early casualty, followed soon after by dictation.[84] As *Promethea* wears on, though, a positive model for writing sound affects does shimmer into view. This model leans away from language (academic or otherwise) and toward the visual arts for their ability to capture the gestures and movements of "action-filled bodies."[85] Contemplating Promethea, the narrator sighs, "I want to make a sort of vast frieze," before adding, "I would have liked … so much to film Eternity … every instant with its radiant procession of reminiscences!"[86] The types of visual art that the narrator invokes here mirror each other: the frieze is a band of panels inscribed horizontally across the face of a building, and cinematographic film is a spool of frames that could in theory "proceed" for Eternity.

The narrator's overtures to the visual arts are mitigated by her continued commitment to the page as the site of inscription. While she might "want" to carve Promethea in stone or "like" to write her in light, the challenge that she has set for herself is to discover a way to write her in ink. The trick is finding a way to subsume the visual element into language. What is afoot here is a complex experiment in synesthesia: by appealing to the visual arts in language, the narrator hopes to create in the reader the sensory effect of hearing sound. Throughout the course of the novel, the narrator toys with techniques that recall the writing experiments of the Symbolists and their progeny, the Surrealists. Take, for example, the method of automatic writing by which the narrator traces out the sounds of Promethea's body as the graphic play of an unbroken horizontal line. "I have often put my left hand between her breasts and with the rapid motions of my docile right hand it was written. I am only that cardiograph."[87] Another strategy, less built out but still apparent, takes a cue from grapheme-color synesthesia, the sensory phenomenon that inspired Rimbaud's sonnet "Voyelles." There exists a "book of Promethea's heart," says the narrator, that bears "a name composed of several different colored words."[88] That these experiments in drawing and dying ultimately fail to organize into a structured set of literary protocols does not mean they are without value. *Promethea* is a logbook of tests that, taken together, suggest that writing aloud depends on the swapping out of imagery for imaging.

Barthes's meditation on writing aloud comes to a similar conclusion. In the closing lines of *The Pleasure of the Text*, Barthes proposes the cinematic close-up as one form of writing aloud:

> A certain art of singing can give an idea of this vocal writing; but since melody is dead, we may find it more easily today at the cinema. In fact, it suffices that the cinema captures the sound of speech *close up* (this is, in fact, the generalized definition of the "grain" of writing) and make us hear in their materiality, their sensuality, the breath, the gutturals, the fleshiness of the lips, a whole presence of the human muzzle (that the voice, that writing, be as fresh, supple, lubricated, delicately granular and vibrant as an animal's muzzle), to succeed in shifting the signified a great distance.[89]

Barthes's declaration that "cinema captures the sound of speech *close up*" is ultimately enigmatic. When we go looking for a concrete example, are we in pursuit of a close-up shot of the mouth in motion, something like a cinematic version of the fast-moving contortions of "Mouth" in Sam Beckett's *Not I* (Cixous's favorite of his plays)?[90] Or are we on the lookout for a scene in which actors are closely miked, but not clearly in shot? Put another way, which sensory apparatus does the acoustic close-up play on: the eye or the ear? Of course, this is a trick question. Like the synesthete who hears color or sketches sound, Barthes's acoustic close-up depends on a cross-sensory operation by which we "hear" the granularity of the voice through our eyes and "see" its fleshliness through our ears. Although Barthes nominates the filmic image as a paradigmatic form of writing aloud, we do not have to proceed to the darkened space of the cinema to achieve its effect. Whether they are writing in light, ink, or stone, what matters is that the writer court a synesthetic effect—that they imbricate the sensory apparatuses of eye and ear in such a way as to produce the effect of a body in sound.

Two Lessons in Laughter

In closing, I want to introduce and remark upon two art objects that use cross-sensory, cross-media tactics to successfully stage laughter as a material sound affect. The first is *Hysteria* (1997), an eight-minute video artwork by the British artist Sam Taylor-Johnson (née Taylor-Wood). *Hysteria* is comprised of one unbroken, closely framed shot of a woman caught in the throes of a sustained bodily spasm that alternately codes as laughter and crying. The camera does not leave the woman's face. It does, however, make slight adjustments in distance and position. Because the woman is in constant and often violent motion—her head thrown way back, her mouth agape, her uvula quaking—this minimal camerawork is almost imperceptible. We register it as a kind of mutter, a background noise that in its persistence suggests a fussiness, even an obsessiveness, on behalf of the filmmaker. Perhaps I sense this visual effect aurally because of the startling soundscape of the video itself. For while at least one reviewer has suggested that the woman is "miming" laughter (itself an interesting conceit), *Hysteria* is a silent film.[91] The removal of the sound element calls attention to the sight of sound, which is to say, the sight of the body in sound. To borrow from Barthes, *Hysteria* brings to our eyes that fleshly *something* that comes directly from the woman's body; "the cavities, the muscles, the membranes, the cartilages," these are all on vivid display.

Now freely available online as an eight-minute digital video, *Hysteria* was originally shot on 16 mm color film and displayed as a single screen projection at the White Cube gallery in London. In 2008, the first major US museum exhibit of Sam Taylor-Johnson's work opened at The Museum of Contemporary Art in Cleveland, Ohio. The curator, Margo A. Crutchfield, chose to install the majority of Taylor-Johnson's video artwork in darkened spaces that recall the cinematic experience. The exception was *Hysteria*, a looped version of which was projected onto a thin screen that hung suspended from the ceiling of the well-lit gallery space. Crutchfield's staging of *Hysteria* made of it a floating portrait, an effect that was amplified by her mounting of Taylor-Johnson's *Suspended* series, a set of photographic self-portraits that depict the artist in various states of acrobatic suspension, on a nearby gallery wall. These curatorial cues, combined with the video's soundlessness, provoke the museumgoer into locating *Hysteria* in the uncanny, squinted spaces between film, photograph, and painting. Is it a still-life in motion? An animated photograph? A work of "deaf cinema," to borrow Michel Chion's term?[92] We expect photographs to stay still and color film to emit sound, and when *Hysteria* does neither, the effect is a confusion not only of media, but of sensation. This sensory confusion is in fact a return of sensation that triggers a heightened attention to the materiality of the screen's surface. Unsure what we are looking at, we study the grain of the image—the wet twitch of the woman's vocal cords and the inky black of her surrounds—to ascertain its material provenance. The muted laugh demands that we examine the texture to the image, "in order to make us feel objects, to make a stone feel stony."[93]

The second artifact is Lorrie Moore's short story "Real Estate" (1998), or more precisely, its opening two and a half pages. The story is a meditation on marriage and death. It centers on Ruth, a woman who is dying of cancer and whose marriage died long ago, a casualty of her husband's infidelity. Moore is quick to furnish us with these two details, which Ruth thinks together in the story's first few paragraphs. "It must be, Ruth thought, that she was going to die in the spring ... Of course, it had always been in the spring that she discovered her husband's affairs."[94] It is some combination of the two, the arrival of death and the departure of love, that causes Ruth (or is it the page itself) to break into a laugh that is as closely framed and as relentless as that of Sam Taylor-Johnson's *Hysteria*. The lead-up line is innocuous enough, it reads: "There had been a parade of flings—in the end they'd made her laugh."[95] What follows is a solid block of 982 "Ha!"s, each typed just like that: Ha! The geometric stacks of Ha!'s hit the eye with a visual energy similar to that of a Bridget Riley painting. The dizzying optics causes the eye to buzz and hum; the material grain of the page rises to the fore for a moment and then slips back behind the grid of three vertical lines that (used to) form the exclamatory "Ha!"

Bridget Riley described her compositional practice as one based in rhythm and repetition. "Rhythm and repetition are at the root of movement," she explains. "They create a situation within which the most simple, basic forms start to become visually active. By massing them and repeating them they become more fully present."[96] An identical principle is at work in Moore's Ha-block, which produces through repetition a visual rhythm that we receive through our eyes. Each Ha! is a heartbeat, perhaps, or a strum notation. The suspicion that these Ha!s bear traces of sound is reinforced by the story's epigraph, which is a lyric excised from "Glitter and be Gay," the coloratura aria from Leonard Bernstein's operetta *Candide*. A darkly comic showpiece about the seductive lure and seedy underbelly of the world of property, "Glitter and be Gay," is sung by Cunégonde, Candide's love interest. The aria contains sung strings of laughter that are articulated in the musical score as a series of punctuated Ha!s. When performed, these Ha!s trill with a velocity that causes the word to reverse back on itself to become an "Ah!" which is to say, a sob. It's clear that in "Real Estate," Moore is not trying to offer a direct transcription of Bernstein's aria: her Ha!s outstrip his at a ratio of approximately four to one (the final count is 982 to 226). A relationship between the two does exist, however. How could it not? To see Moore's unforgiving Ha-block is to hear the ghostly trace of Cunégonde's run of laughs—it is to hear a soundless music.

Both *Hysteria* and "Real Estate" take crosscuts at the problem of writing aloud by rendering laughter's sonic properties as a visual trace. Sound is not absented so much as it is translated into an optical effect that makes us increasingly aware of and involved in the materiality of the art object—we touch with our eyes the grain of the page, the pixels of the screen. If we build an intimacy with the material body of the text instead of directly with the laughing women, this is because both scenes of laughter traffic in affects instead of emotions. In the moment immediately preceding her laughter, Ruth tries and fails to describe the feeling that occupies her in terms of emotion, "What she was feeling was too strange, too contrary, too isolated for a mere emotion," she states.[97] The Ha-block outplays "mere" emotion. Like Cunégode's folded laugh-sob ("Ha-Ah") it has a complex affective density that cannot be read but can be seen and may be heard. When asked about the Ha-block, Moore explained: "I needed enough so that it registered as a scream."[98] Her note suggests that there are (at least) two possible ways of understanding the laugh section. You can *read* all 932 words, one after another, as we are taught to do in school. Or, you can *look* at the Ha-block as you would a painting or a photograph. It is the second operation, Moore suggests, that would allow us to hear the affective timbre of this laugh that is also a scream.

Let me return, for a moment, to the tail end of Bridget Riley's statement about rhythm and repetition in which she proposes that it is by "massing [basic forms] and repeating them they become more fully present."[99] Writing aloud, finally, is the art of presence. This is the project that *The Book of Promethea* sets itself; to find a way to present (to make present) Promethea, raw and bleeding, on the page. Although the narrator knows that the art of presence has something to do with sound and vision and laughter, she cannot work out how to make the three work together successfully. As working examples of writing aloud, *Hysteria* and "Real Estate" together suggest that the art of presence depends on the cultivation of a different durational structure that never ends or completes itself, and that flickers at the edge of absence. Taylor-Johnson's looped video is gossamer thin and literally infinite, and Moore's Ha-block is designed to be taken in at a glance, but its optical effect is that of the gestalt: to look at it is to experience that blotchy sensation of blacking out as white space and black ink rapidly switch cut at the fore of your vision. This flickering sensation is theorized by Jean Luc Nancy in his essay, "Laughter, Presence," in which he proposes that "presence does not belong to imitation ... but to the quite different logic of presentation itself. Presentation desires to be presented *in its very disappearance*."[100] Presence, in other words, is an infinite process of arrival.

As his title suggests, laughter holds a privileged place in Nancy's investigation into what he calls the "erotico-aesthetics" of the art of presence. Nancy's description of laughter sounds like a remix of *Promethea*'s narrator and Barthes circa 1970:

> Laughter is the sound of a voice that is not a voice, that is not the voice it is. It is the material and the timbre of the voice, and it is not the voice. It is between the color of the voice, its modulation (or its modeledness) and its articulation. Laughter laughs a voice without the qualities of a voice. It is like the very substance of the voice, indeed, like its subject, but a substance that disappears in presenting itself.[101]

Nancy's essay helps us understand why it is that in chasing down a working example of writing aloud we once again found ourselves at the foot of laughter. His figuration of laughter as "pure presentation" depends upon his logic that the art of presence is always a disappearing act. *Hysteria* and "Real Estate" show us how writing aloud performs this vanishing trick: both pieces are high-wire acts of suspension—they slip in the gaps between the senses (and media) of sight and sound, between joy and joylessness, between presence and absence. To present laughter, finally, is to write in disappearing ink.

Notes

1 Hélène Cixous, "The Book as One of Its Own Characters," *New Literary History* 33, no. 3 (2002): 432.
2 Hélène Cixous, "Conclusion: Ay yay! The cry of literature," in *Ways of Re-Thinking Literature*, ed. Tom Bishop and Donatien Grau (London and New York: Routledge, 2018), 208.
3 Hélène Cixous, "The Laugh of the Medusa," *Signs* 1, no. 4 (Summer 1976): n. 878.
4 Ibid.
5 Hélène Cixous and Michel Foucault, "Marguerite Duras," in *Foucault at the Movies*, ed. Clare O'Farrell (New York: Columbia University Press, 2018), 124.
6 The term "sound body" belongs to Deborah Kapchan, who defines it as "a resonant body that is porous, that transforms according to the vibrations of its environment, and correspondingly transforms that environment." Deborah Kapchan, "Body," in *Keywords in Sound Studies*, ed. David Novak and Matt Sakakeeny (Durham, NC: Duke University Press, 2015), 38.
7 Cixous and Foucault, "Marguerite Duras," 130.
8 Ibid., 131.
9 Marguerite Duras, *Destroy, She Said: A Novel*, trans. Barbara Bray (New York: Grove Press, 1986), 85.
10 Duras, *Destroy, She Said*, 85.
11 Cixous and Foucault, "Marguerite Duras," 131.
12 Ibid.

13 Ibid., 124.
14 Ian Blyth with Susan Sellers, *Hélène Cixous: Live Theory* (London; New York: Continuum Books, 2004), 50.
15 Cixous and Foucault, "Marguerite Duras," 134. Emphasis my own.
16 B. Ruby Rich, "In the Name of Feminist Film Criticism," in *Issues in Feminist Film Criticism* ed. Patricia Erens (Bloomington: Indiana University Press, 1990), 282.
17 See Frances Gray, *Women and Laughter* (Charlottesville: University Press of Virginia, 1994); Kathleen Rowe, *The Unruly Woman; Gender and the Genres of Laughter* (Austin: University of Texas Press, 1995); Domnica Radulescu, *Women's Comedic Art as Social Revolution. Five Performers and the Lessons of Their Subversive Humor* (Jefferson, NC: McFarland & Company, Inc., 2012).
18 Parvulescu, *Laughter*, 117.
19 Hélène Cixous and McQuillan, "You race towards that secret, which escapes: An Interview With Hélène Cixous," *Oxford Literary Review* 24 (2002): 186–7.
20 "Medusa's Head" is the title of a 1922 essay by Freud in which he, like Perseus before him, averts his gaze from Medusa's living, laughing body to instead pose her decapitated head as an emblem of (the male fear of) castration. See Sigmund Freud, "Medusa's Head," in *The Standard Edition of the Complete Psychological Works of Sigmund Freud, Volume XVIII (1920–1922): Beyond the Pleasure Principle, Group Psychology and Other Works*, trans. James Strachey (London: The Hogarth Press, 1955), 273–4.
21 Cixous, "Laugh of the Medusa," 885.
22 Hélène Cixous and Mirielle Calle-Gruber, *Hélène Cixous, Rootprints: Memory and Life Writing*, trans. Eric Prenowitz (London; New York: Routledge, 1997), 18.
23 Parvulescu, *Laughter*, 111.
24 Walter Gershon, "Vibrational Affect Sound Theory and Practice in Qualitative Research," *Cultural Studies Critical Methodologies* 13, no. 4 (2013): 257. See also Marie Thompson and Ian Biddle, *Sound Music Affect: Theorizing Sonic Experience* (New York: Bloomsbury Academic, 2013).
25 Ryan Bishop, "The Force of Noise, or Touching Music: The Tele-Haptics of Stockhausen's 'Helicopter String Quartet,'" *SubStance* 40, no. 3 (2011): 27.
26 Sedgwick, *Touching Feeling*, 14.
27 Hélène Cixous, "Castration or Decapitation?" *Signs* 7, no. 1 (Autumn 1981): 54.
28 Verena Andermatt Conley, *Hélène Cixous: Writing the Feminine* (Lincoln, Nebraska: University of Nebraska Press, 1984), 146.
29 Conley, *Hélène Cixous*, 146.
30 Cixous, "Laugh of the Medusa," 882.
31 Hélène Cixous, "Sorties: Out and Out: Attacks/Ways Out/Forays," in Hélène Cixous and Catherine Clement, *The Newly Born Woman*, trans. Betsy Wing (Minneapolis: University of Minnesota Press, 1986), 93.

32 Blyth and Sellers, *Live Theory*, 44; Hélène Cixous, *Angst* (New York: Riverrun Press, 1985), 218–19.
33 Hélène Cixous, *The Book of Promethea*, trans. Betsy Wing (Lincoln, NE: The University of Nebraska, 1991), xiii.
34 Roland Barthes, *The Pleasure of the Text*, trans. Richard Howard (New York: Hill and Wang, 1998), 66–7.
35 Kaja Silverman, The *Acoustic Mirror: The Female Voice in Psychoanalysis and Cinema* (Bloomington: Indiana University Press, 1988), 87.
36 Cixous, *The Book of Promethea*, xiii.
37 Barthes, *The Pleasure of the Text*, 66.
38 Rebecca Lentjes, "Against the Grain," *VAN Magazine*, July 6, 2017, https://van-us.atavist.com/against-the-grain.
39 Barthes, "The Grain of Voice," 182; Barthes, *The Pleasure of the Text*, 66.
40 Roland Barthes, "The Third Meaning" in *Image-Music-Text*, 54.
41 Barthes, *The Pleasure of the Text*, 61.
42 Barthes, "Grain," 189. As an example of such squeamishness, Jonathan Dunsby cites the scholar John Daverio's passing off of Barthes's scholarship as "sensitive if eccentric." Writes Dunsby, "Daverio, Schumann's foremost English-language spokesperson of modern times, always shied away, it may be thought out of embarrassment, from Barthes's attempt to explain his engagement with Schumann as one not of contemplation but of desire." See Jonathan Dunsby, "Roland Barthes and the Grain of Panzéra's Voice," *Journal of the Royal Musical Association* 134, no. 1 (2009): 48.
43 Barthes, "The Grain of the Voice," 180.
44 Barthes, "The Third Meaning," 65.
45 Barthes, "The Grain of the Voice," 181.
46 Ibid.
47 Cixous, *The Book of Promethea*, 3.
48 Ibid., 12.
49 Ibid., 5, 6, 111.
50 Ibid., 5–6.
51 Ibid., 5.
52 Ibid., 16.
53 Ibid., 14.
54 Ibid., 15.
55 Sissel Lie, "Medusa's Laughter and the Hows and Whys of Writing According to Hélène Cixous," in *Emergent Writing Methodologies in Feminist Studies*, ed. Mona Livholts (New York: Routledge, 2012), 44.
56 Cixous, *The Book of Promethea*, 15.
57 Ibid., 73.

58 Ibid., 152.
59 Ibid., 111.
60 Ibid., 91.
61 Ibid., 92.
62 Ibid., 40.
63 Barthes, *The Pleasure of the Text*, 67.
64 Cixous, *The Book of Promethea*, 23-4.
65 Ibid., 154-5.
66 Ibid., 5.
67 Ibid., 24.
68 See Karen Barad's "self-touching electron" in "Quantum Entanglements and Hauntological Relations of Inheritance: Dis/continuities, SpaceTime Enfoldings, and Justice-to-Come," *Derrida Today* 3, no. 2 (2010): 240-68. See also Brinkema, *The Forms of the Affects*.
69 Brennan, *The Transmission of Affect*, 1.
70 Cixous, *The Book of Promethea*, 18.
71 Ibid., 9.
72 Calle-Gruber, "Hélène Cixous: Music Forever or Short Treatise on a Poetics for a Story to be Sung," 76.
73 Cixous, "Laugh of the Medusa," 882.
74 Gilles Deleuze, "Hélène Cixous, or, Writing in Strobe," in *Desert Islands and Other Texts, 1953-1974*, trans. Betsy Wing (Los Angeles: Semiotext(e), 2004), 230.
75 Michael Naas, "Flicker 1: Reflections on Photography and Literature in the Works of Hélène Cixous," *Mosaic: An Interdisciplinary Critical Journal* 47, no. 4 (2014): 33.
76 Jacques Derrida, "Foreword," in *The Hélène Cixous Reader*, ed. Susan Sellers (London; New York: Routledge, 2003), vii.
77 Ibid.
78 Laurent Milesi, "Translator's Note," in Hélène Cixous, *Tomb(e)*, trans. Laurent Milesi (Calcutta: Seagull Books, 2014), vii.
79 Derrida, "Foreword," vii.
80 Lernout, Geert, *The French Joyce* (Ann Arbor: University of Michigan Press, 1993), 51.
81 Cixous and Calle-Gruber, *Rootprints*, 27.
82 Cixous, "The Laugh of the Medusa," 875.
83 See the chapter titled "Writing with the Voice of the Other" in Susan Sellers, *Hélène Cixous: Authorship, Autobiography, and Love* (Cambridge: Polity Press, 1996); also, H. Jill Scott, "Subjectivities of Proximity in Hélène Cixous's *Book of Promethea*," *World Literature Today* 69, no. 1 (1995): 29-34. Note, too, Lynn Keller Pernod's periodization of Cixous's body of work into three periods: "in the first period texts seem to be essential self-referential and caught in a web of Freudian

dream analysis … A second period produces texts that are basically focused on 'the other.'" Lynn Kettler Penrod, *Hélène Cixous: Twayne's World Authors Series* (New York: Twayne Publishers, 1996), 39.

84 Barthes, "The Grain of the Voice," 180. In France, dictation is a school exercise (*la dictée*) designed to test the competency of students' spelling and grammar.
85 Cixous, *The Book of Promethea*, 17.
86 Ibid., 111.
87 Ibid., 53.
88 Ibid., 98.
89 Barthes, *The Pleasure of the Text*, 67.
90 Cixous has this to say about *Not I*: "If I was asked to choose a text of Beckett's for all, for all that, I would certainly not do so but if I did, it would be *Not I*." See Hélène Cixous, *Zero's Neighbour Sam Beckett*, trans. Laurent Milesi (Cambridge: Polity Press, 2010), 48.
91 Simon Hattenstone, "There's Something about Sam," *The Guardian*, November 28, 2009, https://www.theguardian.com/artanddesign/2009/nov/28/sam-taylor-wood-interview.
92 Michel Chion, *The Voice in Cinema*, trans. Claudia Gorbman (New York: Columbia University Press, 1999), 7.
93 Victor Shklovsky, *Theory of Prose*, trans. Benjamin Sher (Illinois: Dalkey Archive Press, 1998), 6.
94 Lorrie Moore, *Birds of America* (New York: Picador, 1998), 77.
95 Ibid.
96 Bridget Riley, cited by Brett Baker, "Bridget Riley: Repetition, Rhythm, & Learning to Look," *Painter's Table*, October 31, 2012, https://www.painters-table.com/blog/bridget-riley-repetition-rhythm-learning-look-video#:~:text=In%20the%20first%20video%20Riley,they%20become%20more%20fully%20present.
97 Moore, *Birds of America*, 77.
98 Email correspondence with the author.
99 Riley, "Bridget Riley: Repetition, Rhythm, & Learning to Look."
100 Jean-Luc Nancy, "Wild Laughter in the Throat of Death," *MLA* 102, no. 4 (1987): 728.
101 Nancy, *The Birth to Presence*, 388.

4

Atomic Laughter

President Harry Truman on 6 August, 1945, announcing the bombing of Hiroshima: "We have spent more than two billion dollars on the greatest scientific gamble in history and we have won."

Figure 2 "Atomic Laughter" by Andreas Müller-Pohle © 2002. Reproduced with the permission of the artist.

In 2002, a Parisian gallery housed an art installation by the Berlin-based photographer Andreas Müller-Pohle. The work, titled *Atomic Laughter*, consisted of eleven portrait photographs that told in sequence the story of a laugh. With eyes squeezed shut, nose bunched, and mouth stretched wide, the first five frames depicted a man caught in laughter's throes. The next six showed the suppression of the same—the man's eyes open to fix steadily on the camera, his facial muscles firm into a grimace, and his lips pull into the oval shape of speech. The subject of the artwork is President Harry Truman, the date of capture August 6, 1945. The blurred black-and-white grain of the photographs hints at their provenance—these are the moments immediately preceding Truman's radio announcement of the Hiroshima bombing. Given its context, it is tempting to read Truman's laughter as indexing a particular feeling or emotion—the glint of superiority at a war finally won, perhaps, or the surge of relief at a gamble gone good. Put aside the diagnostic *why* of humor studies for a moment, though, and an alternate reading falls into view, one that the artist himself urges us to consider.

In a 2003 lecture, Müller-Pohle invited the audience to conceive of Truman's laughter as a creative gesture. "It was not Truman who decided to drop the atom bomb on Hiroshima and Nagasaki," he explains, "but rather the apparatus he lent his face to. By unintentionally showing his 'true' face … Truman breaks the political code and turns into an involuntary artist."[1] Rooted in art and affect rather than science and statistics, Truman's impromptu laughter is a subversive gesture that scrambles the "political codes" of progressive humanism to transmit, albeit just for a moment, a different type of "truth." Viewed from this canted angle, *Atomic Laughter* can be seen as containing the traces of two explosions: the deadly atomic flash that flattened Hiroshima, and the creative burst of affect that crumples Truman's face. In this chapter, I use Müller-Pohle's title, "atomic laughter," to refer to a mutant strain of laughter that emerged in a subset of literary and philosophical texts following the Hiroshima and Nagasaki attacks. As its name suggests, atomic laughter shares genetic similarities with the atom bomb: it arrives on the page (or screen) as a shattering agent that obliterates humanist orders and principles. Decimation is but its first function, however. As Müller-Pohle demonstrates, atomic laughter is also a creative practice that breaches the locked logic of political rationalism to produce an affect-charged outside to Enlightenment discourse.

Up until this point, *Posthumorism* has focused on how individual authors have used laughter as a tool to inscribe affects in language—indeed, what I've proposed so far is something like an auteur theory of writing laughter, in which each author's own idiosyncratic signature bears out in how they figure laughter. This chapter behaves differently. Atomic laughter does not belong to a single author and so cannot be analyzed in such terms. Instead, it has multiple agents, all of whom contribute to a rescaled affectology that takes the planet, not the human, as its primary unit of measurement. Atomic laughter derives from two different literary traditions, French poststructuralist theory and American black humor, both of which develop it as a means of coming to terms with and imagining a way past the epistemological and ontological fallout of the atomic bomb. Instead of grafting poststructuralism over American black humor, or vice versa, I offer here an exploratory ethnography of atomic laughter as it moves across and between theoretical and literary bodies. Falling in step with its object, the chapter drifts back and forth between France and America before dilating further to meditate upon the global dimensions of our planet. Drawing on Kostas Axelos and Édouard Glissant's theories of globality and Relation, my closing argument is that atomic laughter is the affective embodiment of planetary thought.

Atomic Laughter

Let us return, then, to the beginning. On the morning of 6 August 1945, President Harry S. Truman announced the bombing of Hiroshima to a dazed and disconcerted world. While the official purpose of the speech was to announce and justify an act of war, its larger project was to formally introduce the atomic bomb to the American people as a natural and inevitable part of human history. This double motivation is responsible for the speech's tonal dissonance, which sits somewhere between the flat reportage of a military operation and the effluvious introduction of a debutante. Truman rattles off a few statistics before arriving at his pitch: "It is an atomic bomb. It is a harnessing of the basic power of the universe. The force from which the sun draws its power has been loosed against those who brought war to the Far East."[2] Having established the bomb as the ultimate natural resource, Truman goes on to note the exceptional teamwork that went into its development, and invites his listeners to marvel at "the achievement of scientific brains in putting together infinitely complex pieces of knowledge held by many men in different fields of science into a workable plan."[3] In this way, Truman proposes the bomb as the crowning demonstration of the Enlightenment principles of scientific rationalism, democratic procedure, and human progress.

Not all his listeners, though, were convinced. Writing a few years later, Georges Bataille denounced Truman's speech as a con designed to conceal the bomb's radical alterity. The occasion for Bataille's writing was the book publication of John Hersey's *Hiroshima*, a 31,000-word report on the Hiroshima attack that had first appeared in *The New Yorker* in 1946. Widely read by the American public, *Hiroshima* conveyed for the first time the horror of atomic violence as it was experienced by six survivors. Viewed from Japanese soil rather than the American laboratory, which is to say, in practice rather than in theory, the bomb appeared not as a rational object of scientific knowledge, but as an unintelligible and alien force that moved through the city according to its own capricious logic. The city and its residents, utterly unprepared for the attack, were thrown into "weird and illogical confusion." Some bodies were vaporized into "vague human silhouettes," while others were barely touched.[4] For Bataille, Hersey's style of reporting, which strung together eye-witness accounts of the bomb's detonation, emphasized the isolated incomprehension of those caught in the scene. "The individual in the streets of Hiroshima learned nothing from the colossal explosion. He submitted to it like an animal, not even knowing its gigantic scope."[5]

Reading Truman's speech and Hersey's *Hiroshima* side by side, Bataille recognized the fatal damage nuclear violence has caused the Enlightenment project. In the figure of the bomb, atomized individualism culminates in impersonal mass death; progressive humanism culminates in the total finitude of humankind; and rational calculation culminates in the production of an alien weapon whose "weird" destructive path specialists could neither predict nor control. However, as Bataille was quick to point out, the bomb also cleared a path for the inauguration of a new philosophical framework, one that might avoid its predecessor's genocidal trajectory. Bataille called this post-nuclear, post-Enlightenment disposition a "sovereign sensibility," and listed as its key characteristic a refusal to subordinate the present to the future. He saw a version of it in the "animal stupor" of those caught in the immense nuclear flash of the Hiroshima attack who, deprived as they were of "a passage into the future," were caught too in a heightened experience of the present.[6] Bataille hoped to parlay the stunned atemporality of the nuclear survivor into a freedom from the world of activity, which he described as "an old sponge of anxiety … whose movements lead to destruction."[7] The sweaty-palmed release of Big Boy over Hiroshima was one such example of this fearful orientation toward the future.

Crucially for the purposes of this chapter, Bataille associated the "man of sovereign sensibility" with a particular vocal effect that he described in the Hiroshima essay as a "cry of the instant." Bataille imagined the cry of the instant as a nonviolent version of the atomic blast that manages to make the leap out of the dead ends of Enlightenment thought without annihilating a population. What hurtles through the air is not intense thermal radiation but an expansive cry that testifies to the world's radical openness as it goes. Writes Bataille: "If there is no salvation and if the rationalized future of the world cannot alter the world's being open to all that is possible—then nothing counts more than this cry, which fills the air like the wind or the light and, however powerless, leaves no room for fear, that is to say, for worrying about the future."[8] Elsewhere and often, Bataille figures the cry of the instant as a cry of laughter, as Derrida explains, Bataille's "thinking of the instant, which he calls sovereignty" has to do with "laughter, bursts of laughter; that's the instant."[9]

Bataille was not the only cultural figure to find philosophical value in the bomb. In a late interview that was published in *Le Monde* in 1980, Michel Foucault invoked the image of atomic annihilation as the ground from which to imagine a new, non-hierarchical style of thought. His lyrical description of this new disposition is worth citing in full for its similarities to Bataille's sovereign cry:

> The last man, when radiation has finally reduced his last enemy to ashes, will sit down behind some rickety table and begin the trial of the individual responsible. I can't help but dream of a kind of criticism that would not try to judge, but to bring an oeuvre, a book, a sentence, an idea to life; it would light fires, watch the grass grow, listen to the wind, and catch the sea-foam in the breeze and scatter it. It would multiply, not judgments, but signs of existence; it would summon them, drag them from their sleep. Perhaps it would invent them—all the better. All the better. Criticism that hands down sentences sends me to sleep; I'd like a criticism of scintillating leaps of the imagination.[10]

To imagine criticism unleashed from the chokehold of hierarchical thought, Foucault borrows tropes and techniques from literature—figurative language, mounting rhythms, and arcing cadences—to fling his imagination into unclear and uncleared terrain. No longer shackled to the "rickety table" of judgment, Foucault's post-atomic thought is free to experiment with unrestricted styles of movement that are in the service of life, not death. As Bataille's cry "fills the air like the wind or the light," so Foucault draws on elemental imagery to emphasize the clean, open-aired "leaps" that post-atomic thought can make.

Foucault's acrobatic style of post-nuclear thought reappeared elsewhere in his work in the form of a laugh. In an essay titled "The Laugh of Michel Foucault," Michel de Certeau declared laughter to be Foucault's "philosophical signature" and the basis of his critical discourse. In de Certeau's account, Foucault's laugh was synonymous with his style of thought:

> Something that exceeds the thinkable and opens the possibility of 'thinking otherwise' bursts in through comical, incongruous, or paradoxical half-openings of discourse. The philosopher, overtaken by laughter, seized by an irony of things equivalent to an illumination, is not the author but the *witness of these flashes* traversing and transgressing the gridding of discourses effected by established systems of reason.[11]

Reading de Certeau's piece in the shadow of Bataille's Hiroshima essay helps highlight its atomic undercurrents. Like the nuclear survivor, the philosopher here bears "witness" to catastrophic "flashes" that illuminate the fissured ground in which discourse takes root. Seized by the fallout of this blast, the philosopher (both Bataille's "man of the instant" and Foucault's post-atomic thinker) bursts into an activating cry of laughter that overruns existing discourse to provide "a new tone, a new way of looking, a new way of doing."[12]

Foucault's atomic laughter finds its most explicit expression in his Preface to *The Order of Things*, in which he famously credited the book's birth to a "shattering" laughter that accompanied his reading of a fictional taxonomy by Jorge Luis Borges:

> This book first arose out of a passage of Borges, out of the laughter that shattered, as I read the passage, all the familiar landscapes of my thought—*our* thought, the thought that bears the stamp of our age and our geography—breaking up all the ordered surfaces and all the planes with which we are accustomed to tame the wild profusion of existing things, and continuing long afterwards to disturb and threaten with collapse our age-old distinction between the Same and the Other.[13]

The twin operations of atomic laughter are here clearly on display. First, Foucault's shatters the structural bases of humanist thought. As nuclear survivors stepped out of the rubble to see their houses, neighborhoods, and cities razed to the ground, Foucault wrestles his attention from Borges' book to see that the "familiar landscapes" that constituted his self, his imagined community, and his epoch have been obliterated. But atomic laughter is also a creative force that prompts Foucault to imagine a radically different set of terms by which to arrange and assemble "things." Reading this passage closely, the transformative effect of atomic laughter falls into view: it transfigures Foucault's specular "I" into a speculative "our," and in so doing pushes him outward into the uncertain, communal ground that lies between reading and writing, between Borges and Foucault, between Self and Other.

With Bataille and Foucault in hand, we can now refine our definition of atomic laughter. The gesture of atomic laughter is a "scintillating," "great," or "impossible" leap that hooks thought up with its constitutive outside. It is tempting to stop here so that we might leave atomic laughter forever caught in the gesture of a leap, but as *Thelma and Louise* taught us some years ago, to freeze a jump at its apex is to render it a utopian and suicidal gesture. To activate atomic laughter's creative capacities, we must let it complete its bound into the black. Both Bataille and Foucault knew this and were committed to describing what lay on the other side of atomic laughter. For Bataille, the "cry of the instant" opened onto a radical present, one that was unhinged from past actions or future concerns. Foucault, for his part, described thought's outside in spatial rather than temporal terms:

The passage from Borges kept me laughing a long time, though not without a certain uneasiness that I found hard to shake off. Perhaps because there arose in its wake the suspicion that there is a worse kind of disorder than that of the incongruous, the linking together of things that are inappropriate; I mean the disorder in which fragments of a large number of possible orders glitter separately in the dimension, without law or geometry, of the *heteroclite*.[14]

As it turns out, the "empty space" that swells between Borges's taxonomic classes, that gap between language and world that prompted Foucault's laughter in the first place, is not empty at all; rather, it is a densely populated zone teeming with things. Foucault testified to his laughing revelation of this heteroclite zone with the fervor of the recently converted. He invited his reader to envision this space, as if in picturing the absolute dispersion of its contents, we too would be transformed.

So, atomic laughter performs a double movement. First, it acts as a shattering agent that levels humanism. Second, it models an adventurous, nomadic style of thought that leaps through but does not close those gaps that de Certeau described as the "paradoxical half-openings in discourse."[15] As we trace the operations of various bursts of atomic laughter we shall see this gap take on different guises: the gap between language and world into which Foucault, laughing, casts himself; the gap between expectation and reality that constitutes the incongruity-resolution theory of humor; the gap between emotion and affect that grounds Massumi's affect theory; the gap between dialectical poles that Kostas Axelos calls the "interlude"; and, of course, the fictional missile gap that propelled real American Cold War policy. For it was not only in pockets of French thought that the bomb's philosophical ramifications were felt and atomic laughter's critical potential tested. In the American context, the question of how to think that which obliterated the very foundations of thought was written up as black humor. In what follows, I argue that atomic laughter found a permanent home in the decidedly American strain of black humor that emerged in the wake of the Japanese bombings. It is here that its twin operations—to flatten and to leap—are fleshed out in their most compelling form.

A Comedy of Surfaces

The question of how to make sense of the atom bomb, of how to think through that which obliterated the very foundations of Western thought, registered in the American consciousness as an aesthetic problem. In his exhaustive retrospective on American reactions to atomic warfare, Paul Boyer details the struggle among US writers and artists to respond creatively to the bomb:

> How was one to respond imaginatively to Hiroshima and Nagasaki and, still more, to the prospect of world holocaust? The question haunted writers in 1945, and it would continue to do so. As one linguistic specialist asked in 1965: "Is it possible that in spite of our vast and ever-growing vocabulary we have finally created an object that transcends all possible description?"[16]

Boyer is attentive here to the scale of the bomb's destructive capacity. How does one stretch the parameters of one's mind to imagine "world holocaust"? As an example of the bomb's aesthetic fallout, Boyer alights upon Pat Frank's *Mr. Adam* (1946) and Ward Moore's *Greener Than You Think* (1947), two post-Hiroshima apocalyptic narratives that share a sardonic humor and a "feverish, surreal style." Boyer is visibly rankled by the authors' decision to treat "the most sobering theme imaginable" with humor, but his ire is reserved for *Mr. Adam*, which he describes as a "justifiably forgotten novel" that, when faced with the trauma of the bomb, can "manage only an ill-assorted mixture of satire, rather leering humor, and occasional nihilistic flashes."[17]

But what if that which Boyer takes to be a failed attempt at "light-hearted social satire" is in fact an early sign that satire itself was undergoing a mutation? In 1965, Bantam Books published *Black Humor*, a paperback anthology that featured short selections by Terry Southern, Joseph Heller, and Thomas Pynchon, among others. In his foreword, which is itself much anthologized, Bruce Jay Friedman announced a changing of the guard: satire was out, and an "ill-assorted" and peculiarly American style of comedy was firming up in its place, a "one-foot-in-the-asylum style of fiction" that he famously codified as black humor. Confronted with an increasingly absurd political reality where the threat of apocalypse hung squarely in the balance, the moralizing language of satire ceased to function. "The black humorist," observes Friedman, "has had to discover new land, invent a new currency, a new set of filters, has had to sail into darker waters somewhere out beyond satire."[18] A decade later, Linda Barnes elaborated on this distinction, noting that "whereas satire, being moralistic, aims to correct by holding within brackets a vision of what should be, Black Humor does not tell us how to live; its concern is rather with perception and mediation, forging through surface reality to present life as it is."[19]

In their figuring of the black humorist as a nomadic explorer of surfaces rather than an excavator of moral depths, Friedman and Barnes cut to the aesthetic and philosophical heart of the mode. The primary characteristic of black humor is *flatness*. This flatness is expressed most profoundly in black humor's particular style of comedy, in which a library fine and a decapitation have propensity to hold equal narrative and moral weight, but it registers, too, in the mode's very form and structure. In 1968, Max Schulz provided a list of black humor's various tropes, citing its "one-dimensional characters, wasteland settings, and disjunctive and a-temporal narrative structures."[20] Cut loose from the ponderous chains of psychic depth, the "one-dimensional" character is set in flight across the newly open, traversable terrain of its decimated "wasteland setting." In every case, black humor's flat surfaces facilitate adventure and movement; flattened characters skim the flattened surface of a flattened world. This compulsion to move laterally and at speed extends too to the reader: black humor's "disjunctive narrative structure," reflected in its early romance with the anthology format, encourages the reader to skate across and between episodes rather than through and down into them.

In *The Logic of Sense*, Gilles Deleuze argues for a distinction between irony and humor that maps usefully onto the distinction that I am making (via Barnes and Friedman) between satire and black humor. For Deleuze, irony is a style of intellectual movement that climbs vertically up and down the pole of an assumed Truth, the foundation of which is the rational subject. Humor, in contrast, is a lateral "adventure" that renounces the "art of depths and heights" in favor of the cultivation of relation; it is "the art of surfaces and of the complex relation between the two surfaces."[21] Irony and humor each bear philosophical freight. While "irony is a co-extensiveness of being with the individual, or of the I with representation, humor is the co-extensiveness of sense with nonsense."[22] Like Bataille's laughter, Deleuze's "humor" overruns the dialectic; sense and nonsense rush freely into one another, and all receptacles (the "I" included) are abandoned. In his recent book on comedy and philosophy, Russell Ford describes Deleuze's humor as a procedure that "propels thinking to 'the surface,' the name that Deleuze gives to the domain of thinking that is populated with both ideas and things and that is no longer coordinated by a desire to secure the legitimate authority of the former over the latter."[23] In its style and direction of movement, Deleuze's humor is similar to the atomic laughter that overwhelms Foucault at the beginning of *The Order of Things*; here, too, thought is freed from the individual and pitched into a heteroclite zone where order cannot go.

Flattened comedy, the philosophical value of which is parsed by Deleuze above, is black humor's first characteristic. But black humor does not only flatten; it also builds. Its second characteristic is an affirmative laughter that is both internal to and produced by the work. Critics writing in the 1960s understood black humor's laughter as essentially reactive and nonproductive. In 1965, for example, Leslie Fiedler declared black humor to be a last resort: "You can't fight or cry or shout or pound the table. The only response to the world that is left is laughter."[24] Morris Dickstein offers a similar diagnosis, "Black humor," he asserts, "is pitched at the breaking point where moral anguish explodes into a mixture of comedy and terror, where things are so bad you might as well laugh."[25] And yet, as Dickstein's language inadvertently suggests, what black humor's laughter bears witness to is the explosion of morality into a heightened mix of affects. Deleuze discusses this process in a 1973 essay titled "Nomadic Thought":

> Whoever reads Nietzsche without laughing, and laughing heartily and often and sometimes hysterically, is almost not reading Nietzsche at all. This is true not only for Nietzsche, but for all the authors who comprise the same horizon of our counter-culture. What shows us our decadence and degeneracy is the way we feel the need to read in them anguish, solitude, guilt, the drama of communication, the whole tragedy of interiority. Even Max Brod tells us how the audience would laugh hysterically when Kafka read *The Trial*. And Beckett, I mean, it is difficult not to laugh when you read him, moving from one joyful moment to the next. Laughter, not the signifier. What springs from great books is schizo-laughter or revolutionary joy, not the anguish of our pathetic narcissism, not the terror of our guilt […] You cannot help but laugh when you mix up the codes. If you put thought in relation to the outside, Dionysian moments of laughter will erupt, and this is thinking in clear air.[26]

Atomic laughter does not index a personal emotion: my anguish, my narcissism, my guilt. Instead, it abdicates absolutely from the tragedy of interiority so that it might open itself to everything that stands outside the closed borders of the self, which is to say, the comedy of everything else.

It can be no surprise that Deleuze's recuperation of laughter coincided with the boom in American black humor. In *Nihil Unbound* (2007), Ray Brassier calls nihilism "not an existential quandary but a speculative opportunity," and it is in American black humor that these speculative opportunities are given literary form.[27] In the remainder of this chapter, I look to two black humor texts that are routinely tagged as nihilistic, Kurt Vonnegut's *Cat's Cradle* (1963) and Stanley Kubrick's *Dr. Strangelove, or, How I Learned to Stop Worrying and Love The Bomb* (1964). Published within a year of one another, the atom bomb stands at the center of both texts as the ugly culmination of a modern temperament obsessed with social domination and scientific absolutism. Both texts adopt an aesthetics and comedy of flatness to collapse the hierarchies and binaries that constitute Western thought and build in their place, by way of atomic laughter, a counter style of thought that is based in affect and relation, instead of reason and isolation. Although the texts work toward similar ends, Kubrick organizes his film around the political paradoxes of Cold War nuclear policy, whereas Vonnegut treats the bomb as a philosophical axis upon which a rotation from a tragic Western-Christian humanism to a comic poetics of Relation may be enacted.

Laughing in the (Missile) Gap

Two months after *Dr. Strangelove*'s release, renowned political correspondent Hans J. Morgenthau published an article entitled "The Four Paradoxes of Nuclear Strategy" in which he located a troublesome gap between Enlightenment thought and Cold War policies.

> While our conditions of life have drastically changed under the impact of the nuclear age, we still live in our thoughts and act through our institutions in an age that has passed. There exists, then, a gap between what we think about our social, political, and philosophical problems and the objective conditions which the nuclear age has created.[28]

Morgenthau refers to this gap between outdated structures of thought and the nuclear reality of global extinction as "the fatal flaw" that engendered the four paradoxes of his title.[29] In interviews, Kubrick repeatedly explained that his impetus in making *Dr. Strangelove* was a fascination with precisely this flawed logic that fueled American foreign policy. "I was struck by the paradoxes of every variation of the problem from one extreme to the other, from the paradoxes of unilateral disarmament to the first strike."[30] For Morgenthau, the paradoxes of mutually assured destruction can be resolved in two possible ways: the acceptance of total political impotence, or the unleashing of total global annihilation. Kubrick offers a different strategy: instead of trying to reconcile or synthesize the paradox, we can occupy it with laughter. "The things you laugh at most [in *Dr. Strangelove*]," Kubrick told an interviewer in 1963, "are really the heart of the paradoxical postures that make a nuclear war possible."[31]

The comic occupation of a gap between thought and action corresponds with the incongruity-resolution theory of humor, which was first formulated during the Enlightenment and remains the dominant paradigm in humor studies today. In its earliest form, the theory did not include the second stage of resolution. Writing in 1779, James Beattie suggested that "laughter arises from the view of two or more inconsistent, unsuitable, or incongruous parts or circumstances, considered as united in one complex object or assemblage, or as acquiring a sort of mutual relation from the peculiar manner in which the mind takes notice of them."[32] For Beattie, an incongruity creates a field of uncertainty in which laughter enters to create unexpected or "peculiar" forms of relation: precisely the operations that we here associate with atomic laughter. Within the decade, though, Beattie's theory had been overshadowed by the work of Immanuel Kant, whose commentary on humor in *The Critique of Judgment* (1790) is routinely acknowledged as the origin of the incongruity-resolution theory. Kant argues that our laughter stems not from the experience of uncertainty, but from our triumphant self-inoculation against the same. Our laughter is the happy return to order, signaling as it does the "restoration of equilibrium."[33] Taking their cue from Kant, modern incongruity-resolution theorists posit humor as a reasoning game that invites us to reconcile paradoxical gaps with a preexisting masternarrative of reason.

The fixation with closing gaps in a bid for mastery and progress is directly satirized in *Dr. Strangelove*, as the President's military advisors rush to close presumed gaps between Russian and American military clout at the expense of humanity's survival. Henry Kissinger's dark premonition of a "missile gap" in *The Necessity for Choice* (1960) is extrapolated in *Dr. Strangelove* as President Muffley (Peter Sellers) is warned first of a "Doomsday gap" ("preposterous!" he splutters) and then of a "mine-shaft gap" in reference to Dr. Strangelove's suggestion of a post-nuclear survival strategy based on the relocation of men and women underground.[34] The latter is announced in the penultimate line of the film, moments before the interior scene fades into a symphonic montage of exploding bombs. The reasoning game of incongruity-resolution humor, thus exaggerated, becomes a hysterical intolerance of gaps that fuels the inexorable passage to global annihilation. Kubrick's intervention is to show how cultivating a different type of laughter, that which I call atomic laughter, may get us out of this predicament. Kubrick replaces the malfunctioning incongruity theory, which states that we laugh at the pleasure of resolution, with black humor, which states that we laugh at the pleasure of difference. As per the mode, Kubrick retains the comedy of paradoxes, incongruities, and gaps but does away with the drive toward synthesis that we associate with the rationalism of traditional narrative forms. The film teems with unresolvable paradoxes that encourage the audience to fill gaps not with reason but with laughter. Colonel Bat Guano won't shoot a Coke Machine to save the world ("That's private property!") and General Ripper (Sterling Hayden) is willing to have every atom of his body infiltrated by nuclear radiation but refuses to drink a glass of water for fear of "Commie" contamination.

Dr. Strangelove's famous culminating scene recognizes the necessary conjunction of this flattened humor with the creative gesture of atomic laughter. Somewhere over Russia, Major T.J. "King" Kong (Slim Pickens) straddles a nuclear warhead as he frantically scrambles to fix the malfunctioning bomb release mechanism of his B-52. Abruptly, the bomb bay doors open and Kong shouts in triumph, unaware that his misguided heroics have triggered Russia's Doomsday Machine and will directly lead to the extinction of all life on Earth. This scene is most often read by critics as a symbolic implosion of America's frontier spirit in an act of irrevocable global violence.[35] However, if we take the naturalistic sound design of the scene as a cue and pay close attention to the shifting sonic registers of Kong's cry, a different reading becomes possible. Erupting literally at the limits of life and language, Kong's atomic laughter skids between human howl, animal yowl, and mechanical screech. Its emotional parameters are equally illegible: the sound vibrates in an indistinct zone that lies somewhere between terror, exuberance, horror, and joy. The ontological and affective capaciousness of Kong's cry is intensified by the gigantic scale of the panoramic backdrop, which sets his falling body against the vast open plains of Russian airspace. It is hard not to think here of Deleuze's description of atomic laughter as the orotund sound of radical exteriority: "If you put thought in relation to the outside, Dionysian moments of laughter will erupt, and this is thinking in clear air."[36]

To think in clear air is to think outside the mind. Glossing Deleuze, Mieke Taat explains that bursts of atomic laughter "do not spring from some inner or internalized source, but are simply the production of flows on the surface of a body."[37] There is, in other words, an affective truth as well as a rational one, or, as Kubrick famously noted, "sometimes the truth of the thing is not so much in the think of it, but in the feel of it."[38] In his book *The Kubrick Façade*, Jason Sperb uses this quote to make the compelling argument that Kubrick's work be understood in terms of surfaces rather than depths, which is to say, in terms of affects and sensations rather than rational argumentation. Sperb proposes that "Kubrick's films progressively advocate that we start—as much as one can—outside the mind entirely, at the preconscious sensory level of sight and sound."[39] Kubrick's films, in other words, make thought's constitutive outside their central theme, and in so doing compel us to "unthink the mind" by propelling us "into an unthought realm where mutual experience and interaction exist."[40] Of all the cinematic images in Kubrick's catalogue, none is more ripe for conceiving of this *unthought realm* than Kong's laughing descent. As Sperb notes, its "naturalistic emphasis seems to point away from verbal or explicit narrating of any kind. The event is the event."[41]

Representing a euphoric loss of physical and ontological control, Kong's suicide-event must be compared with that of the cigar-chewing and stony-faced General Ripper, whose paranoid fantasies of hygienic enclosure and "purity of essence" causes him to launch the nuclear attack against Russia.[42] We have said that the atomic bomb represents the bottoming out of Enlightenment principles; the apogee of humanism is the end of humanity. General Ripper is the personification of these values pushed to their perverse limits. Convinced that a "monstrously conceived" Communist plot to pollute the national water supply is underway, Ripper is in a perpetual state of fear that the Russians will somehow, through contamination, "sap and impurify our precious bodily fluids." As the film progresses, Ripper recedes into smaller and smaller spaces. He seals off his base, barricades his office, and finally locks himself in the tiny bathroom that adjoins his office, where, terrified that he will be forced under torture to reveal the military codes that would issue the stand-down order on Kong's plane, Ripper ensures his own silence by putting a bullet in his brain. That Ripper's suicidal management of his own silence takes place in a bathroom, a private space reserved for the maintenance of bodily integrity, reflects his commitment to preserving a particular conceptualization of the monadic self, whose continued existence depends on its sealed containment. The two suicides thereby stand in opposition: Ripper's silent, meticulous, and private self-termination against Kong's hyper-physical and public self-detonation.

Kong's atomic laughter implicates the audience in the film's project of thinking otherwise. How are we to hear it? To watch the bomb-drop scene and accept that it is both horror and humor, a scene of terrifying global annihilation and the hub of a laughing community, requires a repudiation of the type of either/or thinking that Kubrick implies brought about the communicative impasse of the Cold War in the first place. Critics writing about *Dr. Strangelove* upon its release identified the activating effect the film had on its audience—Lewis Mumford, for example, described the film as "the first break in the catatonic cold war trance that has so long held our country in its rigid grip."[43] Writing for *Sight and Sound*, Tom Milne suggested that in order to appreciate *Dr. Strangelove*, which he describes as "the most hilariously funny and the most nightmarish film of the year," an audience would have to cultivate a certain affective uncertainty.[44] Life magazine's Loudon Wainwright zeroed in further on the film's activating agent: "Had I suddenly arrived—after prolonged laughter—at a glimpse of some awful truth?" he asks.[45]

Wainwright here suspects that his laughter is raw material; it is his responsibility to hear in it the sound of a new and unexpected "truth" that is produced on the affective surfaces of the body rather than in the seat of the brain. Taken together, these reviews suggest that to laugh along with Kong (with Kubrick) is to cease any attempt to measure or fix the parameters of his scream. The tight spaces of the cockpit, the bounded subject, the frame of the film itself, all are shattered: Kong's laughter explodes laterally out across the Russian skies and skids through the surfaces of our screens, impelling us too to become impassioned.

Thinking surfaces instead of heights—laterally instead of hierarchically, affectively rather than rationally—lends itself to a planetary ethics. In *Dr. Strangelove*, the Russian Ambassador is the first character to conceive of nuclear war not in terms of human statistics but as an ecological disaster. Announcing the existence of the Doomsday Machine, he declares that the bombs will destroy "everything on the surface of the globe." The bomb threatens global annihilation, but it also highlights the fragile interconnectivity of all life on earth. Lewis Mumford identified this new global consciousness in the wake of the bomb. "For the first time, mankind exists as a self-conscious collective entity," he remarked in 1955, before calling for an all-encompassing, ecological attentiveness to "all forms of organic partnership between the millions of species that add to the vitality and wealth of the earth."[46] We have said that atomic laughter is a positive incarnation of the bomb: it activates our capacity to think globally without imposing universalisms or destroying the world. In the final section of this chapter, I complete the gesture of atomic laughter by connecting it to the art of planetary thinking as it is theorized by the Greek French philosopher Kostas Axelos and the Martinican poet and scholar Édouard Glissant. Planetary thinking is a conceptual apparatus that enacts a similar style and movement of thought to atomic laughter, operating as it does on the surface and in "clear air."

Planetary Thinking

The last piece of my argument is this: atomic laughter is the affective embodiment of planetary thinking. The descriptive language used by our authors to limn atomic laughter suggests that they have long intuited its planetary dimensions. We sense the world's vast scope in Deleuze's Dionysian burst into open air and in Bataille and Foucault's nimble cries that travel along the elemental channels of air, wind, and fire. And, of course, the bomb-drop scene from *Dr. Strangelove* offers a powerful visual of the planetary coordinates of atomic laughter: *this is thinking in clear air*. The connection between atomic laughter and planetary thinking cuts both ways. As artists and philosophers use scaled-up natural images to figure atomic laughter, so Kostas Axelos's theory of planetary thinking is underwritten by a dialectic-bursting laughter. Axelos's landmark book *Towards Planetary Thought* was released in 1964, the same year as *Dr. Strangelove*. In his review of the book, Henri Lefebvre describes the enigmatic laughter that suffuses Axelos's prose:

> The writings of Kostas Axelos happen to irritate many readers, exasperating some of them. And furthermore, one never knows, in reading him, exactly where and when we encounter an essential thought or mere wordplay. Axelos knows this. Behind his ambiguity, we glimpse his laughter, the laughter of the Sphinx before the young Oedipus (reader). A demon of dialectics, he uses and abuses this game.[47]

As with the black humorist, Axelos refuses to enforce a distinction between the "essential thought" from "mere" play, and his laughter leaps from this flattened zone. For Lefebvre, Axelos's laughter is a sign that the dialectic's guarantee has been revoked.

Drawing on Heraclitus, Nietzsche, and Heidegger, Axelos is a philosopher of play. He conceives of the world (*le monde*) as a self-sustaining game that plays itself out in a perpetual process of becoming. It is time, Axelos says, for us to construe of the "World as the space-time of the Open, the adventure of errancy, the game of itinerance," and to adapt our thinking and our language accordingly.[48] Planetary thought is open, adventurous, playful, and itinerant; it spins perpetually between the poles of the dialectic and so never arrives at an answer, never reaches the shore. (I think here of Friedman's description of the black humorist as a castaway, sailing away from satire into darker waters). As Axelos puts it, "Nothing is ever quite elucidated. Prelude, development and—especially—finale remain problematical. We are always embarked and under way. We are—and what we are not is too—in the interlude."[49] Planetary thought knows that everything that happens happens in the interlude, in the "gap" that opens between Man and World, between One and All, between Self and Other. Attuned, finally, to the relational, rotational game of the world, man would be inoculated against his drive toward annihilation. He would learn instead "to see being and things simultaneously from close up and far away, large and small, in their and in our wandering (*errance*), in the great World which is at the same time small, where there are no victors."[50] This paradoxical double vision is the ethical heart of planetary thinking—it is how we embrace totality without becoming totalitarian, conceive of unity without resorting to homogenizing universals, and think relation without slipping into relativism.

Like Foucault's post-nuclear criticism, Axelos's planetary thought remains speculative. To hear the tale of errant global thought told in the present tense, we must enlist Édouard Glissant, for whom the thinking of an identity that extends itself through, rather than exists in violent opposition to, the Other has long been underway in the "explosive region" of the Caribbean. The dynamic processes of creolization, like planetary thinking and like atomic laughter, resists the theoretician's urge to hierarchize or synthesize. Because of this resistance, it plays out as a deeply unpredictable process with unforeseeable results; it "opens on a radically new dimension of reality … [it] does not produce direct synthesis, but *resultantes* results: something else, another way."[51] In his *Poetics of Relation*, Glissant builds out a vision of what this "something else" might look like, in terms that are strikingly similar to those used by Axelos:

> the poetics of Relation remains forever conjectural and presupposes no ideological stability. It is against the comfortable assurances linked to the supposed excellence of a language. A poetics that is latent, open, multi-lingual in intention, directly in contact with everything possible. Theoretician thought, focused on the basic and fundamental, and allying these with what is true, shies away from these uncertain paths.[52]

If the poetics of Relation was a gesture, it might look something like the wide-open cry and wing-spanned arms of Kong as he falls clean through the Russian skies. Expansive and without guarantee, the poetics of Relation sits in contrast to classical thinking, which is risk-averse and so prefers its critical objects, its identities, and its World to be stable, fixed, and finite.

Because so much is at stake in the question of *how* precisely we are to achieve this mutation in thought, it's worth pausing here to clarify the relationship that exists between the poetics of Relation and classical thought. Glissant is careful to show that the former is not held in opposition to the latter but is rather its rebellious offspring. As the violent oppositional logic of colonialism provides the ground upon which creolization might emerge, so everywhere "the ontological obsession with knowledge" will give "way to the enjoyment of a relation."[53] Glissant suggests that this radical transformation in how we conceive of Self, Other, and World can be understood as a seismic shift from a tragic to a comic worldview. Classical thought constitutes identity through its violent opposition to and the absolute exclusion of the Other. Such oppositional thinking bases its systems of community and kinship on the filiation model, which refuses the cultural legitimacy of any form of relation save that between father and son. As the structural seed of classical identity, the "chain of filiation" imposes linearity on everything it touches, from legitimate bloodlines and arrow-like geographical conquest, to the steady march of scientific progress and chronological time. Any rupture in these chains engenders tragedy, which Glissant describes as the "quest for legitimacy and its reestablishment."[54] In contrast, the poetics of Relation is an essentially comic practice that gives up the clean lines and ratified roots of the filiation model in favor of an entangled state of coexistence that Joseph Meeker has elsewhere described as a "gigantic comic drama."[55]

A Gigantic Comic Drama

Published one year before *Dr. Strangelove's* cinematic release, Kurt Vonnegut' *Cat's Cradle* is a blackly humorous meditation on planetary thinking that enacts through an atomic laughter the necessary leap from the grisly dead-ends of the Age of Reason to the gigantic comic drama of the Age of Relation. As *Poetics of Relation* pushes through and past a malfunctioning Western Christian discourse to discover a Creole-inspired poetics of Relation, *Cat's Cradle* functions as a conversion narrative that pushes past the tragedy of the filiation model to build a comic poetics of Relation based in atomic laughter. The book opens with our protagonist Jonah (formerly John)'s announcement of his conversion to Bokononism, a religion native to the small Caribbean island of San Lorenzo where most of the narrative action takes place. The book we hold in our hands is evidence of this conversion—it is a Bokononist mutation of Jonah's formerly "Christian" book about the lives of "important Americans" on the day of the Hiroshima attack. On the first page of the novel, Jonah explains the transformative impact his renunciation of Western Christian humanism has had on his project:

> When I was a much younger man, I began to collect material for a book to be called *The Day the World Ended*.
> The book was to be factual.
> The book was to be an account of what important Americans had done on the day when the first atomic bomb was dropped on Hiroshima, Japan.
> It was to be a Christian book. I was a Christian then.
> I am a Bokononist now.
> I would have been a Bokononist then, if there had been anyone to teach me the bittersweet lies of Bokononism. But Bokononism was unknown beyond the

gravel beaches and coral knives that ring this little island in the Caribbean Sea, the Republic of San Lorenzo.

We Bokononists believe that humanity is organized into teams, teams that do God's Will without ever discovering what they are doing. Such a team is called a *karass* by Bokonon, and the instrument, the *kan-kan* that brought me into my own particular *karass* was the book I never finished, the book to be called *The Day the World Ended*.[56]

Newcomers to Vonnegut's novel might be excused in reading this passage as a set of binary oppositions. We rack them up in our minds: *The Day the World Ended* versus *Cat's Cradle*, Christianity versus Bokononism, factuality versus "bittersweet lies," the progressive narrative of scientific rationalism (as manifested in the atomic bomb) versus undulating *karasses* that cleave together "without ever discovering what they are doing," and "important Americans" against humanity in its entirety.

One critic who certainly read these couplets as oppositional pairs is Fredric Jameson, who in his *Archaeologies of the Future* lambasted *Cat's Cradle* for peddling in racist, sophomoric binaries:

> [The] displacement of the action from upstate New York to the Caribbean, from dehumanized American scientists to the joyous and skeptical religious practices of Bokononism, suggests a scarcely disguised meditation on the relationship between American power and the Third World, between repression and scientific knowledge in the capitalist world, and a nostalgic and primitivistic evocation of the more genuine human possibilities available in an older and simpler culture.[57]

In reading the novel as a set of oversimplified opposites, however, Jameson paves over the enigmatic gap that holds each dyad in tension. As the title of his rejected Master's thesis, "Fluctuations between Good and Evil in Simple Tasks," suggests, Vonnegut is interested in the state of flux that vibrates in the gap between a binary's poles.[58] *Cat's Cradle* suggests that Jonah has not simply exchanged Christianity for Bokononism, but has instead passed through the one to attain the other. The opening passage states this Glissantian idea plainly: the "Christian," "factual," "history" of "important people" is not only the philosophical opposite of Bokononism, but also how Jonah is able to attain Bokononism. "The instrument, the *kan-kan*, that brought me into my own particular *karass*," Jonah reminds us, "was the book I never finished, the book to be called The Day the World Ended."[59]

The Day the World Ended was to be an ode to filiation. Its paternal centerpiece was Felix Hoenikker who as the progenitor of three children, the atom bomb, and the world-ending biochemical weapon that will be accidentally unleashed into the ocean at the end of the novel, was three times a father—sanguine, scientific, and divine. Vonnegut weaves together these paternal valences to confer upon Felix the absolute sovereign power of the Father. In an early scene, Jonah makes a pilgrimage to photograph Felix's gravestone in the hopes that it will serve as a dramatic frontispiece for his book-in-progress. As it turns out, the towering alabaster column marked Hoenikker that dominates the cemetery grounds was erected in memory to Emily Hoenikker, Felix's wife. Felix's own tombstone is somewhat less eye-catching. Writes Jonah, "His memorial—as specified in his will, I later discovered—was a marble cube forty centimeters on each side. 'FATHER,' it said."[60] The unusual shape of the monument is one example of many in which the three streams of Felix's claim to fatherhood intersect. A cube, if unfolded, becomes a tesseract. Erected on the family plot, Felix's monument is a mathematically condensed Christian crucifix; a neat conflation of his parental-conjugal role, his scientific prowess, and his divine paternalism. The terse epigraph helps sustain the threaded nature of Hoenniker's paternalism: we ask, "Father to whom, and to what?"

Despite being dead for the entirety of the novel, Felix's absolute grip on the world's fate does not weaken. The chain of filiation sees his deadly final creation—icenine—pass through his three children's hands before slipping into the ocean, where it hurtles through the world's moisture atoms and leaves in its wake a frozen planet. Jonah describes the global shutting down of motion and relation at the end of the novel. "There were no smells. There was no movement. Every step I took made a gravelly squeak in blue-white frost. And every squeak was echoed loudly. The season of locking was over. The earth was locked up tight. It was winter, now and forever."[61] Crucially, icenine kills not by annihilating bodies but the relations between bodies. Asa Breed, an associate of Hoenikker tells Jonah that icenine obliterates the "gaps" between hydrogen molecules, causing water to "stack and lock in an orderly, rigid way."[62] Later, Breed suggests that icenine's apocalyptic activity reflects the scientist's role in the age of progress. The scientist, Breed says, is "supposed to fill the little gaps" in knowledge.[63] The chaining effect of filiation is therefore dramatized in the apocalyptic chain reaction of icenine through the world's waters, which literally halts movement and destroys the relations between people, animals and things. As Breed puts it, "When [the rain] fell, it would freeze into hard little hob-nails of icenine—and that would be the end of the world!"[64] Here, as in *Dr. Strangelove*, the Western intolerance for gaps results in world death.

on the surface, in the expanse, weaving our imaginary structures and not filling up the voids of a science, but rather as we go along, removing boxes that are too full so that in the end we can imagine infinite volumes."[78] Atomic laughter is an embodiment of this infinite movement. It escapes the grip of the sciences to act as a creative, communal movement that vibrates through and dislodges the grouting between these chains, these blocks. This, too, is how scholar Patrick O'Neill describes the reader of Black Humor in his landmark text *Comedy of Entropy*: "Like Maxwell's Demon," O'Neill writes, "[the reader] industriously sets to work, assiduously sorting molecules, generating energy, reversing entropy. And as he works he laughs, for his work is play."[79]

In both Kubrick and Vonnegut's blackly humorous texts, humanism skids to its final, fatal culmination—the flattening of life and difference—in atomic decimation and the molecular compactness of an icenine death, respectively. In both cases, the apocalyptic event of "flattening" sees the obliteration of humanism and its attendant icons—filiation, linearity, reason. And in both cases, this philosophical terminus becomes the occasion for an unbounded atomic laughter. Major Kong and Julian Castle's laughter is the noise of philosophical conversion, as the tragic heaviness of being is transfigured into the errant joy of comic becoming. This new philosophical mode is founded on nomadism and errantry instead of a quarantined and "pure" universal Being, which in *Dr. Strangelove* and *Cat's Cradle* meets its own suicidal end in the clean, cloistered spaces of General Ripper's bathroom and the molecular compactness of an icenine death. Calling upon the laughter that spills over the borders of texts, a readerly laughter, as evidence for a poetics of Relation may seem theoretically crude. Perhaps it seems so because it is impossible to map. Infinite and noncalculable, it exists beyond the texts in the embodied communities that form, however momentarily, around them. It is precisely in these unsteady zones of readerly laughter that resistance against the universalizing, annihilating maxims of a Western-Christian humanism becomes possible. Like the Bokononist karass, these laughing communities perpetually form and un-form across multiple times and spaces to embody the planetary principles of a new philosophical framework, a poetics of Relation.

Notes

1   Andréas Müller-Pohle, e-mail message to author, March 11, 2013. The original lecture was delivered in German, in Bucharest in 2003. Translation is my own.

2   Harry Truman, "August 6, 1945: Statement by the President Announcing the Use of the A-Bomb at Hiroshima," *Miller Center*, last modified October 4, 2019, https://millercenter.org/the-presidency/presidential-speeches/august-6-1945-statement-president-announcing-use-bomb.
3   Ibid.
4   John Hersey, *Hiroshima* (1946; New York: Knopf, 1985), 30, 96.
5   Georges Bataille, "Concerning the Accounts Given By the Residents of Hiroshima," *American Imago* 48, no. 4 (1991): 500.
6   Ibid.
7   Ibid., 513.
8   Ibid.
9   Jacques Derrida, "Derrida's Response to Hent de Vries," in *Augustine and Postmodernism: Confessions and Circumfession*, ed. John D. Caputo and Michael J. Scanlon (Bloomington: Indiana University Press, 2005), 89.
10 Michel Foucault, "The Masked Philosopher," in *Ethics: Subjectivity and Truth*, ed. Paul Rabinow (New York: The New Press, 1997), 323.
11 Michel de Certeau, "The Laugh of Michel Foucault," in *Heterologies: Discourse on the Other* (Minneapolis: University of Minnesota Press, 1986), 194. Emphasis my own.
12 Foucault, "The Masked Philosopher," 327. It is this cataclysmic glare that Akira Mizuta Lippit theorizes in *Atomic Light (Shadow Optics)* (Minneapolis: University of Minnesota Press, 2005).
13 Foucault, *The Order of Things*, xvi.
14 Ibid., xix.
15 de Certeau, "The Laugh of Michel Foucault," 194.
16 Paul Boyer, *By The Bomb's Early Light: American Thought and Culture at the Dawn of the Atomic Age* (Chapel Hill: The University of North Carolina Press, 1994), 250.
17 Ibid., 261.
18 Bruce Jay Friedman, "Foreword: *Black Humor*," in *Black Humor: Critical Essays*, ed. Alan R. Pratt (New York: Garland Publishing, Inc., 1993), x.
19 Linda Barnes, *The Dialectics of Black Humor: Process and Product* (Frankfurt: Peter Lang, 1978), 25.
20 Max F. Schulz, "Pop, Op, and Black Humor: The Aesthetics of Anxiety," *College English* 30, no. 3 (1968): 272.
21 Gilles Deleuze, *The Logic of Sense* (New York: Columbia University Press, 1990), 9, 248.
22 Ibid., 141.
23 Russell Ford, "Humor, Law, and Jurisprudence: On Deleuze's Political Philosophy," *Angelaki: Journal of the Theoretical Humanities* 21, no. 3 (2016): 98.
24 Leslie Fiedler quoted in Leonard Feinberg, *The Secret of Humour* (Amsterdam, Netherlands: Rodopi, 1978), 156.

25 Morris Dickstein, *Gates of Eden: American Culture in the Sixties* (Cambridge, MA.: Harvard University Press, 1997), 97.
26 Gilles Deleuze, "Nomadic Thought," in *Desert Islands*, 257–8.
27 Ray Brassier, *Nihil Unbound: Enlightenment and Extinction* (New York: Palgrave MacMillan, 2007), xi.
28 Hans. J. Morgenthau, "The Four Paradoxes of Nuclear Strategy," *The American Political Science Review* 58, no. 1 (1964): 23.
29 "The commitment to the use of force, nuclear or otherwise, paralyzed by the fear of having to use it; the search for a nuclear strategy which would avoid the predictable consequences of nuclear war; the pursuit of a nuclear armaments race joined with attempts to stop it; the pursuit of an alliance policy which the availability of nuclear weapons has rendered obsolete. All these paradoxes result from the contrast between traditional attitudes and the possibility of nuclear war and from the fruitless attempts to reconcile the two," Morgenthau, "The Four Paradoxes," 23.
30 Stanley Kubrick, "How I Learned to Stop Worrying and Love the Cinema," *Films and Filming* 9 (1963): 12.
31 Joseph Gelmis, "The Film Director as Superstar: Stanley Kubrick," in *Stanley Kubrick: Interviews*, ed. Gene D Phillips (Mississippi: University Press of Mississippi, 2001), 309.
32 Graeme Ritchie, *The Linguistic Analysis of Jokes* (London: Routledge, 2004), 124.
33 Immanuel Kant, *Critique of Judgment* (New York: Cosimo Books, 2007), 133.
34 Henry Kissinger, *The Necessity for Choice: Prospects of American Foreign Policy* (New York: Harper, 1961).
35 Charles Maland, "Dr. Strangelove: Nightmare Comedy and the Ideology of Liberal Consensus," *American Quarterly* 31, no. 5 (1979). There have been various cultural reiterations of the scene, including a "riding the couch" *Simpsons* gag, and a 2012 album track by American post-punk band The Offspring, called "Slim Pickens Does the Right Thing And Rides The Bomb Straight To Hell."
36 Deleuze, "Nomadic Thought," 258.
37 Ibid., 260.
38 As quoted in Piers Bizony, *2001: Filming the Future* (London: Aurum Press, 1994), 137.
39 Jason Sperb, *The Kubrick Façade: Faces and Voices in the Films of Stanley Kubrick* (Oxford: Scarecrow Press, 2006), 7.
40 Ibid., 5.
41 Ibid., 75.
42 All dialogue has been transcribed from the film. Stanley Kubrick, *Dr. Strangelove or: How I Learned to Stop Worrying and Love the Bomb* (Culver City, CA.: Columbia, 1964).
43 Lewis Mumford, "'Strangelove' Reactions," *New York Times* (March 1, 1964): 8.

44 Tom Milne, "Dr. Strangelove: Monthly Film Bulletin," *Sight and Sound* 33 (Winter): 37.
45 Loudon Wainwright, "The Strange Case of Dr. Strangelove," *Life* (March 13, 1964): 15.
46 Lewis Mumford, *Interpretations and Forecasts: 1922-1972* (New York: Harcourt Brace Jovanovich, 1973), 461, 465.
47 Henri Lefebvre, "Review of Kostas Axelos's *Toward Planetary Thought*," in *State, Space, World: Selected Essays*, ed. Neil Brenner and Stuart Elden (Minneapolis: Minnesota University Press, 2009), 255.
48 Kostas Axelos, "The World: Being Becoming Totality," trans. Gerald Moore, *Environment and Planning D: Society and Space* 24 (2006): 644.
49 Kostas Axelos, "Planetary Interlude," *Yale French Studies* 41 (1968): 11.
50 Ibid., 13.
51 Édouard Glissant, "Creolization in the Making of the Americas," *Caribbean Quarterly* 54, no. 1 and 2 (2008): 83.
52 Édouard Glissant, *Poetics of Relation*, trans. Betsy Wing (Ann Arbor: The University of Michigan Press, 2010), 32.
53 Ibid., 19.
54 Ibid., 52.
55 Joseph Meeker, *The Comedy of Survival: Literary Ecology and a Play Ethic* (Tucson: University of Arizona Press, 1997), 33.
56 Kurt Vonnegut, *Cat's Cradle* (New York: Dial Press Trade Paperbacks, 1991), 1-2.
57 Fredric Jameson, *Archaeologies of the Future: The Desire Called Utopia and Other Science Fictions* (New York: Verso Books, 2005), 269.
58 See also Vonnegut's "Address at Rededication of Wheaton College Library, 1973," in which he discusses the pitfalls of considering life in terms of pure category divisions: "I am not pure. We are not pure. Our nation is not pure. And I insist that at the core of the American tragedy, best exemplified by the massacre of civilians at My Lai, is the illusion [..] that in the war between good and evil we are always … on the side of good" in *Wampeters, Foma & Granfalloons (Opinions)* (Seymour Lawrence: Delacorte Press, 1974), 213-4.
59 Vonnegut, *Cat's Cradle*, 2.
60 Ibid., 62.
61 Ibid., 269.
62 Ibid., 44.
63 Ibid., 42.
64 Ibid., 50.
65 Ibid., vii.
66 Ibid.
67 Ibid., 2.

68 Foucault, *Order of Things*, xvii.
69 Vonnegut, *Cat's Cradle*, 2.
70 Todd Davis, *Kurt Vonnegut's Crusade or, How a Postmodern Harlequin Preached a New Kind of Humanism* (New York: State of New York Press, 2006), 63.
71 Vonnegut, *Cat's Cradle*, 52.
72 Ibid., 160.
73 Ibid., 161.
74 Ibid., 162.
75 Harry James Cargus, "Are There Things a Novelist Shouldn't Joke About? An Interview with Kurt Vonnegut," *Christian Century* (November 24, 1976): 1048–50.
76 William Allen, *Conversations with Kurt Vonnegut* (Jackson: University Press of Mississippi, 1988), 91.
77 Friedman, "Foreword," x.
78 Glissant, *Poetics of Relation*, 207.
79 Patrick O'Neill, *The Comedy of Entropy: Humour, Narrative, Reading* (Toronto: University of Toronto Press, 1990), 125.

Digital Posthumorism

Vwhdfd: LOL^{LOL^{LOL^{LOL^{LOL^{LOL}}}}}
mrburt: lol, lol, lol,
lickthecowhappy: Seriously. At that point why not type "hahahaha

"What I think of when someone texts "lolololol" instead of just "lol"." *Reddit*, 2013.

In May 1989, the online newsletter *FidoNews* published a dictionary of fifty-one initialisms and emoticons that were then in active use on the FidoNet bulletin board system. This unassuming entry is now widely recognized as the first recorded occurrence of "LOL," which appears alongside other graphical representations of laughter that include the "laugh face" (:D), the "mischievous smile" (:>), and the more expressive "LMTO—Laughing My Tush Off."[1] This early archive of e-laughter is fascinating for how it is framed by its author, L. Edel, who proffers it as part of a new, experimental language capable of translating feelings and gestures into text-based forms. Edel highlights the inherently "artistic" nature of these "icons," which they "hope [will] make for more 'colorful communicating'" online.[2] Written fifteen years later, the same spirit of creative play is at work in the top two comments featured in my epigraph, both of which parody the previous generation's emphasis on compression. The first uses superscript to imagine "LOL" raised to its own exponential power; the second uses the comma to carve its content into discrete bits.

Since its coinage in the early 1980s, "LOL" has undergone several mutations in both meaning and form. Perhaps most importantly, the initialism *LOL* (pronounced L. O. L.) has gradually been replaced by the acronym *lol* (pronounced as a single word, "lol"). This grammatical and graphical shift— from initialism to acronym, from capital to lowercase letters—indicates a more profound shift in what the word means and how it communicates. While *LOL* meant that the user was literally "laughing out loud" (as per Edel's dictionary), *lol* is used to express all manner of feelings and actions, from extreme joy to quiet indignation.³ I'm particularly interested, though, in one variant of e-laughter: the extended run of "lololol" that has become commonplace in digital communication. Here, the user takes advantage of the physical proximity of the l and o keys, rubbing a finger across the two to produce a solid block of text. If we were to remain faithful to the logic of the initialism, we would read this as either "laughing out loud out loud out loud" or as "laughing out laughing out laughing out loud." More likely, though, is that we understand the user's stretching out of the word as indicating a certain intensity, not in their laughter or even their amusement, per say, but in their gesture of typing. This idea—that what "lololol" registers is not laughter, but the fleshly encounter between finger pad and keyboard—provides an answer to the question posed by the beleaguered writer of the third comment in my epigraph. "Seriously. At that point, why not write 'hahahaha.'"⁴ Seriously: because the ergonomics of the QWERTY keyboard are such that striking h-a-h-a-h-a requires the arched hand of a pianist, whereas lololol is produced by the pushing of a single digit across a proximate zone.

The Czech philosopher and media theorist Vilém Flusser can help us understand what is at stake in the swapping out of these two gestures. In the mid-1980s, Flusser wrote several essays theorizing the gesture of writing, and, relatedly, the gesture of typewriting, both of which he understood as acts of inscription where "the one writing is pressing a virtuality hidden within him out through numerous layers of resistance."⁵ For Flusser, our gesture of writing structures how we exist in and experience the world. But, as he observes in "The Gesture of Writing," this style of inscription is on the cusp of being replaced by a new mode of writing that is tuned to the technical universe of electronic media. "The problems lying before us demand that we think in codes and gestures far more refined, exact, and fertile than those of the alphabet," he advises, "We need to think in video, in analog and digital models and programs, in multidimensional codes."⁶ Flusser's theory of gestures is also a theory of affect, which he understands as an aesthetic process by which nebulous "states of mind" are given gestural form; as he explains it, "affect releases states of mind from their original contexts and allows them to become formal (aesthetic)—to take the form of gestures."⁷ It is with an eye on the relationships among gesture, affect, and form that I ask: what happens when posthumorist practice goes online? What does born-digital laughter look like, and what can it tell us about how affects gather and disperse in digital environments? Finally, what does it mean that modernist experiments in writing laughter terminate here, in the decentralized spaces of the World Wide Web?

Our probe into digital posthumorism has two main exhibits. Exhibit A is the frictive palindrome "lololol," which in its very form suggests both tactility and the possibility of infinity. Exhibit B is the laugh-loop video, a curious artifact from the internet's history that follows Flusser's injunction to leave the alphabet behind: it exemplifies *thinking in video*. There are two key variants of the laugh-loop video: the laughter reaction GIF and the phenomenon of "ten-hour YouTube." At first glance, these two examples might seem diametrically opposed. The reaction GIF is by nature small, portable, and infinitely reusable. Ten-hour YouTube, by contrast, is unapologetically elephantine. As we shall see, though, both operate according to the posthumorist formula of tactility + infinity = the transmission of affect. The laugh-loop video is, I wager, the natural successor to all the various forms of posthumorist laughter that this book has brought to light, from Robert Smithson's ha ha-crystal to the atomic laughter of American black humor. The leap from these avant-garde experiments in writing laughter to the "vernacular creativity" of Reddit threads and YouTube videos is not as dramatic as it might seem.[8] With *Posthumorism* at my back, I understand the laugh-loop video as the contemporary incarnation of a digital posthumorism that made its debut in 1970s and 1980s science fiction. A rough prehistory of the laugh-loop video includes William S. Burroughs's tape recorder experiments and the cyberpunk writings of Harlan Ellison and William Gibson. In the spirit of posthumorism, then, I'm interested here in how the laugh-loop's unique formal capacities—both on the page and on the screen—enable it to carry and conduct affect as a pure, impersonal gesture.

**

Type "laughter" (or "lol" or "haha") into any GIF repository and you will be met with a vast gallery of people, animals, and cartoon creatures caught in the gesture of laughter. These are reaction GIFs, a subgenre of the GIF format that loops a single gesture—a snicker, a side-eye, a bite of a sandwich—as a small, portable file that users can then embed in any number of contexts.[9] Much has been written about the GIF as a cultural device, with scholars paying special attention to how it gives form to emotions in a digital environment. Typical of such work is a 2017 essay by Kate Miltner and Tim Highfield, in which the authors marvel at the creativity with which users deploy GIFs "as a proxy for, or expression of, emotion and/or affect."[10] For others, though, the GIF's proxy status is cause for concern. As Lauren Michele Jackson and Laurence Scott have each argued, to use a reaction GIF is to participate in the outsourcing of emotional labor.¹¹ The GIF's subjects (who, as Jackson points out, are disproportionately Black) are conscripted to body forth feeling so that the user doesn't have to; this is what Scott means when he says that the GIF carries with it a "frisson of ghostly possession."¹² This same gothic sensibility undergirds Slavok Žižek's critique of another affect machine—canned laughter—which he deems "unsettling" because it reveals that "my most intimate feelings can be radically externalized. I can literally laugh and cry through another."¹³

Žižek doesn't use the word "affect" in his essay, however, his realization that one's "most intimate feelings" can be loosed from the individual human body recalls affect as it has been theorized both in this book and in the field generally. Interestingly, though, Žižek reverses affect's timeline as it was first proposed by Brian Massumi. Here, affect does not precede emotion, rather, Žižek's internal emotions are "radically externalized" as affect. The implication is that the sound engineer's "Laff Box" has the capacity to transform personal emotion into impersonal affect, and that it does so through the gesture of the loop. (The looping here is twofold: the looped audio track in turn creates a feedback loop between Žižek and the unseen laugher.) The GIF is and does the same thing. It is a technological device that transforms emotion into affect through the sheer strength of its looping form. Watch a GIF for long enough, and this operation becomes visible; as Maria Poulaki explains, "[After multiple watching] the 'attraction' is no longer a happening or event but the 'attractor' of a system emerging in time and qualitatively altering its components, in the sense that the central gesture or event becomes a less significant fractal of its own self-similar architecture building up in time."¹⁴ What Poulaki is describing here is something similar to *gestalt looking* as I theorized it in Chapter 1—the GIF's emergent causality makes it possible for the viewer to mark a difference between its signifying content (the gesture it depicts) and its non-signifying form (the "self-similar architecture" of the loop's infinite duration).

My argument here is that the loop's form *is* the taking place of affect, which is close to but different from that of artist and curator Sally McKay, for whom the GIF's reflexive looping point enacts the famous gap between emotion and affect that grounds Brian Massumi's affect theory. Following Massumi's description of affect as a "temporal sink," McKay suggests that "in animated GIFs, the gaps in action between frames … are small enough to suggest motion, but large enough to create a perceptible gap, which means there is plenty of time for the affect to take hold."¹⁵ For McKay, the GIF's intermittency creates the conditions of possibility for affect to "take hold." In my formulation, though, its looped structure *directly produces* affects and puts them on display, at the expense of the internal emotions that are felt by either the GIF's subject or its user. It is not a coincidence, I think, that the GIF operates through the posthumorist tactics of fragmentation and extension that we remember from the drug writings of Walter Benjamin, Henri Michaux, and William James. Fragmentation: it clips the gesture from its narrative context to make of it a fragment. Extension: it loops the gesture ad infinitum. These two operations combine to make of the GIF an affect machine that, in media theorist Hampus Hagman's words, "is not a matter of communicating a particular content, but of showing movement as a medium of communicability as such. In itself, it is pure becoming and process."[16]

In this book, I've argued that laughter is a useful case study for registering some of the ways in which language (both literary and cinematic) can be made to carry and conduct affects. In the case of the reaction GIF, one might argue that the laughter element is irrelevant. While those that depict laughter certainly constitute a prominent type, it would not seem they are formally different from any other reaction GIF. Why then should we spotlight the laughter reaction GIF in particular? To answer this question, it helps to remember the distinction between our two key terms. Every reaction GIF is *affectological*, because its formal architecture is such that it transmits affects, untranslated, from point A to point B. The laughter reaction GIF, though, is both *affectological* and uniquely *posthumorist*, because it participates in the modernist tradition of using laughter as a technique for disrupting humanist logics.

To better see its posthumorist coordinates, I'll spend the last few pages locating the laughter reaction GIF as part of a longer history of looping laughter. This history mirrors the same tussle between emotion and affect that has served as the structural seed of every chapter of this book. On the one hand, there is canned laughter, which made its televisual debut on the *Hank McCune Show* in September 1950. Following Žižek and so many others, I understand the laugh track as a regulating device that enforces a standardized "sense of humor" to structure the inner emotional lives of its listeners. On the other, we have a set of posthumorist practices that make subversive use of the laugh-loop to carry and conduct the material stuff of affect. As we have come to expect, these experiments come at the expense of the bounded individual, whose internal coherence dissolves in the presence of affect. The experience of the laugh-loop, like the experience of all posthumorist laughter, is marked by its tactility and infinity—it is both of the flesh and out of time, simultaneously intimate and inhuman.

***

If the first technician of canned laughter was the famed sound engineer Charles Douglass, then the first technician of the posthumorist laugh-loop was William S. Burroughs. Burroughs never discussed canned laughter directly in his work, but "Genial," the young assassin that appears briefly in the opening scenes of his 1962 novel *The Ticket That Exploded*, suggests that he understood the violence inherent in the laugh track. A man has been found hanged inside his home, and police believe that Genial is to blame. In a pivotal scene, Inspector Lee discusses Genial with a fellow officer:

> "Did you interview a young man named Terrence Weld in this connection?"
> "Young 'Genial'? Yes I interviewed that specimen."
> "He was genial?"
> "Impeccably so. I considered him directly responsible for Harrison's death. When I told him so he said
> "'What and me so young?'
> "Exactly. And then he laughed."
> "Interesting sound."
> "Very."
> "You recorded it?"
> "Of course."
> "Rather stupid on his part wouldn't you say so?"
> "Not stupid exactly. He simply doesn't think the way we do. Perhaps he can't help laughing like that even when it would seem to be very much to his disadvantage to do so."
> "I would suggest that 'Genial' is that laugh ... only existence 'Genial' has."
> "Infectious laughter what? Yes he's a disease ... a virus."[17]

The officers' speculations are based on what they already know about the Nova Mob, a dispersed rebel organization that has developed a means of splicing together different body sounds—heartbeats, breath, bowel movements, and yes, laughter—to create biological weapons that upon playback induce in their listener intense physical reactions, from orgasm to death. "Genial," Lee believes, is one such weapon: it quite literally *is* a looped laugh that can manifest in any number of bodies, organic or otherwise.

What's interesting is how this conversation proceeds. Notice how, over the course of just a few utterances, the officers demarcate a line between the "genial" Terrence Weld and the pure strain of laughter that they eventually dub "Genial." The grammatical rotation from adjective ("he's genial") to noun ("Genial") signals a movement away from the emotive individual and toward unmanned affect, a shift that both men regard with horror. In the spirit of the humor studies scholar, the second officer works furiously to map the errant laugh back on to a pathologized laugher; he cannot bring himself to give up the possessive pronoun when he submits his diagnosis that *"he's* a disease.. a virus." In *Ticket*'s dystopian world, the laugh loop is clearly something to fear—Genial is it made flesh and made fatal—and yet, at the same time as he was writing, Burroughs himself was experimenting with the subversive potential of capturing, weaponizing, and deploying non-signifying registers of the voice. In *The Electronic Revolution*, the long essay that represents the culmination of his tape recorder experiments, Burroughs speculated about the revolutionary possibility of body tapes: "Could laugh tapes, sneeze tapes, hiccough tapes, cough tapes, give rise to laughing, sneezing, hiccoughing, and coughing?"[18] And if so, what then?

As the analog era drew to a close, the laugh track escaped magnetic tape and migrated across media in search of the digital. We find one of the first literary treatments of an explicitly digital laugh-loop in a short story by Harlan Ellison that was published as part of his 1988 collection *Angry Candy*. The story opens with the protagonist's discovery that a recording of his dead Aunt Babe's laughter is being put to "indiscriminate use" as the laugh track on shows ranging from *Maude* to *M*A*S*H*.[19] With the help of a mysterious sound engineer, Babe's nephew concocts a plan to free her from her servitude as a "video galley slave."[20] Implementing a series of digital processes that we recognize today as prototypes of digital mapping and printing. the two men extract the "electronic code" of Aunt Babe's laugh from its master tape and digitize it as a "moebius loop" program, which they then use to rebuild her body, section by section.[21] The engineer describes the latter half of the process:

> Now I feed her into the computer, digitally encode her so she never diminishes. Slick, right? Then I feed in a program that … gets a simulation mapping for the instrument that produced that sound; in other words, your aunt's throat and tongue and palate and teeth and larynx and all that. Now comes the tricky part. I build a program that postulates an actual physical *situation*, a terrain, a *place* where that voice exists. And I send the computer on a search to bring me back everything that comprises that place.[22]

Uncanning Aunt Babe is an explicitly material and materializing process. Wally Modisett, the sound engineer, reverse-engineers the non-signifying sounds of her laugh to build back her body piece by piece—larynx, palate, teeth, and tongue—and with it, her subjectivity. This fantasy of reembodiment is also a fantasy of connectivity. Newly digitized, Aunt Babe locates "pathways in the microwave comm-system" that allow her to slip between and hijack the feeds of any and all televisual broadcasts."[23] Modisett contemplates this limitless digital landscape with an ecstatic reverence that we recognize from the posthumorists that came before him; the narrator observes that Modisett "[basked] in the unalloyed joy of having tapped a line into some Elsewhere."[24]

While Modisett finds posthumorist pleasure in both the uncanny materiality of Aunt Babe's laughter and the radical "Elsewhere" to which it provides access, Aunt Babe's nephew Angelo's motivations are quite different. A sitcom writer by trade, Angelo mourns what he sees as the slow debasement of comedy in the age of corporate greed. The greatest laughs, he remembers, were those "unduplicable originals" that television executives had "kidnapped off radio shows from the Forties and Fifties," and planted alongside "weary sitcom minutiae" in order to hawk their product.[25] Angelo's nostalgia for the 1950s as a Golden Era where one's personhood, like one's laughter, still had the capacity to be both unduplicable and original, is the engine for the story's plot, which hinges on his belief that Aunt Babe's laughter is an expression of her personal taste, and so proof of her personhood. To Angelo's mind, the primary act of dehumanization is that Aunt Babe is being forced to work, against her will and against her tastes, by a television network. In step with his 1950s nostalgia, Angelo's horror carries with it white supremacist undertones. What is under threat here for Angelo is not only Aunt Babe's claim to personal freedom, but also her claim to whiteness (she is, or was, of Italian American Jewish descent). He longs to free her from her state as a "beanfield slave" so that she might "bound free like a snow rabbit, to vanish into great white spaces."[26] Of course, this grasping dream of "great white spaces" cannot coexist alongside posthumorism, which aims to destroy the very underpinnings of that which Angelo seeks to preserve.

A similar romance between the laugh track and the digital can be found in *Neuromancer*, William Gibson's classic cyberpunk novel. There, too, we get a version of the laugh-loop that flirts with posthumorism whilst remaining firmly within the trappings of a (white, male) liberal humanism; as Kate Hayles wrote over twenty years ago, "the erasure of embodiment is a feature in common to *both* the liberal humanist subject and the cybernetic posthuman."[27] Our "cybernetic posthuman" in *Neuromancer* is a hacker named McCoy Pauley who, like Aunt Babe, is dead long before the story begins. And, like Aunt Babe, aspects of McCoy – his skillset and a copy of his personality – have been archived for use by others, this time as a hardwired ROM construct nicknamed "The Dixie Flatline." The prerecording that is The Dixie Flatline has one unusual quirk: it laughs. Or, almost. Our protagonist, Case, describes Dixie's laugh as an "eerie nonlaugh" that elicits from him a strong bodily reaction.[28] Four times the construct laughs, and four times Case flinches:

"When the construct laughed, it came through as something else, not laughter, but a stab of cold down Case's spine."
"The ugly laughter sensation rattled down Case's spine."
"The construct approximated laughter. Case winced at the sensation."
"'Fuck off,' Case said, and flipped, cutting off the torn-fingernail edge of the Flatline's laughter."[29]

Like Case and all the other "console cowboys" that populate the Sprawl, Dixie Flatline uses its access to global networks to hack and hijack informational flow.[30] Its nonlaugh, though, hacks and hijacks the very logic of the novel, which depends upon (and is famous for) Gibson's figuring of cyberspace as an immaterial frontier where the body cannot go. Case only hears Flatline's laughter when he is "jacked in," and yet each time his response to it is markedly visceral—he is stabbed and rattled, he winces and recoils.[31] These moments are destabilizing because they puncture the liberal humanist dream of disembodiment that powers both the novel's plot and its pleasures. Dixie Flatline's laughter is thus simultaneously infinite and tactile; it is an immortal loop that triggers the reentry of the "meat" into cyberspace.

In these two literary depictions of the laugh track, advancements in digital technologies have created the conditions for a prerecorded laugh to jump from its magnetic tape loop, take on embodied coordinates, and move out into the smooth, networked spaces of the digital. "Going digital" in both cases is an explicitly corporeal process that returns to the prerecorded laugh a fleshy vitality, and with it the capacity for improvisation and exploit. At first glance, the informational drift of cyberspace appears to be one more version of the thickened "Elsewhere" into which the posthumorist dives. On closer inspection, though, we see that Ellison and Gibson's digital landscapes retain the infrastructure of humanism that posthumorism seeks to explode. The stories' shared commitment to the liberal humanist subject means that neither can qualify as properly posthumorist, although they still have something to tell us about how laughter might move as an affect through digital space.

These literary experiments in digitizing and looping laughter edge us closer to the properly posthumorist practice of the laugh-loop GIF. Its immediate predecessor, though, is a batch of YouTube videos that proliferated between 2009 and 2012 and played a starring role in two viral fads—ten-minute YouTube and ten-hour YouTube. To think through these phenomena I'll use a clutch of videos that sample the same four-second clip from *Jurassic Park* in which Jeff Goldblum's character half-laughs, half-snarls at his fellow scientists. In 2009,

YouTuber FireMaster7001 uploaded a twenty-seven-second loop of the clip titled "Jeff Goldblum … laughing?"[32] Boasting nearly 1.2 million views, the post spawned a cottage industry of Goldblum laugh-loops that engaged with his laugh in new and experimental ways. Some users imagined Goldblum's laugh zipping through the "comm system" (to borrow from Harlan Ellison) to cameo in other iconic scenes from twentieth-century pop culture, for example, "Jeff Goldblum Laughs at Lois Lane" and "Jeff Goldblum Laughs at Predator."[33] Others focused on or tinkered with the laugh itself. A 2014 video shows a violinist discussing its melodic properties with a technical rigor usually reserved for Brahms or Liszt ("Alan Reads Sheet Music Episode 01: Jeff Goldblum Laugh").[34] Another user reverses the laugh and lets it run, looped, for ten minutes ("Jeff Goldblum's Laugh REVERSED").[35]

The ten-minute running time is important. In 2011, ten-minute YouTube became its own genre, with users posting short content looped to run the full length of the platform's upload limit. The most popular subgenre of these was the ten-minute laugh-loop video, in which a diverse array of actors, from K-pop stars to a stop-motion orange, were conscripted to laugh over and over again for ten-minutes straight.[36] Perhaps unsurprisingly, "Jeff Goldblum Laughs for 10 Minutes" remains the most watched of these, clocking in at around 600,000 views.[37] As ten-minute YouTube was gaining steam, changes in the platform's rules allowed selected users to publish files that were up to ten hours long.[38] The first ten-hour video was uploaded in April 2011 by user Neh1ppe. Titled "Nyan Cat 10 Hours," it looped the then-viral "Nyan Cat" clip for ten hours straight, and in so doing established some of the conventions of the genre, from its lo-fi presentation to the tongue-in-cheek literalness of its titles.[39] The ten-hour video, like its ten-minute counterpart, was presented to viewers as an endurance test—can *you* sit through the whole thing? While the original post is no longer available to view, its influence on meme culture is apparent in the slew of ten-hour videos that were published in its wake; as Chloe Lizotte explains in her recent essay on the phenomenon, "the absurdity of the bloated duration, and a sudden glee at the possibilities it suggested sparked a new wave of Insane Editions—including ten-hour vlogs documenting those who took on the challenge of watching them."[40]

The first ten-hour laugh-loop video was uploaded by Henry Kingston in January 2012. Titled "Crazy Old Italian Man Laughing," it depicts a nameless man whose shoulders slope down to fill the bottom of the frame.[41] He says, "Do you know how I'm supposed to laugh?" before bursting into a bout of laughter that runs for twenty seconds and is looped for ten hours, as per the genre's conventions. As the laugh-loop fad took hold, videos began to appear with the precipitating joke already cropped out—this is the case for most that followed, with subjects ranging from the famous (Hillary Clinton, Kawhi Leonard) to the fictional (Voldemort, Tom from *Tom and Jerry*) to the nonhuman ("Shark Laugh – 10 hours"). Uploaded in June 2018, "Jeff Goldblum Laugh 10 hours" was uncharacteristically late to the party, but in both its content and comments the video is exemplary of the subgenre.⁴² As we shall see, it is in the comments section that the posthumorist elements of the format become most clear.

There is remarkable consistency across ten-hour YouTubes comments, which fall into one of two categories. First, there are those that draw attention to the genre's maximalism, usually by jokingly suggesting that there are some parts that are better than others, when of course the looped structure makes such gradations impossible. Comments like "I especially love the bit at 4:01:27" or "I like the part when he laughs" recur across several different videos.⁴³ As these comments make plain, the ten-hour laugh-loop video has neither plot nor story; it is this a-narrative "frictionlessness," to borrow from Jason Eppink, that user Gaz lampoons when he describes the Jeff Goldblum video as a "bit boring for first couple of hours imo but then it really pulls you in with the character development and sub plots."⁴⁴ If Bataille's affectology compacts linear time into one "solidified instant," then the ten-hour laugh-loop video stretches time until it thins and snaps altogether.⁴⁵ This temporal deformation is part of the subgenre's appeal, as Tim Highfield explains it to reporter Abby Ohlheiser, "set the loop going and there's no real idea of time passing, it's the same clip over and over again."⁴⁶ But the loop's atemporality has another effect. Boosted out of linear time, the laugh sample takes on its own uncanny materiality—it thickens into a milieu in which the viewer becomes enmeshed.⁴⁷ This is what Chloe Lizotte means when she writes that ten-hour YouTube's extreme repetitiveness "strips [its sample] of a beginning or an ending and turns it into an immersive texture."⁴⁸

While this first set of comments gesture to the ten-hour laugh-loop's deformation of time and its subsequent tactility, the second set gesture to its deformation of emotion and its subsequent affectivity. (Notice that we have found our way back to Sedgwick's formula of touching + feeling). These users try to maximize the format's maximalism by concocting extreme viewing conditions – it's LOL to the exponential power of LOL. Suggestions range from playing the video in multiple tabs to changing the audio speed settings. The effect in every case is the mutation of the videos' emotive content. In the case of "Tidus Laugh 10 HOURS," for example, a consensus is reached that "if you adjust the speed to 0.5 it becomes all too clear that he was actually crying from intense pain."⁴⁹ Of Jeff Goldblum, user Gibran writes, "He's literally DYING in .25x speed!" Other commenters offer alternative interpretations of the feelings that power and are produced by the laugh-loop. "[It] made me cry. it's really sentimental," observes user Yung Boike; "This is what joy sounds like," reflects Maxeffect N7. Intense pain, sentimentality, joy—while users agree that the laugh loop is expressive, there is no consensus as to *what* it is expressing, although it's worth noting that not one comment refers to the laugh's original, humorous context. In fact, the above comments suggest that the laugh, by way of its intensive looping, has escaped both the filmic body (*Jurassic Park*) and the individual human body (Jeff Goldblum). If the transmissible affects of "joy" and "sentiment" belong to anyone, it is not Jeff Goldblum nor the character he plays, but the insistently looping form of the video itself.

***

In his famous SF story "What Dead Men Tell" (1949), Theodore Sturgeon imagines his protagonist trapped in a Möbius topography that appears as an endlessly repeating series of corridors that shiver with quantum possibility. The floor, the narrator notices, "was smooth, solid, for all its slight yielding; but in addition there was a sensation of movement in it, as if its surface were composed of myriads of microscopic eddies in violent, tiny motion."[50] (Laughter, it seems, is never far away—the protagonist awakens in this impossible place after a strange encounter with a man who may or may not be Conrad Veidt, the rictus-faced star of the 1928 silent film *The Man Who Laughs*.) The narrative is propelled by the protagonist's increasingly desperate attempts to determine his position and direction—is he inside or outside, before or after, then or now? Eventually, he realizes he is being subjected to a test. Through dazzling powers of deduction, he correctly identifies the environment's geometry, which earns him release from its looping structure and, as it turns out, immortality. Even the floor's molecular instability is finally accounted for; its surface has been painted with a special substance to help stabilize the test's conditions.

As in Sturgeon's story, digital posthumorism projects the Möbius strip as a livable environment. Our first clue that the laugh-loop is this particular *type* of loop is Aunt Babe, whose digitization as a "moebius loop" program is an important plot point in Ellison's "Laugh Track." "I put her on an endless loop," Wally Modiscott explains, barely containing his excitement, "but not just *any* kind of normal standard endless loop … A moebius loop."[51] The Möbius strip's defining feature is that it is unorientable: it is a single twisted surface without boundary. Aunt Babe uses this quality to elude the studio executives, who "pulled the tape [and] tried to find her, but she was gone, skipping off across the similarity matrix like Bambi."[52] A similar issue is at work in Gibson's cyberspace, where the Dixie Flatline's laughter causes the neat binary of inside/outside to fold in on itself; subjected to the looped laugh, Case is no longer sure if he is flesh or code. If Ellison and Gibson describe a Möbius environment, then ten-hour YouTube enacts one. Caught in the "immersive texture" of the digital laugh-loop, all our measuring devices break down; like Sturgeon's narrator, we can no longer orient ourselves in space or time.[53] Unlike Sturgeon's story, though, there is a third unorientable point—that of affect. There is no one way of narrativizing the feelings that the digital laugh-loop emits and provokes; they slip off Robert Plutchik's wheel of emotions as if it, too, had been twisted and looped. What the laugh-loop makes tangible, finally, is the topologically unorientable forms of affects themselves, in which Self and Other, body and mind, inside and outside, and then and now fold in on, literally *become*, one another. It is in these curved arms that this book comes to rest.

Notes

1 L. Edel, "Mo_Icons_Please," *FidoNews: International FidoNet Association* Newsletter 6, no. 19 (1989), http://www.textfiles.com/fidonet-on-the-internet/878889/fido0619.txt.
2 Ibid.
3 It's interesting to note that for Wayne Pearson, a Calgary engineer who in 2002 claimed to have coined the term. the term "Laugh Out Loud" means something very specific: the somewhat foolish experience of laughing out loud when you are conversing online but are physically alone. For a discussion of the changing cultural meanings of lol, see, Gretchen McCulloch, *Because Internet: Understanding the New Rules of Language* (New York: Riverhead Books, 2019), 139–50.
4 Lickthecowhappy, "What I think when someone texts 'lolololo.' instead of just 'lol.'" *Reddit*, 2013. https://www.reddit.com/r/funny/comments/104as1/what_i_think_of_when_someone_texts_lololol=l/".
5 Vilém Flusser, *Gestures* (Minneapolis: University of Minnesota Press, 2007), 22.
6 Ibid., 25.
7 Ibid., 6.
8 Henry Jenkins, "'Vernacular Creativity': An Interview with Jean Burgess (Part One)," *Confessions of an ACA Fan*. October 7, 2007, http://henryjenkins.org/blog/2007/10/vernacular_creativity_an_inter.html.
9 Short for Graphical Interchange Format, the GIF might depict anything from a flashing "Under Construction" sign (a regular sight in the early days of the World

Wide Web) to a few frames of a film or television show (as is common today). For an authoritative history of the GIF, see Jason Eppink, "A Brief History of the GIF (So Far)," *Journal of Visual Culture* 13, no. 3 (2014): 298.

10 Kate N. Miltner and Tim Highfield, "Never Gonna GIF You Up: Analyzing the Cultural Significance of the Animated GIF," *Social Media + Society* 3, no. 3 (2017): 5.

11 Lauren Michele Jackson, "We Need To Talk about Digital Blackface in Reaction GIFS," *Teen Vogue*, August 2, 2017, https://www.teenvogue.com/story/digital-blackface-reaction-gifs; and Laurence Scott, "GIFS Are Glorious, GIFs Are Perverse," *Wired*, March 2, 2020, https://www.wired.com/story/gifs-are-glorious-gifs-are-perverse/.

12 Scott, "GIFS Are Glorious." See also Monica Torres's argument that the GIF of dash-cam footage depicting the 2014 murder of Laquan McDonald "re-enacts the spectacle for our consumption, puppets made to rise and fall, victims without sanctuary" in Monica Torres, "Instant Replay," *Real Life*, November 22, 2016, https://reallifemag.com/instant-replay/.

13 Slavoj Žižek, "Will You Laugh for Me, Please?" *In These Times*, July 18, 2003, https://inthesetimes.com/article/will-you-laugh-for-me-please

14 Maria Poulaki, "Featuring shortness in online loop cultures," *Empedocles: European Journal for the Philosophy of Communication* 5, no. 1 (2015): 93.

15 Sally McKay, "The Affect of Animated GIFs (Tom Moody, Petra Cortright, Lorna Mills)," *ArtFCity*, July 16, 2016, http://artfcity.com/2018/07/16/the-affect-of-animated-gifs-tom-moody-petra-cortright-lorna-mills/.

16 Hampus Hagman, "The Digital Gesture: Rediscovering Cinematic Movement through Gifs," cited by Dominik Maeder and Daniela Wentz, "Digital Seriality as Structure and Process," *Eludamos* 8, no. 1 (2014): 143.

17 William S. Burroughs, *The Ticket That Exploded* (New York: Grove Atlantic, 2011), 16.

18 William S. Burroughs, *Word Virus: The William S. Burroughs Reader*, ed. James Grauerholz and Ira Silverberg (New York: Grove Press, 1998), 300.

19 Harlan Ellison, *Angry Candy* (Boston; New York: Houghton Mifflin Company, 1988), 180.

20 Ibid.

21 Ibid., 191, 190.

22 Ibid., 190.

23 Ibid., 194.

24 Ibid., 193.

25 Ibid., 185, 179.

26 Ibid., 180.

27 Hayles, *How We Became Posthuman*, 4.

28 William Gibson, *Neuromancer* (New York: Ace Books, 2000), 197.

29 Ibid., 104, 128, 163, 209.
30 Ibid., 28.
31 Ibid., 65.
32 "Jeff Goldblum ... laughing? (The Original Video)," *YouTube*, uploaded by FireMaster7001, February 22, 2009, https://www.youtube.com/watch?v=JlOx9738iyw.
33 See "Jeff Goldblum Laughs at Lois Lane," *YouTube*, uploaded by Jeff Goldblum, March 11, 2013, https://www.youtube.com/watch?v=6bwJiXUNiFA and "Jeff Goldblum Laughs at Predator," *YouTube*, uploaded by Jeff Goldblum, March 13, 2013, https://www.youtube.com/watch?v=JnvtVGQ0cYY.
34 "Alan Reads Sheet Music Episode 01: Jeff Goldblum Laugh," *YouTube*, uploaded by Curious Quail, October 20, 2014, https://www.youtube.com/watch?v=s8VRgV4DXnE.
35 "Jeff Goldblum's laugh – REVERSED," *YouTube*, uploaded by Aaron Ludwig, November 26, 2014, https://www.youtube.com/watch?v=dL4lxOaAIBU.
36 See "10 minutes RyeoWook's laugh," *YouTube*, uploaded by Q501Q, January 11, 2013, https://www.youtube.com/watch?v=Lgvvk4fECKo&t=1s; "Annoying Orange laughing 10 minutes," *YouTube*, uploaded by d0nth4v34nyv1d5, June 5, 2011, https://www.youtube.com/watch?v=FqVpzT2oaGA.
37 "Jeff Goldblum Laughs for 10 Minutes," *YouTube*, uploaded by IzzyMaiden, July 9, 2011, https://www.youtube.com/watch?v=lS9D6w1GzGY.
38 Joshua Siegel and Doug Mayle, "Up, Up and Away – Long videos for more users," *YouTube Official Blog*, December 9, 2010, https://blog.youtube/news-and-events/up-up-and-away-long-videos-for-more.
39 Cited in Chloe Lizotte, "Ten-Hour YouTube," *Screen Slate*, May 19, 2020, https://www.screenslate.com/articles/ten-hour-youtube.
40 Ibid.
41 "Crazy Old Laughing Italian Man for 10 Hours," *YouTube*, uploaded by Henry Kingston, January 30, 2012, https://www.youtube.com/watch?v=oWrGG9OmB_8.
42 "Jeff Goldblum Laugh 10 hours," *YouTube*, uploaded by JuciyMiddle, June 13, 2018, https://www.youtube.com/watch?v=QWy_zcmopoQ.
43 All comments are from "Jeff Goldblum Laugh 10 hours."
44 Eppink, "A Brief History of the GIF (So Far)," 303.
45 Bataille, *Literature and Evil*, 161.
46 Tim Highfield quoted in Abby Ohlheiser, "The mesmerizing lost art of the 10-hour YouTube loop, 2011's weirdest video trend," *The Washington Post*, June 3, 2016, https://www.washingtonpost.com/news/the-intersect/wp/2016/06/03/the-mesmerizing-lost-art-of-the-10-hour-youtube-loop-2011s-weirdest-video-trend.
47 I've written about this before in "Laughter Without Humor: On the Laugh-Loop GIF," *The Atlantic*, July 17, 2013, https://www.theatlantic.com/technology/archive/2013/07/laughter-without-humor-on-the-laugh-loop-gif/277853/.

48 Lizotte, "Ten-Hour YouTube."
49 "Tidus Laugh 10 HOURS," *YouTube*, uploaded by AuronSuper95, April 23, 2012, https://www.youtube.com/watch?v=-lfiTebewnc.
50 Theodore Sturgeon, "What Dead Men Tell," in *The Perfect Host Volume V: The Complete Stories of Theodore Sturgeon*, ed. Paul Williams (Berkeley: North Atlantic Books, 1998), 326.
51 Ellison, *Angry Candy*, 190.
52 Ibid., 194.
53 Lizotte, "Ten-Hour YouTube," https://www.screenslate.com/articles/ten-hour-youtube.

Bibliography

"10 minutes RyeoWook's laugh." *YouTube*, uploaded by Q501Q. January 11, 2013. https://www.youtube.com/watch?v=Lgvvk4fECKo&t=1s.

Ahmed, Sara. 2010. *The Promise of Happiness*. Durham, NC: Duke University Press.

"Alan Reads Sheet Music Episode 01: Jeff Goldblum Laugh." *YouTube*, uploaded by Curious Quail. October 20, 2014. https://www.youtube.com/watch?v=s8VRgV4DXnE.

Allen, William. 1988. *Conversations with Kurt Vonnegut*. Jackson: University Press of Mississippi.

"Annoying Orange laughing 10 minutes." *YouTube*, uploaded by d0nth4v34nyv1d5. June 5, 2011. https://www.youtube.com/watch?v=FqVpzT2oaGA.

Aristotle. 1902. *Poetics of Aristotle*. Translated by S. H. Butcher. New York: MacMillan.

Aristotle. 1961. *Parts of Animals*. Cambridge, MA: Harvard University Press.

Armstrong, Martin. 1928. *Laughing: An Essay*. New York: Harper and Brothers.

Attardo, Salvatore. 2014. *Encyclopedia of Humor Studies*. Texas A&M University: Sage Publications.

Axelos, Kostas. 1968. "Planetary Interlude." Translated by Sally Hess. *Yale French Studies* 41: 6–18.

Axelos, Kostas. 2006. "The World: Being Becoming Totality." Translated by Gerald Moore. *Environment and Planning D: Society and Space* 24: 643–51.

Bakhtin Mikhail. 1984. *Rabelais and His World*. Translated by Hélène Iswolsky. Indiana: Indiana University Press.

Barad, Karen. 2007. *Meeting the Universe Halfway: Quantum Physics and the Entanglement of Matter*. Durham: Duke University Press.

Barad, Karen. 2010. "Quantum Entanglements and Hauntological Relations of Inheritance: Dis/continuities, SpaceTime Enfoldings, and Justice-to-Come." *Derrida Today* 3, no.2: 240–68.

Barnes, Djuna. 1937. *Nightwood*. New York: Harcourt, Brace.

Barnes, Linda. 1978. *The Dialectics of Black Humor: Process and Product*. Frankfurt: Peter Lang.

Barthes, Roland. 1972. "The Metaphor of the Eye." In *Roland Barthes Critical Essays*, translated by Richard Howard, 239–48. Evanston: Northwestern University Press.

Barthes, Roland. 1978. "The Grain of the Voice." In *Image-Music-Text*, translated by Stephen Heath, 179–89. New York: Hill and Wang.

Barthes, Roland. 1978. "The Third Meaning." In *Image-Music-Text*, translated by Stephen Heath, 52–68. New York: Hill and Wang.

Barthes, Roland. 1989. "Outcomes of the Text." In *The Rustle of Language*, translated by Richard Howard, 238–49. Berkeley and Los Angeles, California: University of California Press.

Barthes, Roland. 1998. *The Pleasure of the Text*. Translated by Richard Howard. New York: Hill and Wang.

Barthes, Roland. 2010. *Roland Barthes by Roland Barthes*. Translated by Richard Howard. New York: Hill and Wang.

Bataille, Georges. 1986. *Eroticism: Death and Sensuality*. Translated by Mary Dalwood. San Francisco, CA: City Lights Books.

Bataille, Georges. 1987. *Story of the Eye by Lord Auche*. Translated by Joachim Neugroschel. San Francisco: City Lights Books.

Bataille, Georges. 1991. "Concerning the Accounts Given by the Residents of Hiroshima." Translated by Alan Keenan. *American Imago* 48, no. 4 (Winter): 497–514.

Bataille, Georges. 1994. "Surrealism and How It Differs from Exceptionalism." In *The Absence of Myth: Writings on Surrealism*, translated and edited by Michael Richardson, 57–67. London; New York: Verso Books.

Bataille, Georges. 2001. *The Unfinished System of Non-Knowledge*. Translated by Michelle Kendall and Stuart Kendall. Minneapolis: University of Minnesota Press.

Bataille, Georges. 2011. *Guilty*. Translated by Stuart Kendall. Albany, NY: SUNY Press.

Bataille, Georges. 2013. "The 'Old Mole' and the Prefix Sur in the Words Surhomme [Superman] and Surrealist." In *Visions of Excess: Selected Writings, 1927–1939*, edited and translated by Allan Stoekl, 32–44. Minneapolis: University of Minnesota Press.

Bataille, Georges. 2014. *Inner Experience*. Translated by Stuart Kendall. Albany, NY: SUNY Press.

Bataille, Georges. 2015. *On Nietzsche*. Translated by Stuart Kendall. Albany, NY: SUNY Press.

Benjamin, Walter. 1999. *The Arcades Project*. Translated by Howard Eiland and Kevin McLaughlin. Cambridge, MA: Harvard University Press.

Benjamin, Walter. 2006. *On Hashish*. Edited by Howard Eiland and Others. Cambridge, MA: Belknap Press of Harvard University Press.

Bergson, Henri. 2012. *Laughter: An Essay on the Meaning of the Comic*. Scotts Valley, CA: CreateSpace Independent Publishing Platform.

Berlant, Lauren. 2011. *Cruel Optimism*. Durham: Duke University Press.

Bishop, Ryan. 2011. "The Force of Noise, or Touching Music: The Tele-Haptics of Stockhausen's 'Helicopter String Quartet.'" *SubStance* 40, no. 3: 25–40.

Bizony, Piers. 1994. *2001: Filming the Future*. London: Aurum Press.

Black, Donald. 1982. "Pathological Laughter: A Review of the Literature." *Journal of Nervous and Mental Disease* 170, no. 2: 67–71.

Blyth, Ian, with Susan Sellers. 2004. *Hélène Cixous: Live Theory*. London; New York: Continuum Books.

Bok, Christian. 2002. *Pataphysics: The Poetics of an Imaginary Science*. Evanston, IL: Northwestern University Press.

Boldt-Irons, Leslie Anne. 1995. "Sacrifice and Violence in Bataille's Erotic Fiction: Reflections from/upon the *Mise en Abime*." In *Bataille: Writing the Sacred*, edited by Carolyn Bailey Gill, 91–104. London and New York: Routledge.

Borsch-Jacobson, Mikkel. 1987. "The Laughter of Being." *MLN* 102, no. 4: 737–60.

Bown, Alfie. 2019. *In the Event of Laughter: Psychoanalysis, Literature*. New York; London: Bloomsbury.

Boyer, Paul. 1994. *By the Bomb's Early Light: American Thought and Culture at the Dawn of the Atomic Age*. Chapel Hill: The University of North Carolina Press.

Boym, Svetlana. 2007. *The Off-Modern*. New York: Bloomsbury Academic.

Bradway, Tyler. 2013. "'Permeable We!': Affect and the Ethics of Intersubjectivity in Eve Sedgwick's A Dialogue on Love." *GLQ: A Journal of Lesbian and Gay Studies* 19, no. 1: 79–110.

Brassier, Ray. 2007. *Nihil Unbound: Enlightenment and Extinction*. New York: Palgrave MacMillan.

Brennan, Teresa. 2004. *The Transmission of Affect*. Ithaca, NY: Cornell University Press.

Breton, André. 1972. *Manifestoes of Surrealism*. Translated by Richard Seaver and Helen R. Lane. Ann Arbor: Ann Arbor Paperbacks.

Breton, André. 1978. "What Is Surrealism?" In *What Is Surrealism? Selected Writings*, edited by Franklin Rosemont, 151–87. New York: Monad.

Breton, André. 1997. "Lightning Rod." In *Anthology of Black Humor*, edited by Mark Polizzotti, xiii–xix. San Francisco: City Lights Books.

Brinkema, Eugenie. 2014. *The Forms of the Affects*. Durham, NC: Duke University Press.

Broome, Peter. 1977. *Henri Michaux*. London: Athlone Press.

Brottman, Mikita. 2012. *Funny Peculiar: Gershon Legman and the Psychopathology of Humor*. New York: Routledge.

Browder, Clifford. 1967. *André Breton: Arbiter of Surrealism*. Geneva: Librairie Droz.

Burroughs, William S. 1998. *Word Virus: The William S. Burroughs Reader*. Edited by James Grauerholz and Ira Silverberg. New York: Grove Press.

Burroughs, William S. 2011. *The Ticket That Exploded*. New York: Grove Atlantic.

Butler, Judith. 2009. *Frames of War: When Is Life Grievable?* London; New York: Verso.

Butler, Judith. 2009. *Precarious Life: The Powers of Mourning and Violence*. London; New York: Verso.

Calle-Gruber, Mireille. 1999. "Hélène Cixous: Music Forever or Short Treatise on a Poetics for a Story to Be Sung." In *Hélène Cixous: Critical Impressions*, edited by Lee. A. Jacobus and Regina Barreca, 75–90. Amsterdam: Gordon and Breach Publishers.

Cargus, Harry James. 1976. "Are There Things a Novelist Shouldn't Joke About? An Interview with Kurt Vonnegut." *Christian Century*, November 24: 1048–50.

Caws, Mary Ann. 2001. *Manifesto: A Century of Isms*. Lincoln, NE: University of Nebraska Press.

Chion, Michel. 1999. *The Voice in Cinema*. Translated by Claudia Gorbman. New York: Columbia University Press.

Cixous, Hélène. 1976. "The Laugh of the Medusa." Translated by Keith Cohen and Paula Cohen. *Signs* 1, no. 4 (Summer): 875–93.

Cixous, Hélène. 1981. "Castration or Decapitation?" Translated by Annette Kuhn. *Signs* 7, no. 1 (Autumn): 41–55.

Cixous, Hélène. 1985. *Angst*. Translated by Jo Levy. New York: Riverrun Press.

Cixous, Hélène. 1986. "Sorties: Out and Out: Attacks/Ways Out/Forays." In *Hélène Cixous and Catherine Clement, The Newly Born Woman*, translated by Betsy Wing, 63–129. Minneapolis: University of Minnesota Press.

Cixous, Hélène. 1991. *The Book of Promethea*. Translated by Betsy Wing. Lincoln, NE: The University of Nebraska.

Cixous, Hélène. 2002. "The Book as One of Its Own Characters." *New Literary History* 33, no. 3: 403–34.

Cixous, Hélène. 2010. *Zero's Neighbour: Sam Beckett*. Translated by Laurent Milesi. Cambridge: Polity Press.

Cixous, Hélène. 2018. "Conclusion: Ay yay! The cry of literature." In *Ways of Re-Thinking Literature*, edited by Tom Bishop and Donatien Grau, 199–217. London and New York: Routledge.

Cixous, Hélène and Mirielle Calle-Gruber. 1997. *Hélène Cixous, Rootprints: Memory and Life Writing*. Translated by Eric Prenowitz. London; New York: Routledge.

Cixous, Hélène and McQuillan. 2002. "'You Race towards That Secret, Which Escapes': An Interview with Hélène Cixous." *Oxford Literary Review* 24: 185–201.

Cixous, Hélène and Michel Foucault. 2018. "Marguerite Duras: Memory without Remembering." In *Foucault at the Movies*, translated and edited by Clare O'Farrell, 123–34. New York: Columbia University Press.

Clement, Catherine. 1994. *Syncope: The Philosophy of Rapture*. Translated by Deirdre M. Mahoney and Sally O'Driscoll. Minneapolis: University of Minnesota Press.

Cohen Shabot, Sara. 2007. "The Grotesque Body: Fleshing Out of the Subject." In *The Shock of the Other: Situating Alterities*, edited by Silke Horstkotte and Esther Peeren, 57–68. New York: Rodopi.

Conley, Verena Andermatt. 1984. *Hélène Cixous: Writing the Feminine*. Lincoln, Nebraska: University of Nebraska Press.

"Crazy Old Laughing Italian Man for 10 Hours." *YouTube*, uploaded by Henry Kingston. January 30, 2012. https://www.youtube.com/watch?v=oWrGG9OmB_8.

Darwin, Charles. 1897. *The Expression of the Emotions in Man and Animals*. New York: D. Appleton and Company.

Daumal, René. 2012. "Pataphysics and the Revelation of Laughter." In *Pataphysical Essays*, translated by Thomas Vosteen, 2–15. Cambridge, MA: Wakefield Press.

Davis, Todd. 2006. *Kurt Vonnegut's Crusade or, How a Postmodern Harlequin Preached a New Kind of Humanism*. New York: State of New York Press.

Davis, Diane. 2000. Breaking Up (at) Totality: A Rhetoric of Laughter. Carbondale and Edwardsville: Southern Illinois University Press.

de Certeau, Michel. 1986. "The Laugh of Michel Foucault." In *Heterologies: Discourse on the Other*, translated by Brian Massumi, 193–8. Minneapolis: University of Minnesota Press.

Deleuze, Gilles. 1990. *The Logic of Sense*. Edited by Constantin V. Boundas and translated by Mark Lester with Charles Stivale. New York: Columbia University Press.

Deleuze, Gilles. 1998. "He Stuttered." In *Essays Critical and Clinical*, translated by Daniel W. Smith and Michael A. Greco, 107–14. London; New York: Verso Books.

Deleuze, Gilles. 2004. "Hélène Cixous, or, Writing in Strobe." In *Desert Islands and Other Texts, 1953–1974*, translated by Betsy Wing, 230–1. Los Angeles: Semiotext(e).

Deleuze, Gilles. 2004. "Nomadic Thought." In *Desert Islands and Other Texts, 1953–1974*, translated by Betsy Wing, 252–61. Los Angeles: Semiotext(e).

Deleuze, Gilles. 2005. *Cinema II: The Time Image*. Translated by Hugh Tomlinson and Robert Caleta. New York: Continuum Books.

Deleuze, Gilles and Félix Guattari. 1994. *What Is Philosophy?* Translated by Hugh Tomlinson and Graham Burchell. New York: Columbia University Press.

Deleuze, Gilles and Félix Guattari. 2004. *Anti-Oedipus: Capitalism and Schizophrenia*. Translated by Robert Hurley, Mark Seem and Helen R. Lane. New York: Continuum Books.

Derrida, Jacques. 1978. "From Restricted to General Economy." In *Writing and Difference*, translated by Alan Bass, 317–50. Chicago: The University of Chicago Press.

Derrida, Jacques. 2003. "Foreword." In *The Hélène Cixous Reader*, edited by Susan Sellers, vi–xiv. London; New York: Routledge.

Derrida, Jacques. 2005. "Derrida's Response to Hent de Vries." In *Augustine and Postmodernism: Confessions and Circumfession*, edited by John D. Caputo and Michael J. Scanlon, 88–90. Bloomington: Indiana University Press.

Dickstein, Morris. 1997. *Gates of Eden: American Culture in the Sixties*. Cambridge, MA: Harvard University Press.

Dunsby, Jonathan. 2009. "Roland Barthes and the Grain of Panzéra's Voice." *Journal of the Royal Musical Association* 134, no. 1: 113–32.

Duras, Marguerite. 1986. *Destroy, She Said: A Novel*. Translated by Barbara Bray. New York: Grove Press.

Edel, L. 1989. "Mo_Icons_Please." *FidoNews: International FidoNet Association Newsletter* 6, no. 19. http://www.textfiles.com/fidonet-on-the-internet/878889/fido0619.txt.

Ellison, Harlan. 1988. *Angry Candy*. Boston; New York: Houghton Mifflin Company.

Eng, David L. and David Kazanjian. 2003. *Loss: The Politics of Mourning*. Berkeley: University of California Press.

Eppink, Jason. 2014. "A Brief History of the GIF (So Far)." *Journal of Visual Culture* 13, no. 3: 298–306.

Faulkner, Joanne. 2010. *Dead Letters to Nietzsche, or, the Necromantic Art of Reading Philosophy*. Athens, OH: Ohio University Press.

Feinberg, Leonard. 1978. *The Secret of Humour*. Amsterdam, Netherlands: Rodopi.

Flusser, Vilém. 2014. *Gestures*. Minneapolis: University of Minnesota Press.

Ford, Russell. 2016, "Humor, Law, and Jurisprudence: On Deleuze's Political Philosophy." *Angelaki: Journal of the Theoretical Humanities* 21, no. 3: 89–102.

Foucault, Michel. 1994. *The Order of Things: An Archaeology of the Human Sciences*. New York: Vintage Books.
Foucault, Michel. 1997. "The Masked Philosopher." In *Ethics: Subjectivity and Truth: The Essential Works of Michel Foucault, Vol. 1*, edited by Paul Rabinow and translated by Robert Hurley and Others, 321–8. New York: The New Press.
Freud, Sigmund. 1928. "Humour." In *The International Journal of Psychoanalysis* 9 (January): 1–6.
Freud, Sigmund. 1955. "Medusa's Head." In *The Standard Edition of the Complete Psychological Works of Sigmund Freud, Volume XVIII (1920–1922): Beyond the Pleasure Principle, Group Psychology and Other Works*, translated by James Strachey, 273–4. London: The Hogarth Press.
Freud, Sigmund. 2003. *The Joke and Its Relation to the Unconscious*. New York: Penguin Classics.
Friedman, Bruce Jay. 1993. "Foreward: *Black Humor*." In *Black Humor: Critical Essays*, edited by Alan R. Pratt. New York: Garland Publishing, Inc.
Friedman, Susan. 2018. *Planetary Modernisms: Provocations on Modernity across Time*. New York: Columbia University Press.
Galloway, Alexander R. and Eugene Thacker. 2007. *The Exploit: A Theory of Networks*. Minneapolis: University of Minnesota Press.
Gelmis, Joseph. 2001. "The Film Director as Superstar: Stanley Kubrick." In *Stanley Kubrick: Interviews*, edited by Gene D. Phillips, 80–104. Mississippi: University Press of Mississippi.
Gershon, Walter. 2013. "Vibrational Affect Sound Theory and Practice in Qualitative Research." *Cultural Studies, Critical Methodologies* 13, no. 4: 257–62.
Gibson, William. 2000. *Neuromancer*. New York: Ace Books.
Glissant, Édouard. 2008. "Creolization in the Making of the Americas." *Caribbean Quarterly* 54, no. 1/2 (March–June): 81–9.
Glissant, Édouard. 2010. *Poetics of Relation*. Translated by Betsy Wing. Ann Arbor: The University of Michigan Press.
Gray, Frances. 1994. *Women and Laughter*. Charlottesville: University Press of Virginia.
Greenberg, Jonathan. 2006. "Nathanael West and the Mystery of Feeling." *Modern Fiction Studies* 52, no. 3: 588–612.
Gregg, Melissa and Gregory J. Seigworth. 2010. "An Inventory of Shimmers." In *The Affect Theory Reader*, edited by Melissa Gregg and Gregory J. Seigworth, 1–28. Durham, NC: Duke University Press.
Hagman, Hampus. 2014. "The Digital Gesture: Rediscovering Cinematic Movement through Gifs." Cited in Dominik Maeder and Daniela Wentz, "Digital Seriality as Structure and Process." *Eludamos* 8, no.1: 129–49.
Halberstam, Jack. 2012. "The Power of Unknowing." In *The Critical Pulse*, edited by Jeffrey Williams and Heather Steffen, 264–70. New York: Columbia University Press.
Halberstam, Jack and Tavia Nyong'o. 2018. "Introduction: Theory in the Wild." *The South Atlantic Quarterly* 117, no. 3 (July): 453–64.

Haraway, Donna. 1994. "A Game of Cat's Cradle: Science Studies, Feminist Theory, Cultural Studies." *Configurations* 2, no. 1: 59–71.

Haraway, Donna. 2016. *Staying with the Trouble: Making Kin in the Chthulucene*. Durham, NC: Duke University Press.

Harman, Graham. 2012. *Weird Realism: Lovecraft and Philosophy*. Washington USA; Winchester UK: Zero Books.

Hattenstone, Simon. 2009. "There's Something about Sam." *The Guardian*, November 28. https://www.theguardian.com/artanddesign/2009/nov/28/sam-taylor-wood-interview.

Hayles, N. Katherine. 1999. *How We Became Posthuman: Virtual Bodies in Cybernetics, Literature, and Informatics*. Chicago: University of Chicago Press.

Hazlitt, William. 1903. "On Wit and Humour." In *The Selected Writings of William Hazlitt*, edited by A.R. Waller and Arnold Glover, 5–29. London: J. M. Dent & Co.

Hegel, Georg Wilhelm Friedrich. 1988. *Hegel's Aesthetics Lectures on Fine Art*, Vol. 1. Translated by T.M. Knox. Oxford: Clarendon Press.

Hersey, John. 1985. *Hiroshima*. New York: Knopf.

Hoeveler, Diane. 1996. "This Cosmic Pawnshop We Call Life; Nathanael West, Bergson, Capitalism, and Schizophrenia." *Studies in Short Fiction* 33, no. 3 (Summer): 411–22.

Hollywood, Amy. 2002. *Sensible Ecstasy: Mysticism, Sexual Difference, and the Demands of History*. Chicago: University of Chicago Press.

Horkheimer, Max and Theodor Adorno. 2002. *Dialectic of Enlightenment: Philosophical Fragments*. Translated by Edmund Jephcott. Stanford, CA: Stanford University Press.

Hungerford, Amy. 2008. "On the Period Formerly Known as Contemporary." *American Literary History* 20, no. 1/2 (Spring–Summer): 410–9.

Jackson, Lauren Michele. 2017. "We Need to Talk about Digital Blackface in Reaction GIFS." *Teen Vogue*. August 2. https://www.teenvogue.com/story/digital-blackface-reaction-gifs

Jaffe, Aaron. 2016. "Who's Afraid of the Inhuman Woolf?" *Modernism/Modernity* 23, no. 3: 491–513.

James, William. 1896. "On Some Hegelisms." In *The Will to Believe: And Other Essays in Popular Philosophy*, 263–98. New York: Longmans, Green and Co.

James, William. 2007. *Varieties of Religious Experience*. New York: Cosimo Classics.

Jameson, Fredric. 1993. *Postmodernism, or, the Cultural Logic of Late Capitalism*. New York: Verso Books.

Jameson, Fredric. 2005. *Archaeologies of the Future: The Desire Called Utopia and Other Science Fictions*. New York: Verso Books.

Jarry, Alfred. 1996. *Exploits and Opinions of Dr. Faustroll, Paraphysician: A Neo-Scientific Novel*. Translated by Roger Shattuck. Cambridge, MA: Exact Change.

"Jeff Goldblum ... laughing? (The Original Video)." *YouTube*, uploaded by FireMaster7001. February 20, 2009. https://www.youtube.com/watch?v=JlOx9738iyw.

"Jeff Goldblum Laughs for 10 Minutes." *YouTube*, uploaded by IzzyMaiden. July 9, 2011. https://www.youtube.com/watch?v=lS9D6w1GzGY.

"Jeff Goldblum Laughs at Lois Lane." *YouTube*, uploaded by Jeff Goldblum. March 11, 2013. https://www.youtube.com/watch?v=6bwJiXUNiFA.

"Jeff Goldblum Laughs at Predator." *YouTube*, uploaded by Jeff Goldblum. March 13, 2013. https://www.youtube.com/watch?v=JnvtVGQ0cYY.

"Jeff Goldblum's laugh – REVERSED." *YouTube*, uploaded by Aaron Ludwig. November 26, 2014. https://www.youtube.com/watch?v=dL4IxOaAIBU.

"Jeff Goldblum Laugh 10 hours." *YouTube*, uploaded by JuciyMiddle. June 13, 2018. https://www.youtube.com/watch?v=QWy_zcmopoQ.

Jenkins, Henry. 2007. "'Vernacular Creativity': An Interview with Jean Burgess (Part One)." *Confessions of an ACA Fan*. October 7. http://henryjenkins.org/blog/2007/10/vernacular_creativity_an_inter.html.

Joy, Jenn. 2004. *The Choreographic*. Cambridge, MA: MIT Press.

Kapchan, Deborah. 2015. "Body." In *Keywords in Sound Studies*, edited by David Novak and Matt Sakakeeny, 33–44. Durham: Duke University Press.

Kant, Immanuel. 2007. *Critique of Judgment*. New York: Cosimo Books.

Kendall, Stuart. 2015. "Translator's Introduction: The Wanderer and His Shadow." In *On Nietzsche*, translated by Stuart Kendall, vii–xxx. Albany, NY: SUNY Press, 2015.

Kettler Penrod, Lynn. 1996. *Hélène Cixous: Twayne's World Authors Series*. New York: Twayne Publishers.

Khlebnikov, Velimir. 2010. "Incantation by Laughter." *The International Literary Quarterly* 10 (February). Translated by Charles Bernstein. http://interlitq.org/issue10/velimir_khlebnikov/job.php.

Kimmins, C.W. 1928. *The Springs of Laughter*. London: Methuen & Co., Ltd.

Kissinger, Henry. 1961. *The Necessity for Choice: Prospects of American Foreign Policy*. New York: Harper.

Kohlhaase, Bill. 2016. "Zingerology: Dissecting humor." *Santa Fe: New Mexican*. Last modified September 3. https://www.santafenewmexican.com/pasatiempo/books/zingerology-dissecting-humor/article_3e673cf0-88d0-5057-a286-4decacc896cd.html

Kubrick, Stanley. 1963. "How I Learned to Stop Worrying and Love the Cinema." *Films and Filming* 9 (June): 12–13.

Kubrick, Stanley. 1964. *Dr. Strangelove or: How I Learned to Stop Worrying and Love the Bomb*. Columbia, DVD.

Lefebvre, Henri. 2009. "Review of Kostas Axelos's *Toward Planetary Thought*." In *State, Space, World: Selected Essays*, edited by Neil Brenner and Stuart Elden, 254–8. Minneapolis: Minnesota University Press.

Lentjes, Rebecca. 2017. "Against the Grain." *VAN Magazine*. Last modified July 6. https://van-us.atavist.com/against-the-grain.

Lernout, Geert. 1993. *The French Joyce*. Ann Arbor: University of Michigan Press.

Lewis, Wyndham. 1982. *The Complete Wild Body*. Santa Barbara, CA: Black Sparrow Press.

Leys, Ruth. 2011. "The Turn to Affect: A Critique." *Critical Inquiry* 37, no. 3: 434–72.

Lie, Sissel. 2012. "Medusa's Laughter and the Hows and Whys of Writing According to Hélène Cixous." In *Emergent Writing Methodologies in Feminist Studies*, edited by Mona Livholts, 41–54. New York: Routledge.

Light, James. 1975. "Varieties of Satire in the Art of Nathanael West." *Studies in American Humor* 2, no. 1: 46–60.

Lippit, Akira Mizuta. 2005. *Atomic Light (Shadow Optics)*. Minneapolis: University of Minnesota Press.

Lizotte, Chloe. 2020. "Ten-Hour YouTube." *Screen Slate*, May 19. https://www.screenslate.com/articles/ten-hour-youtube.

Maher, Max. 2019. "Alfie Bown, *In the Event of Laughter: Psychoanalysis, Literature*." *Psychoanalysis and History* 21, no. 1: 115–17.

Maland, Charles. 1979. "Dr. Strangelove: Nightmare Comedy and the Ideology of Liberal Consensus." *American Quarterly*, 31, no. 5: 697–717.

Manning, Erin. 2016. *The Minor Gesture*. Durham: Duke University Press.

Martin, Jay. 1976. "Nathanael West's Burlesque Comedy." *Studies in American Jewish Literature (1975–1979)* 2, no. 1: 6–14.

Massumi, Brian. 2002. *Parables for the Virtual: Movement, Affect, Sensation*. Durham: Duke University Press.

McCulloch, Gretchen. 2019. *Because Internet: Understanding the New Rules of Language*. New York: Riverhead Books.

McDonald, Frances. 2013. "Laughter Without Humor: On the Laugh-Loop GIF." *The Atlantic*, July 17. https://www.theatlantic.com/technology/archive/2013/07/laughter-without-humor-on-the-laugh-loop-gif/277853/.

McKay, Sally. 2016. "The Affect of Animated GIFs (Tom Moody, Petra Cortright, Lorna Mills)." *ArtFCity*. July 16. http://artfcity.com/2018/07/16/the-affect-of-animated-gifs-tom-moody-petra-cortright-lorna-mills/.

Meeker, Joseph. 1997. *The Comedy of Survival: Literary Ecology and a Play Ethic*. Tucson: University of Arizona Press.

Meindl, Dieter. 1996. *American Fiction and the Metaphysics of the Grotesque*. Columbia, MO: University of Missouri Press.

Michaux, Henri. 1963. *Light through Darkness*. New York: The Orion Press.

Michaux, Henri. 1974. *The Major Ordeals of the Mind and the Countless Minor Ones*. New York: Harcourt Brace Jovanovich, Inc.

Milesi, Laurent. 2014. "Translator's Note." In Hélène Cixous, *Tomb(e)*, translated by Laurent Milesi, vii–viii. Calcutta: Seagull Books.

Miller, Henry. 1961. "An Open Letter to Surrealists Everywhere." In *The Cosmological Eye*, 151–96. New York: New Directions Press.

Miller, Tyrus. 1999. *Late Modernism: Politics, Fiction, and the Arts between the World Wars*. Berkeley and Los Angeles: University of California Press.

Milne, Tom. 1964. "Dr. Strangelove: Monthly Film Bulletin." *Sight and Sound* 33 (Winter): 37–8.

Miltner, Kate N. and Tim Highfield. 2017. "Never Gonna GIF You Up: Analyzing the Cultural Significance of the Animated GIF." *Social Media + Society* 3, no. 3: 1–11.

Moore, Lorrie. 1998. *Birds of America*. New York: Picador.

Morgenthau, Hans J. 1964. "The Four Paradoxes of Nuclear Strategy." *The American Political Science Review* 58, no. 1: 23–35.

Morreall, Thomas. 1987. *The Philosophy of Laughter and Humor*. Albany: State University of New York Press.

Morton, Timothy. 2010. *The Ecological Thought*. Cambridge, MA: Harvard University Press.

Mumford, Lewis. 1964. "'Strangelove' Reactions." *The New York Times*. March 1.

Mumford, Lewis. 1973. *Interpretations and Forecasts: 1922–1972*. New York: Harcourt Brace Jovanovich.

Naas, Michael. 2014. "Flicker 1: Reflections on Photography and Literature in the Works of Hélène Cixous." *Mosaic: An Interdisciplinary Critical Journal* 47, no. 4: 27–48.

Nancy, Jean-Luc. 1987. "Wild Laughter in the Throat of Death." *MLA* 102, no. 4 (September): 719–36.

Nancy, Jean-Luc. 1993. *The Birth to Presence*. Stanford, CA: Stanford University Press.

Nancy, Jean-Luc. 2016. *The Disavowed Community*. Translated by Philip Armstrong. New York: Fordham University Press.

Nathanson, Donald L. 1992. *Shame and Pride: Affect, Sex, and the Birth of the Self*. New York; London: W. W. Norton & Company.

Ngai, Sianne. 2005. *Ugly Feelings*. Cambridge, MA: Harvard University Press.

Ngai, Sianne. 2012. *Our Aesthetic Categories: Zany, Cute, Interesting*. Cambridge, MA: Harvard University Press.

Nieland, Justus. 2004. "West's Deadpan: Affect, Slapstick, and Publicity in *Miss Lonelyhearts*." *Novel: A Forum on Fiction* 38, no. 1 (Fall): 57–83.

Nieland, Justus. 2006. "Editor's Introduction: Modernism's Laughter." *Modernist Cultures* 2, no. 2: 80–6.

Nietzsche, Friedrich. 2005. *Thus Spake Zarathustra*. Translated by Graham Parkes. Oxford: Oxford University Press.

O'Neill, Patrick. 1990. *Comedy of Entropy: Humour, Narrative, Reading*. Toronto: University of Toronto Press.

Ohlheiser, Abby. 2016. "The Mesmerizing Lost Art of the 10-hour YouTube Lop, 2011's Weirdest Video Trend." *The Washington Post*, June 3. https://www.washingtonpost.com/news/the-intersect/wp/2016/06/03/the-mesmerizing-lost-art-of-the-10-hour-youtube-loop-2011s-weirdest-video-trend

Parvulescu, Anca. 2010. *Laughter: Notes on a Passion*. Cambridge, MA: MIT Press.

Podhoretz, Norman. 1971. "Nathanael West: A Particular Type of Joking." In *Nathanael West: A Collection of Critical Essays*, edited by Jay Martin, 154–60. New Jersey: Prentice-Hall, Inc.

Polizzotti, Mark. 1995. *Revolution of the Mind: The Life of André Breton*. New York: Farrar, Straus and Giroux.

Poulaki, Maria. 2015. "Featuring Shortness in Online Loop Cultures." *Empedocles: European Journal for the Philosophy of Communication* 5, no. 1: 91–6.
Puar, Jasbir. 2012. "Precarity Talk: A Virtual Roundtable with Lauren Berlant, Judith Butler, Bojana Cvejić, Isabell Lorey, Jasbir Puar, and Ana Vujanović." *The Drama Review* 56, no. 4, 163–77.
Raban, Jonathan. 1971. "A Surfeit of Commodities: The Novels of Nathanael West." In *The American Novel and the Nineteen Twenties*, edited by Malcolm Bradbury, 215–32. London: Edward Arnold.
Radulescu, Domnica. 2012. *Women's Comedic Art as Social Revolution: Five Performers and the Lessons of Their Subversive Humor*. Jefferson, NC: McFarland & Company.
Rich, B. Ruby. 1990. "In the Name of Feminist Film Criticism." In *Issues in Feminist Film Criticism*, edited by Patricia Erens, 268–87. Bloomington: Indiana University Press.
Ritchie, Graeme. 2004. *The Linguistic Analysis of Jokes*. London: Routledge.
Rowe, Kathleen. 1995. *The Unruly Woman; Gender and the Genres of Laughter*. Austin: University of Texas Press.
Rutter, Benjamin. 2010. *Hegel on the Modern Arts*. Cambridge: Cambridge University Press.
Saint-Amour, Paul. 2018. "Weak Theory, Weak Modernism." *Modernism/Modernity* 25, no. 3: 437–59.
Sartre, Jean Paul. 2010. "The New Mystic." In *Critical Essays (Situations 1)*. Translated by Chris Turner, 219–94. Calcutta: Seagull Books.
Schulenberg, David. 1995. "Composition and Improvisation in the School of J.S. Bach." In *Bach Perspectives, Vol. 1*, edited by Russell Stinson, 1–42. Lincoln: University of Nebraska Press.
Schulz, Max F. 1968. "Pop, Op, and Black Humor: The Aesthetics of Anxiety." *College English* 30, no. 3: 230–41.
Schwob, Marcel. 1968. "Laughter." In *Evergreen Review Reader 1957–1966: A Ten-Year Anthology*, edited by Barney Rosset, 299–300. New York: Grove Press.
Scott, H. Jill. 1995. "Subjectivities of Proximity in Hélène Cixous's *Book of Promethea*." *World Literature Today* 69, no. 1 (Winter): 29–34.
Scott, Laurence. 2020. "GIFS Are Glorious, GIFs Are Perverse." *Wired*. March 2. https://www.wired.com/story/gifs-are-glorious-gifs-are-perverse/.
Scruton, Robert. 1987. "Laughter." In *The Philosophy of Laughter and Humor*, edited by John Morreall, 156–71. New York: State University of New York Press.
Sedgwick, Eve Kosofsky. 2003. *Touching Feeling: Affect, Pedagogy, Performance*. Durham, NC: Duke University Press.
Sedgwick, Eve Kosofsky. 2011. *The Weather in Proust*. Edited by Jonathan Goldberg. Durham, NC: Duke University Press.
Sedgwick, Eve Kosofsky and Adam Frank. 1995. "Shame in the Cybernetic Fold: Reading Silvan Tomkins." *Critical Inquiry* 21, no. 2 (Winter): 496–522.
Sellers, Susan. 1996. *Hélène Cixous: Authorship, Autobiography, and Love*. Cambridge: Polity Press.

Shattuck, Roger. 1989. "Introduction: Love and Laughter: Surrealism Reappraised." In *The History of Surrealism*, edited by Maurice Nadeau, 11–34. Cambridge, MA: The Belknap Press of Harvard University.

Shklovsky, Victor. 1998. *Theory of Prose*. Translated by Benjamin Sher. Illinois: Dalkey Archive Press.

Siegel, Joshua and Doug Mayle. 2010. "Up, Up and Away—Long Videos for More Users." *YouTube Official Blog*, December 9. https://blog.youtube/news-and-events/up-up-and-away-long-videos-for-more.

Silverman, Kaja. 1988. *The Acoustic Mirror: The Female Voice in Psychoanalysis and Cinema*. Bloomington: Indiana University Press.

Smithson, Robert. 1996. *Robert Smithson: The Collected Writings*, edited by Jack Flam. Berkeley and Los Angeles: University of California Press.

Sperb, Jason. 2006. *The Kubrick Façade: Faces and Voices in the Films of Stanley Kubrick*. Oxford: Scarecrow Press.

Stevenson, Guy. 2020. "Introduction." *Textual Practice: Anti-Humanist Modernisms* 34, no. 9: 1405–18.

Stewart, Kathleen. 2007. *Ordinary Affects*. Durham, NC: Duke University Press.

Stewart, Kathleen. 2012. "Precarity's Forms," *Cultural Anthropology* 27, no. 3: 518–25.

Sturgeon, Theodore. 1998. "What Dead Men Tell." In *The Perfect Host Volume V: The Complete Stories of Theodore Sturgeon*, edited by Paul Williams, 324–52. Berkeley: North Atlantic Books.

Surya, Michel. 2002. *Georges Bataille: An Intellectual Biography*. New York: Verso.

Terada, Rei. 2001. *Feeling in Theory: Emotion after the Subject*. Cambridge, MA: Harvard University Press.

Thacker, Eugene. 2011. *In the Dust of This Planet*. Washington, USA; Winchester, UK: Zero Books.

Thompson, Marie and Ian Biddle. 2013. *Sound Music Affect: Theorizing Sonic Experience*. New York: Bloomsbury Academic.

"Tidus Laugh 10 HOURS." *YouTube*, uploaded by AuronSuper95. April 23, 2012. https://www.youtube.com/watch?v=-lfiTebewnc.

Torres, Monica. 2016. "Instant Replay." *Real Life*. November 22. https://reallifemag.com/instant-replay/.

Trahair, Lisa. 2007. *The Comedy of Philosophy: Sense and Nonsense in Early Cinematic Slapstick*. Albany, NY: SUNY Press.

Truman, Harry. 2019. "August 6, 1945: Statement by the President Announcing the Use of the A-Bomb at Hiroshima." *Miller Center*. Last modified October 4. https://millercenter.org/the-presidency/presidential-speeches/august-6-1945-statement-president-announcing-use-bomb.

Turner, Christopher. 2005. "Tears of Laughter." *Cabinet: A Quarterly of Art and Culture* 17 (Spring): 69–73.

Vonnegut, Kurt. 1974. *Wampeters, Foma & Granfalloons (Opinions)*. Seymour Lawrence: Delacorte Press.

Vonnegut, Kurt. 2010. *Cat's Cradle*. New York: The Dial Press.

Wainwright, Loudon. 1964. "The Strange Case of Dr. Strangelove." *Life* 56 (March): 13.
Wali, G.M. 1993. "'Fou rire prodromique' heralding a brainstem stroke." *Journal of Neurology, Neurosurgery, and Psychiatry* 56, no. 2 (February): 209–10.
Wallis, Wilson D. 1922. "Why Do We Laugh?" *The Scientific Monthly* 15, no. 4: 343–7.
Weissenborn, Ulrike. 1998. *Just Making Pictures: Hollywood Writers, the Frankfurt School, and Film Theory*. Tübingen: G. Narr.
West, Nathanael. 1975. *The Day of the Locust*. New York: Bantham Books.
West, Nathanael. 1997. *Novels and Other Writings*. Edited by Sacvan Bercovitch. New York: Literary Classics of the United States.
Willett, Cynthia and Julie Willett. 2014. "Going to Bed White and Waking Up Arab: On Xenophobia, Affect Theories of Laughter, and the Social Contagion of the Comic Stage." *Critical Philosophy of Race* 2, no. 1: 84–105.
Williams, Raymond. 1977. *Marxism and Literature*. Oxford: Oxford University Press.
Williams, Raymond. 2020. "Literature and Sociology." In *Culture and Materialism*, 13–34. London: Verso.
Williams, Simon J. 1998. "Bodily Dys-Order: Desire, Excess and the Transgression of Corporeal Boundaries." *Body & Society* 4, no. 2: 59–82.
Wortzel, H.S., T.J. Oster, C.A. Anderson and D.B. Archiniegas. 2008. "Pathological Laughing and Crying: Epidemiology, Pathophysiology and Treatment." *CNS Drugs* 22: 531–45.
Zielinski, Siegfried. 2006. *Deep Time of the Media: Toward an Archaeology of Hearing and Seeing by Technical Means*. Translated by Gloria Custance. Cambridge, MA: MIT Press.
Žižek, Slavoj. 2003. "Will You Laugh for Me, Please?" *In These Times*. July 18. https://inthesetimes.com/article/will-you-laugh-for-me-please.

Index

Adorno, Theodor 38, 42
aesthetic fixity
    in Breton's Surrealism 62, 64
    in *The Day of the Locust* 41–4, 45, 46–8, 54–6
affect
    the body and 79, 89, 129, 146
    in cinema 15–16
    competing definitions of 12–15, 38
    vs. emotion 13–14, 17, 35–9, 61, 70, 146, 147
    as fixed structural relation 13–14, 15
    formal dimensions of 12, 15–16, 20, 23, 68–9
    formlessness of 13, 15
    the gap and 24, 79, 121, 146
    the psychoanalytic subject and 14, 40, 50, 62, 66–7, 96, 100, 104
    sound studies and 91–2. *See also* affect studies; affectology; formless; the gap; temporality of affects
affect studies
    derivation and development 13–16, 38–9, 71, 79
    Flusser and 144
    posthumorism and 13, 15, 20, 38–9, 71, 79
    vagueness in 14–5
affectological techniques
    code-mixing 3, 69–70, 71–4
    extension 8, 10, 19, 29 n.35, 147
    the fragment 8–10, 19, 98, 147
    the gap 18–19, 82
    hypersubstitution 69–70 75–9, 103
    the instant 79–82
    looping 109, 145–55
    mot glissant 69–70, 74–5, 103
    paradox 8, 18, 71, 119, 121, 125–6, 130
    sound affects 27–8, 89, 90–2, 94, 96, 100–2, 104–5
    synesthesia 18, 24–5, 102, 105–6, 110
    the sound image 104–6
    tautology 6, 71
    touch/tactility 10, 70, 92, 93, 96, 100–1, 145, 147, 153
    writing aloud 94–5, 97–101, 106
    zany 5, 10. *See also* infinity
affectology
    atomic laughter and 116
    Bataille's 26, 61, 63, 67–83, 153
    Cixous's 18, 24–5, 87–8, 91, 92–4, 104–6
    contribution to affect studies 19, 20
    definition of 16–17
    digital posthumorism and 147, 153
    écriture feminine and 91, 93, 95
    Ordinary Affects as example of 17–19, 71. *See also* affectological techniques; critical thought (styles of)
Ahmed, Sara 14
American black humor
    atom bomb and 121–5
    Cat's Cradle as example of 132–7
    derivation and definition of 83 n.1, 116, 122
    Dr. Strangelove as example of 125–9
    flatness and 122–4
    vs. incongruity resolution theory 23, 25, 126
    laughter of 27, 123–5
    vs. satire 122, 123
antihumanism
    atomic laughter and 27, 116, 118–21, 137
    Bataille and 67–8, 118–19
    modernism and 10–11, 16
    posthumorist laughter as an expression of 2–11, 21, 23. *See also* inhumanism
Aristotle 20, 46–8, 49
Armstrong, Martin 35–6, 37
atom bomb
    aesthetic fallout of 121–2
    Hersey's *Hiroshima* 117–18

the philosophical possibilities of
116–21
Truman's announcement of 115–16,
117
atomic laughter 11, 23
antihumanism and 27, 116, 118–21, 137
Axelos and 130
in *Cat's Cradle* 132, 135–7
definition and derivation of 27, 115–21
Deleuze and 124–5
in *Dr. Strangelove* 126–30
Foucault's theory of 119–121, 123
Glissant and 130, 136
vs. incongruity-resolution theory 23, 25, 126
planetary thinking and 129–137
post-nuclear thought and 118–21. *See also* laughter (types)
Axelos, Kostas
Lefebvre on 130
planetary thinking and 24, 27, 117, 121, 129–31

Bakhtin, Mikhail 40, 54, 55
Barad, Karen 17, 101
Barnes, Djuna 9, 10
Barnes, Linda 122, 123
Barthes, Roland
affects and 70, 95, 96
on Bataille 70, 73, 77–8, 82
the body in 94–6, 107
on cinema 106
entanglement and 70, 101
the grain of the voice and 26, 94–6, 99, 100, 104–6
on listening 96
materiality and 70, 95, 96, 110
"Outcomes of the Text," 73
The Pleasure of the Text 94–5, 99, 106
Roland Barthes by Roland Barthes 73
the third meaning and 73
writing aloud and 94–5, 96, 99, 100, 106
Bataille, George
affects and 24, 25, 26, 63, 67–83
affectology of 26, 61, 63, 67–83, 153
antihumanism in 67–8, 118
Atheological Summa 20, 26, 62–3, 68, 69, 73, 76, 77–9, 82–3

on the atom bomb 117–18
Barthes on 70, 73, 77–8, 82
and Breton 23, 26, 61, 62, 63
Cixous and 91, 95, 103
code-mixing in 69–70, 71–4
contagion in 67–8, 75–9, 83
Derrida on 67, 68 70, 78, 80–1, 82
entanglement in 67, 71
eroticism 75–6
Freud and 11
Guilty 62, 67, 71, 75, 77, 80
Hegel and 24, 26, 62, 67, 68–9, 75, 123
on Hiroshima 117–18, 119
hypersubstitution in 69–70, 75–9
Inner Experience 62, 68, 70–1, 72–5, 76–8, 80, 82
the instant in 69–70, 79–83, 118, 120, 153
laughter in 11, 16, 23, 24, 61, 62–3, 67–83, 118, 119, 123, 129, 153
On Nietzsche 62, 68, 77
postnuclear thought and 118, 119, 120, 129
prose style of 16, 26, 61, 62, 63, 68–83
Sartre on 70–1, 75, 78, 95
slipping in 69–70, 74–5, 78, 103
The Story of the Eye 62, 77–8
Un Cadavre 63
Baudelaire, Charles 24
Beattie, James 125–6
Beckett, Samuel 106
Benjamin, Walter
drug writings of 7–8, 9, 10, 147
ecstatic laughter and 7, 8
Bergson, Henri 21–2, 47, 49–50, 52, 55
Berlant, Lauren 14
Bernstein, Leonard 108
Bishop, Ryan 91–2
Black, Donald 22
Blyth Ian 89, 94
body
affect and 79, 89, 129, 146
in Barthes 94–6, 107
in Cixous 91, 97–101, 105–6
contagion and 76–7
digital posthumorism and 148–51, 154
horror and 13, 148
laughter and 2–3, 40, 65, 68, 81, 94, 127

Index

sound and 89, 91–2, 107. *See also* grotesque body (Bakhtin); sound body (Kapchan); syncope (Clément); Wild Body (Lewis)
Bok, Christian 7
Boldt-Irons, Leslie Ann 75
Book of Promethea, The (Cixous) 90
    as affectology 96
    materialist reading of 101–6
    Medusa and 98
    metaphor and 101–4
    sound image in 104–6
    Wing on 94
    writing aloud and 97–101
Borges, Jorge Luis 3, 120–1
Bosse-de-Nage (character, *Dr. Faustroll*) 6–7. *See also* laughter (types)
Boyer, Paul 121–2
Boym, Svetlana 25
Brassier, Ray 124
Brennan, Teresa 43, 101
Breton, André
    Anthologie de L'Humour Noir 65
    and Bataille 23, 26, 61, 62, 63
    and Freud 61–2, 66–7
    and Hegel 61, 64–5, 66–7
    and humor noir 23, 26, 31 n.86, 61–2, 63–7
    and laughter 63–4
    "Manifesto of Surrealism," 63
    The Second Surrealist Manifesto 63–4
Brinkema, Eugenie 14, 15–16, 113 n.68
Brissaud, E.W. 22
Brottman, Mikita 53
Browder, Clifford 64
Burroughs, William S. 10, 145
    The Electronic Revolution 149
    The Ticket That Exploded 148–9
Butler, Judith 56–7 n.5

Calle-Gruber, Mirielle 102, 104
canned laughter 7, 44, 46, 146, 147
    in Burroughs 148–9
    in Ellison 149–50, 151
    in Gibson 150–1. *See also* laughter (types)
Cat's Cradle (Vonnegut) 27, 124
    atomic laughter in 132, 135–7
    entanglement in 135

filiation in 133–4, 136
the gap in 133–4, 136
Philip Castle's joke in 135–7
structure of 132–3
world death in 134, 136–7
Chion, Michel 107
cinema
    analysis of affects in 15–16
    Barthes on 106
    the close-up and 106–7
    "deaf cinema" (Chion) 107
    grotesque laughter and 53–4
    synesthesia and 102
Cixous, Hélène
    affectology of 18, 24–5, 87–8, 91–6, 104–6
    Angst 94
    the body in 91, 97–101, 105–6
    The Book of Promethea 20, 25, 27, 90, 94–105, 109
    "Castration or Decapitation?" 89, 92, 94
    on Duras 87–91, 92, 94, 96
    écriture feminine and 87–91, 93, 95–7, 100, 101, 103–4
    on entanglement 89, 92
    on Freud 90
    "The Laugh of the Medusa," 25, 87, 89–90, 93, 98, 104
    laughter in 16, 87–91, 92–6, 98–9, 101–2, 104
    listening and 87–90, 99
    sound affects in 27–8, 89, 90–1, 100–2, 104–5
    materialist reading of 91, 92, 101–2, 104
    Medusa and 23, 25, 89–90, 95, 98
    metaphor in 101–4
    on music 87–9, 92–3, 95, 99, 101
    synesthesia and 18, 24–5, 102, 105–6. *See also* "The Laugh of the Medusa"; Medusa
Clément, Catherine 81
Code-mixing 3, 69–70, 71–4. *See also* affectological techniques
Cold War, the 121, 125–6, 128
comedy
    Aristotle's formulation of 46–7, 48, 49
    Bergson's formulation of 21–2, 49–50
    capitalism and 42, 49

feminism and 90
interpretation and 36, 38. *See also* American black humor; satire
Coppola, Francis Ford 16
Creative-critical 17, 24, 25
    Cixous and 90. *See also* critical thought (styles of)
critical thought (styles of)
    affectology as 16–20
    creative-critical 17, 24, 25, 90
    ethics of unintelligibility 24
    gestalt looking 26, 36–7, 56, 115–8
    minor gesture 25
    planetary thinking 24, 27, 129–32, 136–7
    poetics of Relation 24–5, 131–2, 136–7
    scavenger methodologies 19
    wild theory 3–4

Darwin, Charles 20, 47–8
Daumal, René 7, 9
Davis, Diane D. 19, 25
Davis, Todd 135
The Day of the Locust (West) 20, 23
    aesthetic fixity in 41–3, 46, 48, 54–6
    affect in 26, 37–40, 43, 45, 46–9, 51–3, 56
    critical reception of 24, 37–40
    grotesque laughter in 11, 13, 26, 37–8, 40, 46–56
    ontological precarity in 37, 40, 43–5, 49–53, 56
    postmodernism and 38–9
    self-reflexive laughter in 11, 26, 37, 40, 41–6, 51, 53, 55–6, 61
De Certeau, Michel 119, 121
deaf cinema (Chion) 107
Deleuze, Gilles 31 n.73
    on Cixous 102
    on Dionysian laughter 124, 127, 129
    on the creative stumble 50
    on humor 123
Deleuze, Gilles and Felix Guattari
    on affect 12, 13, 15
    on becoming 40, 50
Derrida, Jacques
    on Bataille 67–8, 70, 78, 80–1, 118
    on Cixous 103
    on laughter 67

pharmakon and 82
"From Restricted to General Economy," 67–8
dialectic (Hegel)
    Axelos and 121, 130
    Bataille and 24, 62, 67–9, 71, 73
    Breton and 64–5
    Deleuze and 123
    the laugh-loop and 155
    posthumorism and 7–9, 13
    Vonnegut and 133
Dickstein, Morris 124
digital posthumorism 27, 143–55
Dionysian laughter 124, 127, 129. *See also* laughter (types)
Dr. Strangelove (Kubrick) 27
    antihumanism of 126–9, 134, 137
    atomic laughter in 126–30
    Cold War policy and 124–7
    incongruity-resolution theory and 126–9, 134, 137
    Kong's laughter in 127–9, 131, 136, 137
    planetary ethics of 129
    Ripper's suicide in 128–9
drug writings 7–8, 9, 10, 147
Duchenne de Boulogne, Guillaume 47–8
Dunsby, Jonathan 112 n.42
Duras, Marguerite
    Destroy, She Said 88–9, 94, 96
    écriture feminine and 87–9
    laughter in 88–9, 90, 94
    sound affects in 88–9, 90, 92, 94, 96

Earl of Shaftesbury 19
écriture feminine
    as affectology 91, 93, 95
    The Book of Promethea as 97, 100–1, 103–4
    critical uptake of 89–90
    Duras as exemplary of 87–9
    sound studies and 95–6
ecstatic laughter 7, 8, 23, 149–50. *See also* laughter (types)
Ellison, Harlan 145, 149–52, 154–5
emoticons 143
emotion
    aesthetics of 47–9, 53
    vs. affect 13–14, 17, 35–9, 40, 56, 61, 70, 146, 147

in affect studies 12–14, 38–9, 79
affectology and 17, 104, 109, 153
canned laughter and 146, 147
Darwin on 20, 47–8
Freud on 66
gestalt looking and 26, 36–7, 56
the GIF and 145–6
in humor studies 22, 27, 36, 56
possessive individual and 4–5, 12, 17, 26, 36, 56, 70, 104, 124
posthumorism and 12, 15, 17, 36, 116
in West 37, 39, 47–9, 56
Eng, David L. 14
entanglement
Barthes and 70, 101
Bataille and 67–8, 71
Cixous and 89, 92
planetary thinking and 129, 132, 135
posthumorism and 13, 20
Eppink, Jason 153
Erasmus 19
ethics of unintelligibility 24. *See also* critical thought (styles of)
excess
affect as 13, 24, 69, 70, 71
Bataille's laughter as 24, 62, 67–9
in Cixous 93–4, 95
the grotesque body as 40. *See also* affectological techniques; code-mixing
exploit (Galloway) 17, 151
extension 8, 10, 19, 29 n.35, 147. *See also* affectological techniques
exteriority
of affects 12, 17
in Deleuze 127–8
in Duras 88–9, 94, 96
in Ellison 149–50
in James 8–9
in Jarry 6, 7
of laughter 10, 67, 93–4, 96, 116, 120–1, 127
in Michaux 8
in Nietzsche 4–5

Faulkner, Joanne 69
Felski, Rita 95
Féré, Charles 22
Fiedler, Leslie 124

Flusser, Vilém 144, 145
Ford, Russell 123
formless
Bataille's *informe* 62
laughter as verbal entropy 2–3
Massumi's theory of affects as 13, 15
Foucault, Michel
on Duras 87–8
laughter of 3, 19, 25, 119–21, 123, 129
The Order of Things 3, 19, 25, 120–1, 123
post-nuclear thought of 3, 10, 119–21, 129, 131, 135
fragment 8–10, 19, 98, 147. *See also* affectological techniques
Frank, Pat 122
Freud, Sigmund 11
on humor 32 n.90, 61–2, 64, 65–7
"On Humour," 61–2, 66
The Joke and Its Relation to the Unconscious 66
on Medusa 90, 111 n.20
Friedman, Bruce Jay 122, 123, 130, 136

Galloway, Alex 17
the gap
as affectological technique 18–19, 82
affect theory and 24, 79, 121, 146
the Cold War and 121, 125–7
the dialectic and 24, 121, 133
incongruity resolution theory and 25, 121, 125–6
the interlude as 130
the loop and 146–7
posthumorism and 24–5
signification and 74–5, 104, 121, 136
synesthesia and 110
in Vonnegut 134–5. *See also* affectological techniques; the middle; the third term
Gershon, Walter 91
gestalt looking 26, 36–7, 56, 115–6. *See also* critical thought (styles of)
gesture
Flusser on 144–5
Manning on 25
Gibson, William 145, 155
Neuromancer 150–1, 155
Glissant, Édouard
on errancy 24

on planetary thinking 24, 27, 117, 129
poetics of relation and 25, 131–2, 133, 136–7
Goldblum, Jeff 151–4
Gorris, Marleen 9, 19
grain of the voice (Barthes) 26, 94–6, 99, 100, 104–6
Greenberg, Jonathan 39–40
Gregg, Melissa 67–8, 69
grotesque body (Bakhtin) 40, 54–5
grotesque laughter 11
    definition of 26, 40
    Harry Greener's (character, *The Day of the Locust*) 51–4, 55
    ontological precarity and 26, 37, 40, 46, 51–4, 55–6, 61. *See also* laughter (types)

Ha-Ha (orthography) 16
    in Jarry 6–7
    in text-speak 144
    in West 26, 37, 45, 46. *See also*, laughter (types)
Hagman, Hampus 147
Halberstam, Jack 3, 19
Haraway, Donna 11, 30 n.54
Hayles, N. Katherine 52, 150
Hegel, G.W.F.
    Bataille and 26, 62, 67, 68–9, 75
    Breton and 64–5, 66, 67
    Cixous and 103
    James on 8–9
    on laughter 65
    on objective humor 31 n.86, 65, 66
Hersey, John 117–8
Highfield, Tim 145, 153
Hiroshima. *See* atom bomb
Hobbes, Thomas 19, 32 n.90
Hollywood, Amy 74
humanism
    cyberpunk and 150, 151
    humor studies and 21, 24
    modernism and 3–5
    world death and 118, 125, 128, 136, 137. *See also* antihumanism; inhumanism
humor studies
    formation as a discipline of 20–1
    Freud's relief theory 65–7

    Hegel's objective humor 64–6
    identifying gestures of 21–2, 23, 35–6
    vs. laughter studies 22–3, 61
    major theories of 21, 32 n.90
    the pathologizing instinct of 22, 35–6, 148–9
    self-reflexive laughter and 26, 37, 61
humor noir 23, 26, 31 n.86, 61–2, 63–7
hypersubstitution 69–70, 75–9, 103. *See also* affectological techniques

incongruity-resolution theory 121
    vs. American black humor 23, 25, 126
    definition and derivation of 21, 32 n.90, 25, 125–6
    Dr. Strangelove as satire of 126–9
    in West 52, 55–6
infinity
    atomic laughter and 137
    in Gibson 155
    in James 8–9
    in Jarry 6–7, 10
    of the looping form 27, 109, 145–7
    in Michaux 8, 29 n.38
    in Smithson 3
inhumanism 5, 10, 29n48. *See also* antihumanism; humanism
Inner Experience (Bataille)
    communication in 58, 82
    laughter in 76, 77
    mot glissant in 74–5
    Rue de Four scene in 72–4, 80–2
    Sartre on 70–1
    the instant 69–70, 79–83, 118, 120, 153. *See also* affectological techniques; temporality of affects
interlude (Axelos) 121, 130. *See also* the gap; middle

Jackson, Lauren Michele 145–6
Jaffe, Aaron 5, 10, 29 n.48
James, William
    on affect 10
    and Hegel 8–9
    laughter of 8–9
    nitrous oxide experiments of 7, 8–9, 31, 147
Jameson, Fredric 38, 58 n.12, 133
Jarry, Alfred 5–7, 10

Kant, Immanuel 32 n.90, 126
Kapchan, Deborah 110 n.6
Kendall, Stuart 73
Kettler Penrod, Lynn 113 n.82
Khlebnikov, Velimir 9
Kimmins, C.W. 21-2
Kissinger, Henry 126
Kristeva, Julia 95, 102
Kubrick, Stanley 2
  Dr. Strangelove 27, 124-9, 130, 131, 134, 137

"The Laugh of the Medusa" (Cixous) 25, 87, 89-90, 93, 98, 104. *See also* Medusa
laugh track. *See* canned laughter
laugh-loop 27, 109, 145-55. *See also* laughter (types)
laughing gas 8
laughter (types)
  atomic laughter 11, 23, 25, 27, 115-37
  Bosse-de-Nage's "Ha-Ha" (*Dr. Faustroll*) 6-7
  canned laughter 7, 44, 46, 146-51
  Dionysian laughter 124, 127, 129
  ecstatic laughter 7, 8, 23, 149-50
  grotesque laughter 11, 26, 37-8, 40, 46-56, 61
  ha-ha-crystal 2-3, 6, 13, 20, 25, 145
  the laugh-loop 27, 109, 145-55
  pataphysical laughter 5-7
  pathological laughter 22, 38, 53, 149
  self-reflexive laughter 11, 26, 37, 40, 41-6, 51, 53, 55-6, 61
laughter studies
  as an alternative to humor studies 23, 61
  canon of 9, 19-20, 26
Lefebvre, Henri 130
Lentjes, Rebecca 95
Lernout, Geert 103
Lewis, Wyndham 11, 20, 58 n.31
Leys, Ruth 79
listening 87-90, 96, 99
Lizotte, Chloe 152, 153
LOL/lol (orthography) 143-4
looping 109, 145-155. *See also* affectological techniques

Manning, Erin 25
Massumi, Brian
  on affect *vs.* emotion 13, 14-5, 68, 95, 121
  "The Autonomy of Affect" 13
  on Jameson 58 n.12
  on liminality of affects 24, 68
  Parables for the Virtual 68
  on timing 24, 79-80, 82, 146
material turn 101
materialism 23, 61, 62
materiality
  of affect 12, 15, 92, 147
  of the body 40, 55, 95
  of language 9, 70, 91, 93, 95-6, 101-4
  of the laugh-loop 149, 150, 153
  of laughter 2, 16, 52, 62, 93, 94, 98, 106-10. *See also* materialism; material turn
McKay, Sally 146
Medusa
  Cixous's treatment of 90, 98
  Freud on 90, 111 n.20
  laughter of 23, 89-90, 95. *See also* "Laugh of the Medusa"
Meeker, Joseph 132
Michaux, Henri
  drug writings of 7, 9, 10, 147
  "Immense Voice," 8
  laughter in 8
the middle
  Bataille's third term 71-3
  in Cixous 100-1, 104-5
  in feminist methodologies 10-11
  in Foucault 120. *See also* critical thought (styles of); the gap; interlude (Axelos); muddle (Haraway)
Milesi, Laurent 103
Miller, Henry 64
Miller, Tyrus 26, 41-2
Miltner, Kate 145
minor gesture (Manning) 25. *See also* critical thought (styles of)
Möbius strip 27, 149, 154-5
modernism
  anti/inhumanism of 5-6, 10-11, 16
  posthumorism and 4-11, 16, 25, 79, 147
Moi, Toril 95

Moore, Lorrie 27, 91, 107–10
Moore, Ward 122
Morgenthau, Hans J. 125
Morton, Timothy 17
mot glissant (Bataille) 69–70, 74–5, 103.
    See also affectological techniques
muddle (Haraway) 11. See also the middle
Müller-Pohle, Andreas 115–16
Mumford, Lewis 128, 129
music 7–9, 92–3, 95, 99, 101
Myers, Forrest 1–2

Nancy, Jean-Luc 82, 109–10
Nass, Michael 102
Ngai, Sianne 5, 15–16
Nieland, Justus 39–40, 53
Nietzsche, Friedrich
    affects in 10
    Axelos and 130
    Bataille and 63, 73
    Deleuze on 124
    laughter in 4–5, 10
    posthumorism and 5, 21, 63
    literary style of 5, 10. See also *Thus Spake Zarathustra*
Nin, Anaïs 64
Nyong'o, Tavia 3

O'Neill, Patrick 137
objective humor (Hegel) 31 n.86, 61, 64–6
ontological precarity
    Abe Kusich and 43–5
    definition of 56–7 n.5
    grotesque laughter and 26, 37, 40, 45, 51–4, 55, 56
    Major Kong and 127–8
    stilling of 40, 43, 44, 46
Ordinary Affects (Stewart)
    affectology of 17–19, 71
    hedging in 18
    remediation in 18
outside. See exteriority

paradox
    in Bataille's affectology 71
    Cold War policy and 125, 139 n.29
    Dr. Strangelove and 125–7
    Foucault's laughter and 119, 121
    incongruity-resolution theory and 126

planetary thinking and 130–1
in Stewart's affectology 18, 71. See also affectological techniques
Park Place Group 2
Parvulescu, Anca 9, 19, 25
    on Bataille 74
    on Cixous 90, 91
pataphysical laughter 5–7. See also laughter (types)
pataphysics 5–7, 8
pathological laughter
    in Burroughs 149
    medical definition of 22
    in West 38, 53. See also laughter (types)
pharmakon (Derrida) 82
planetary thinking 24, 27, 129–32, 136–7.
    See also critical thought (styles of);
    poetics of Relation (Glissant)
poetics of Relation (Glissant) 27, 125, 131–2
    in *Cat's Cradle* 132–7. See also planetary thinking
posthumorism
    affect, and 10, 12–3
    affect studies and 13–16, 20
    critical discourse and 3–4, 10–11, 16, 19
    formalism and 20
    as a gap 24–5
    vs. humor (studies) 20–1, 23, 35–6, 61
    Lewis as exemplary of 11
    modernism and 4–12, 16, 23, 25, 147
    the promise of 23, 24. See also affectology; affectological techniques; posthumorist laughter
posthumorist laughter
    as an affect 12–16, 36
    antihumanism of 2–11, 21, 23
    definition and development of 3, 4–5, 12–3, 27, 145, 147
    as a gap 24–5
    and Hegel's dialectic 7–9, 13, 24, 62, 67–9, 73, 82, 121, 123, 130
    language and 10–11, 16–17
    ontology and 11, 36, 53, 56, 127
    sovereignty and 3–4, 62, 80–1, 118–9.
        See also affectology; affectological techniques; posthumorism
postnuclear thought
    Bataille and 118, 119
    Foucault and 119–21, 129, 131, 135

poststructuralism 14, 39, 56, 116
Poulaki, Maria 146
psychoanalysis
  affect and 40, 50, 96, 100, 104
  affect studies and 14
  humor noir and 66–7
  lack and 62, 111 n.20
Puar, Jasbir 57 n.5

reaction GIFs 145–6, 147
Rich, B. Ruby 90
Riley, Bridget 108, 109

Saint-Amour, Paul 5
Sartre, Jean-Paul 70–1, 75, 78
satire 39, 122–3. *See also* American black humor
scavenger methodologies 19. *See also* critical thought (styles of)
Schulz, Max 123
Schwob, Marcel 7
Scott, Laurence 145–6
Scruton, Roger 22
Sedgwick, Eve K.
  on affect 10–11, 13–14, 79
  literary style of 20
  on touching 10–11, 92, 153
  Touching Feeling 92. *See also* touching feeling
Seigworth, Gregory 67–8, 69
Self-reflexive laughter 11
  Abe Kusich's 43–5, 46
  definition of 26, 37
  stillness and 40, 41–5, 46, 51, 53
  Tod Hackett's 55–6. *See also* laughter (types)
Sellers, Susan 95, 104
Shattuck, Roger 64
Signification 74–5, 104, 121, 136. *See also* the gap
Silverman, Kaja 95
Smithson, Robert
  anti-humanism of 2–3, 9–10
  the ha-ha crystal and 2–3, 6, 13, 20, 25, 145
  on laughter 2, 23
  The Spiral Jetty 3
sound affects
  in Cixous 27–8, 90–1, 100–2, 104–5

  in Duras 89, 94, 96
  formulation of 92. *See also* affectological techniques
sound body (Kapchan) 88
  definition of 110 n.6
sound studies 91–2, 96
Spencer, Herbert 32 n.90
Sperb, Jason 127–8
Stanford Friedman, Susan 5
Stevenson, Guy 5
Stewart, Kathleen 17–19, 20, 71. *See also* *Ordinary Affects* (Stewart)
structuralism 13–14, 15
structures of feeling (Williams) 15
Sturgeon, Theodore 154–5
Surrealism 63–4, 65, 66
syncope (Clément) 81
synesthesia 18, 24–5, 102, 105–6, 110. *See also* affectological techniques

Taat, Mieke 127
tautology 6, 71. *See also* affectological techniques
Taylor-Johnson, Sam 27, 91, 106–7, 108, 109–10
temporality of affects
  Deleuze's stumble and 50
  Hiroshima and 118
  infinity and 27, 109, 145–7
  the instant and 69–70, 79–83, 118, 120, 153
  radical priorness of 79–80, 81
  Žižek on 145. *See also* the instant
ten-hour YouTube 145, 151–4
ten-minute YouTube 151–2
Terada, Rei 39
Thacker, Eugene 17
Thus Spake Zarathustra (Nietzsche) 4–5, 10, 12. *See also* Nietzsche, Friedrich
Tomkins, Silvan 13–14, 79
touch/tactility
  affect as 92
  Barthes on 96
  Bataille and 26, 70
  Cixous and 92–3, 100–1
  digital posthumorism and 151, 153
  Nancy on 82
  posthumorism and 10, 145, 147

sound as 91–2. *See also* affectological techniques; touching feeling (Sedgwick)
touching feeling (Sedgwick) 10, 92, 153
Truman, Harry S. 115–8
Turner, Christopher 47

violence
    Bataille and 69–70, 75, 81
    in *The Book of Promethea* 97, 98
    in *The Day of the Locust* 41, 45
    in *Hysteria* 107
    of laughter 7, 8
    of oppositional thinking 131, 136–7
    of world death 117–18, 127, 134, 136–7
Vonnegut, Kurt 27, 124–5, 132–7. *See also Cat's Cradle*

Wainwright, Loudon 128–9
Wallis, Wilson D. 32 n.94

West, Nathanael 11, 20, 23
    affectology of 24, 26, 37–56. See also *The Day of the Locust*
Wild Body (Lewis) 11. *See also* body
wild theory 3–4. *See also* critical thought (styles of)
Willett, Cynthia 76
Williams, Raymond 13, 15
Wing, Betsy 94
writing affects. *See* affectological techniques
writing aloud 94–5, 97–101, 106. *See also* affectological techniques
writing laughter. *See* affectological techniques

zany 5, 10. *See also* affectological techniques
Zielinski, Siegfried 25
Žižek, Slavok 146, 147

www.ingramcontent.com/pod-product-compliance
Lightning Source LLC
Chambersburg PA
CBHW061835300426
44115CB00013B/2391